THE TRAGEDIES OF SENECA

RENDERED INTO ENGLISH VERSE

By ELLA ISABEL HARRIS

TO PROFESSOR
ALBERT STANBURROUGH COOK

WITH GRATEFUL ACKNOWLEDGEMENT OF WHAT IT OWES TO HIS
CRITICAL SCHOLARSHIP AND LITERARY INSIGHT, THIS TRANSLATION IS
DEDICATED BY THE TRANSLATOR

A Digireads.com Book
Digireads.com Publishing

The Tragedies of Seneca
By Seneca
Translated by Ella Isabel Harris
ISBN 10: 1-4209-4310-3
ISBN 13: 978-1-4209-4310-8

This edition copyright © 2011

Please visit *www.digireads.com*

PREFACE

The student of the English drama finds constant allusion to the influence of Seneca upon the development of English tragedy, but he seldom has such command of Latin as will enable him freely to study Seneca in the original; and should he seek a firsthand knowledge of the Senecan plays and of the nature of their influence, a difficulty is at once presented by the fact that for many years there has been no English translation available, the old translations of 1581 and 1702 having been long out of print. It was my own sense of the need of a sufficiently literal and otherwise adequate translation of the Roman tragedies, while I was engaged in the study and teaching of the later drama, that occasioned the present translation.

In undertaking the work, I was at once met by the question of form. Should the translation be in prose or verse? If in verse, should any attempt be made to render the lyric measures of the choruses? The first question was easily answered, since blank verse has long been accepted as a fairly adequate rendering of the rhythm found in the dramatic portions of the tragedies, and has besides the advantage of being the poetic form most acceptable to English ears for dramatic compositions. The second question was not so easily answered. Ideally the choruses should have been rendered in lyric form; and it was with some regret that the decision was reached that this task was beyond the translator's poetic power, and that blank verse must be retained throughout, or the whole marred by an unsuccessful attempt to transfer into the English the lyric measures of the Latin.

Leo's text is the basis of the present translation, and has on the whole been closely followed, though other readings have occasionally been preferred when the change commended itself to the translator's judgment. It has seemed best not to burden the translation with notes, since it is intended rather for the student of Seneca as an influence on modern drama than of Seneca for himself. For the same reason, any historical or critical introduction, such as those accompanying the volumes of Way's Euripides, has been omitted.

In my work of translation I have to acknowledge my indebtedness to Dr. Albert S. Cook of Yale University, to whom this book is dedicated, and who from its inception has helped me with encouragement and criticism: without his aid and that of my sister, Dr. M. Anstice Harris, of Elmira College, it is doubtful whether the work would have been completed. I have also to express my thanks to those who were good enough to criticize the translation from the point of view of the erudite Latinist: to Dr. Robert S. Radford, of Elmira College, for the examination of *The Trojans and Medea*; to Dr. Hugh M. Kingery, of Wabash College, for the examination of *The Mad Hercules* and *Hercules on Œta*; to Dr. Mortimer Lamson Earle, of Columbia University, for the examination of *Œdipus*; and to Dr. Charles Knapp, also of Columbia University, for the examination of *Phædra* and *Thyestes*. Dr. Charles G. Osgood and Dr. Robert K. Root, of Yale University, have also assisted me with criticism and suggestion.

Two of the plays, *Medea* and *The Trojans*, were published upon their completion by Messrs. Lamson, Wolffe and Company, the copyright later passing into the hands of Messrs. Houghton, Mifflin and Company, who, upon the approval of Professor Palmer of

Harvard University, brought these two plays out as the second in a series of translations inaugurated by Professor Palmer's translation of the *Antigone* of Sophocles. The translations of the other plays included in this volume are now published for the first time.

E. I. H.

The Cottage, Martinsburg, New York:
    July 18, 1904.

CONTENTS

PREFACE 3

MAD HERCULES 7

THE DAUGHTERS OF TROY 40

THE PHŒNICIAN WOMEN 69

MEDEA 86

PHÆDRA 111

ŒDIPUS 142

AGAMEMNON 168

THYESTES 194

HERCULES ON ŒTA 222

OCTAVIA 269

MAD HERCULES

DRAMATIS PERSONÆ

Hercules.
Amphitryon.
Lycus.
Theseus.
Juno.
Megara.
The Children of Hercules.
Chorus of Thebans.

Scene: *Thebes.*

MAD HERCULES

ACT I

Scene I

Juno, alone.

The Thunderer's sister, for that name alone
Is left me, widowed, I am driven forth
From heaven's heights and ever-faithless Jove;
Forced from the sky, have giv'n to concubines
My place, must dwell on earth while they hold heaven.
High in the zenith of the icy north
The star Arcturus guides the Argive fleet;
There where the day grows long with early spring,
The bull that bore away the Tyrian maid
Shines o'er the waves; there the Atlantides,
Aimlessly roaming, feared by ships at sea,
Rise, and Orion, threatening with his sword,
Affrights the gods; there golden Perseus gleams;
There shines the constellation of the twins,
The bright Tyndaridæ—for birth of these
The floating land stood still. And not alone
Do Bacchus and his mother dwell with gods:
Lest any place be free from infamy,
The sky must wear the Gnosian maiden's crown.
But these are ancient griefs that we lament;
How often has the single land of Thebes,
Harsh and detested, full of impious ones,
Made me a stepdame! Jupiter permits
Victorious Alcmena to ascend

25 The skies and hold my place; the promised star
May be the habitation of her son,—
The world at his creation lost a day,
And Phœbus, bidden hold his light concealed
In ocean, slowly lit the western sky.
30 My hatred will not lightly die away,
Enduring anger stirs my wrathful soul;
Anger shall banish peace, my bitter rage
Shall wage eternal war. What war remains?
All fearful things the hostile earth brings forth,
35 Whatever dreadful, savage, harsh, or wild,
Or pestilential thing the sea or air
Creates, has been subdued and overthrown;
He conquers, waxes strong through ills, enjoys
Our anger, into glory turns our hate,
40 And I, in setting all too heavy tasks,
Increase his glory, prove him son of Jove.
Where with near torch the sun at rise and set
Touches at east and west the Ethiop's land,
Fame of his valor spreads, and all the world
45 Proclaim him god; already monsters fail.
A lighter task it is for Hercules
To do my bidding than for me to bid,—
With joy he undertakes to do my will.
What harsh or tyrannous decree can harm
50 This dauntless youth? The things he feared and slew
He bears as weapons, panoplied he comes
With hydra's spoil and lion's. Lands enough
Do not lie open, he has burst apart
Th' infernal monarch's portals, brought to light
55 The wealth of Hades' conquered king; I saw,
Myself I saw him at his father's feet
Lay down the spoils he snatched from night, and death,
And vanquished Dis. Why leads he not in chains
Him who by lot was equal made with Jove?
60 Why rules he not in conquered Erebus?
Why lays he not the Stygian kingdom bare?
'Tis not enough that he returns again,
The federation of the world of shades
Is broken, from the lowest depths a path
65 Leads upward for return, the secret ways
Of cruel death are opened. Ah! and he,
Bold since he burst the prison of the shades,
Now triumphs over me and proudly leads
Through Argive towns the fierce black dog of hell.
70 I've seen the day at sight of Cerberus
Fail and the sun grow fearful, terror woke
In me as well, I saw the threefold head

Of Pluto's vanquished monster, and I feared
Because I had commanded. But too long
75 I linger, grieving over petty ills;
I needs must fear for heav'n, lest he who took
Hell captive should be master of the skies,
And snatch the scepter from his father's hand.
He seeks no quiet pathway to the stars,
80 As Bacchus did, through ruin he would make
His way, would govern in an empty world.
Tried strength he boasts, by bearing up the sky
Learned that he might have gained it by his might:
Upon his head he bore the world nor bent
85 Beneath the burden of its mighty mass;
Lightly upon the neck of Hercules
The vault of heaven rested, on his back
He bore th' unshaken stars, the sky, yea, bore
My weight down-pressing. To the realms above
90 He seeks a path. Up vengeance, up and strike—
Strike him who meditates such wondrous deeds;
Join battle with him, with thine own hand strive,
Why delegate thy wrath? Wild beasts may go,
Eurystheus, wearied, cease to give new toils.
95 Let loose the Titans who dared storm Jove's realm,
Lay wide the hollow peak of Sicily,
Let Doria, trembling underneath the blows,
Set free the buried monster—but him too
Alcides conquered; dost thou seek to find
100 Alcides' peer? There is none but himself.
Alcides now must war against himself.
From lowest depths of Tartarus called forth,
Come, Furies, from your flaming locks, spread fire,
And wield with cruel hand your serpent scourge.
105 Go, proud one, seek thyself a seat in heaven
And scorn thy human lot. Dost thou believe
The gloomy shades and Styx are left behind?
Here will I show thee hell; will call again
Discord from where she lies in deepest gloom,
110 Beyond the place of exile of the damned,
Imprisoned in a mighty mountain cave;
Will drag from lowest depths of Pluto's realm
Whatever there is left; come, loathsome crime,
Impiety that drinks the blood of kin,
115 Fierce frenzy, fury armed against itself—
Here, here, I find my ministers of wrath.
Come then, ye nimble servitors of Dis,
Wave high your glowing torch; Megæra, lead
Thy serpent-crowned and dreadful company;
120 Snatch from the funeral pyre with baleful hand

A huge and glowing brand; haste, seek revenge
For violated Styx; inflame his heart;
Impair his mind; so, fiercer than the fires
Of Ætna's forge he'll rage. But thus to move
125 Alcides, stung with bitter rage and crazed,
First, Juno, thou must be thyself insane.
Why rav'st thou not? Me first, me first o'erwhelm,
Ye sisters, overthrow my reason first,
That something worthy of a stepdame's wrath
130 I may at last attempt. My mind is changed,
With strength unbroken let him come again,
I pray, and see again, unharmed, his sons.
The day is come in which the hated strength
Of Hercules shall even make me glad.
135 Me he o'ercame, himself he shall o'ercome;
Returned from hell shall long again for death.
I glory now that he is son of Jove;
I will assist him, that with steady aim
His shafts may fly; my hand shall hold the bow,
140 Myself will guide the weapons of his rage,
And Hercules, when going forth to war,
Shall have at length my aid; the crime complete,
Then let his father to the skies admit
Those blood-stained hands. The war must be begun,
145 Day dawns and from his golden resting-place
Bright Titan comes.

Scene II

Chorus of Thebans.

The stars are shining only here and there
In heaven, their light is pale; the conquered night
Collects at day's return her wandering fires,
150 Their shining ranks are closed by Lucifer;
The icy constellation of the north,
The Wagoner calls back the light of day;
Already leading forth his azure steeds,
From Œta's summit Titan looks abroad;
155 Already dewy morning stains with red
The brake that Theban mænads gave to fame,
And Phœbus' sister flies—but to return.
Hard toil arises bringing back all cares
And opening every door.
160 The shepherd, having sent his herd afield,
Gathers the grass still sparkling with the rime;
The hornless bullock sports at liberty
About the open meadows, while the dams

Refill their empty udders; aimlessly
In the soft herbage roams the wanton kid;
The Thracian Philomela sits and sings
On topmost bough, exults to spread her wings
In the new sun, near to her querulous nest;
The general chorus of the happy birds
With mingled voices greets the day's return.
When by the breeze the loosened sails are filled,
The sailor trusts his vessel to the winds,
Uncertain of his life. The fisher leans
Above the broken cliff and baits his hook,
Or waits with ready hand to seize the prey—
Fie feels the trembling fish upon his line.
Such tranquil peace is theirs who stainless live
Content at home with little. Boundless hopes
Wander through cities, and unmeasured fears.
At the proud portals, the stern gates of kings,
One sleepless waits; one, covetous of gold,
And poor amid his hoarded wealth, collects
Unending riches; popular applause,
The common voice more fickle than the waves,
Makes one man proud, puffed up with empty air;
Another, basely making merchandise
Of brawling quarrels in the noisy courts,
Sells wrath and empty words for gold. Few know
Repose untroubled; mindful of swift time,
Few use the years that never will return.
While fate permits, live happy; life's swift course
Is quickly run, and by the winged hours
The circle of the flying years is turned;
The cruel sisters ply their wheel, nor turn
Backward their thread; uncertain of their lot,
The race of men are borne by rapid fates
To meet their death, and of their own will seek
The Stygian waves. Alcides, strong of heart,
Too soon thou soughtest out the mournful shade—
The Parcæ come at the appointed hour,
And none may linger when their voice commands,
None stay the fatal day; the urn receives
The fleeting generations. Fair renown
May bear one's name through many distant lands,
And garrulous rumor praise him, to the skies
Advance his glory; in his lofty car
Another rides; me let my native land
Conceal within a safe and unknown home.
He who loves quiet lives to gray old age;
The lowly fortunes of a humble hearth,
Although obscure, are certain. From the heights

He falls who boasts a bolder heart. But see,
Sad, with loose hair, leading her little ones,
Comes Megara; advancing slow with age,
215 Alcides' father follows.

ACT II

Scene I

Amphitryon, Megara, The Children.

Amphitryon. Great ruler of Olympus, Judge of earth,
Put to my heavy grief and misery
At length an end. For me untroubled light
Has never shined, one sorrow's end but marks
220 A step to future ills, straightway new foes
Are ready to be met. But late returned,
His happy home just reached, another foe
Must be subdued; he finds no quiet hour,
None free from toil save while he waits the word.
225 Unfriendly Juno, even from the first,
Pursued him; was his infancy exempt?
He conquered monsters ere he knew their name;
Twin serpents lifted up their crested heads—
The infant crept to meet them, with calm glance
230 And gentle, gazed upon their fiery eyes;
With face serene he grasped their twisted folds
And crushed with tender hand the swelling throats,
And so essayed the Hydra. In the chase
He took the swift wild beast of Mænalus,
235 Whose head was beautiful with branching gold;
The lion, terror of Nemea, groaned,
Crushed by the sinewy hand of Hercules;
The ghastly stables of the Thracian steeds—
Shall I recall them? Or the king who gave
240 Food to those horses? Or shall I recall
The wild Arcadian boar who from the heights
Of wooded Erymanthus caused the groves
Of Arcady to tremble? Or the bull,
The terror of a hundred Cretan towns?
245 Among the far Hesperian herds he slew
Tartessus' three-formed king and drove away
His booty from the farthest west—the slopes
Of Mount Cithæron pasture now those flocks.
When told to seek the land of summer suns
250 And torrid days, the sun-scorched realm, he rent
The hills apart; that barrier broken through,
He made a pathway for the raging seas.

Then the rich groves of the Hesperides
He rifled, from the sleepless dragon bore
255 The golden spoil; then Lerna's snake o'ercame
And forced it learn by fire the way to die.
The foul Stymphalian birds whose outspread wings
Obscured the sky, he sought among the clouds.
He was not conquered by the maiden queen
260 Who near Thermodon rules the virgin troops.
His hand, for every noble work prepared,
Shunned not the loathsome task of making clean
The stables of Augeas.—What avail
These labors? He is absent from a world
265 His hand preserved. The lands that claim him feel
The author of their peace is far away.
Crime, prosperous and happy, now is called
Virtue, the good must pay obedience
To evil doers, might makes right, and fear
270 Is stronger than the law. These eyes have seen
Children, avengers of their father's realm,
Slain by a savage hand, the king himself,
Last son of Cadmus' noble house, I saw
Slain, and the crown that decked his royal head
275 Torn from him. Who has tears enough for Thebes?
Land that abounds in gods, what master now
Is it that makes thee fear? This gracious land,
Out of the fertile bosom of whose fields
The new-born soldiery with drawn swords sprang,
280 Whose walls Jove's son, Amphion, built,—he brought
The stones together by his tuneful songs;
Into whose city from the heavens came,
Not once alone, the father of the gods;
Which has received and borne, and may again
285 (May it not be unlawful so to speak)
Bear gods; this land beneath the shameful yoke
Of tyrants now is bent. O Cadmus' race,
Ophion's hapless seed, how fall'n ye are.
Ye fear a craven exile, one who comes,
290 Shorn of his land, and yet a scourge to ours;
And he who followed up the criminal
By land and sea, whose arm was strong to break
The cruel scepter's might, is now afar
In servitude and bears himself the yoke,
295 While Thebes, the land of Hercules, is ruled
By exiled Lycus. But not long he rules,
Alcides will return and find revenge;
Will suddenly arise to upper day;
Will find or make a path. Return, I pray,
300 Unharmed, a conqueror to thy native Thebes.

Megara. Come forth, my husband, banish with thy hand
The scattered darkness. If no homeward way
Remains and if for thee the road is closed,
Yet break through earth and come, and with thee bring
305 Whate'er black night keeps hid. As thou hast stood
And through the sundered mountains made a way
For ocean's flood, when thy resistless might
Laid open riven Tempe—here and there
The mountain parted yielding to thy breast,
310 And through its broken banks Thessalia's stream
Rushed onward in new channels—seeking thus
Thy parents, children, fatherland, break forth
And with thee bring the buried past; restore
Whatever eager time has borne away
315 In the swift passage of the many years.
Drive forth the people who, forgetting all,
Now fear the light; unworthy spoils are thine,
If nought but what was ordered thou shouldst bring.
Too long I chatter, knowing not our fate.
320 When comes the day that I may once again
Embrace thee, clasp thy hand, nor make complaint
Of thy forgetfulness and slow return?
O ruler of the gods, to thee shall fall
A hundred untamed bulls; to thee be paid,
325 Grain-giver, secret rites, to thee shall wave
The torches in Eleusis' silent groves;
Then shall I deem my brother lives again,
My father flourishes and holds his throne.
If thou art stayed by greater strength than thine,
330 Thee would we follow. Save by thy return
Or drag us with thee—thou wilt drag us down,
Nor any god lift up the weak again.
    Amphitryon. O sharer of our blood, with constancy
Keeping thy faith to great-souled Hercules,
335 Guarding his sons, take courage, have good hope!
He will return, and greater than before
As hitherto he came from easy tasks.
    Megara. The things the wretched wish too eagerly,
They willingly believe.
    Amphitryon. More oft they deem
340 That trouble endless which too much they fear,
And he who fears looks ever for the worst.
    Megara. Buried, submerged, beneath the world shut in,
What pathway has he to the upper day?
    Amphitryon. The same he had when through the arid plain,
345 The sands uncertain, and the stormy sea,
And gulfs that twice withdrew and twice returned,
He found a way when, taken unawares,

He ran aground on Syrtes' shoals and left
His stranded ships and crossed the sea on foot.
350   *Megara.* Unequal fortune rarely spares great worth;
None can with safety long expose himself
To frequent dangers; he who oft escapes
At last must meet misfortune. But behold,
Harsh Lycus comes, with threatening face, and mien
355 Like to his spirit; in his alien hand
He holds the scepter which that hand usurped.

Scene II

Amphitryon, Lycus and his Followers, Megara, The Children.

    Lycus. As king, I hold the rich domain of Thebes,
All lands the deep-soiled Phocian stretches bound,
All that Ismenus waters, and whate'er
360 Cithæron from her lofty summit sees.
Not by the land's old laws do I possess
My home, an idle heir; no noble blood
Nor far-famed race of royal name is mine,
But splendid valor. He who boasts his race
365 Boasts glory not his own. Yet who usurps
A scepter holds it in a trembling hand;
Safety is in the sword alone, it guards
That which is thine against the people's will.
A ruler who is king in alien lands
370 Scarce finds his throne secure. One thing there is
Can make our rule enduring: marriage made
With royal Megara, our newer line
May take its color from her royal race.
Nor do I deem that she will scorn our suit,
375 Yet should she, powerless yet firm, refuse,
The house of Hercules shall be destroyed.
What though the deed cause hatred and reproach
Among the people? He who rules needs first
The strength to bear a people's hate unmoved.
380 Chance gives the opportunity, make trial!
For see she stands, in mourning garments veiled,
Beside the altars of the guardian gods,
While near her Hercules' true father waits.
    Megara. [*Aside*] Scourge and destroyer of our royal race,
385 What unknown evil dost thou now prepare?
    Lycus. O thou who bearest an illustrious name,
Kingly of lineage, for a moment hear
With patient kindliness my words. If hate
Must live eternal in the human heart,

If anger once conceived ne'er leaves the breast,
If happy and unhappy must alike
Bear arms, eternal wars would ruin all;
The devastated fields would lie untilled;
And homes be burned, and nations find a grave
Beneath the ashes. 'Tis expedient
For conquerors to wish for peace restored,
'Tis needful for the conquered:—share our realm,
Accept my hand. With sternly fixed regard,
Why silent stand?

    Megara. And shall I touch the hand
My parents' blood has stained, the hand that slew
My brothers? Sooner will the sun go down
Behind the eastern sky, or rise again
From out the west, and sooner snow and fire
Make peaceful compact; sooner Scylla join
Sicilia and Ausonia; sooner far
Euripus with its swiftly changing tides
Shall wash with listless waves Euboea's shores.
'Tis thou hast taken from me father, realm,
My brothers, home, and country; what remains?
One thing remains more dear than home or realm,
Father or brothers—'tis my hate of thee.
It grieves me that I share it with the land,
Measured by hers, how small a thing is mine.
Rule arrogantly, govern with proud heart,
Th' avenging god pursues the proud man's steps.
I know the Theban realm, what need to speak
Of mothers who have dared and suffered crimes;
Of double guilt, of him who mingled names
Of husband, son and father? Or to name
The brothers' hostile camp, their funeral pyres?
The haughty mother, child of Tantalus,
By sorrows burdened, stands a mournful stone
In Phrygian Sipylos, Cadmus still,
Lifting his head dreadful with serpents' crests,
Goes fleeing through Illyria's realm and leaves
The long trail of his dragging body's length.
Such precedents are thine, bear rule at will,
If but our realm's accustomed fate is thine.

    Lycus. Thou ravest, cease thy savage words, and learn
From thy Alcides how thou shouldst obey
A king's command. Though my victorious hand
Wield here a captured sceptre, though I rule
The lands my arms have conquered without fear
Of law, yet briefly in my own defence
I'd speak. In bloody war thy father died,
Thy brother fell? No bounds are kept by war,

Nor may the drawn sword's fury be restrained
Nor lightly tempered; war delights in blood.
He for his kingdom fought, while we were drawn
440 By base desire? We ask a war's results
And not its cause. But let remembrance die.
When arms are by the victor laid aside
'Tis meet the vanquished also bury hate.
We would not have thee do us reverence
445 With bended knee as sovereign; we rejoice
That with such great-souled courage thou hast borne
Thy ruin; thou art worthy of a king:
Be thou my queen.
    Megara. Throughout my fainting limbs
An icy shudder runs, what sinful words
450 Assail my ears? I was not terrified
When peace was broken and the crash of war
Rang out around the city, that I bore
Fearless, but shudder at this marriage bed.
I feel myself a captive now indeed.
455 Let chains weigh down my limbs, let tardy death
Be brought by creeping famine, nought avails
To overcome my firm fidelity—
Alcides, I will still be thine in death.
    Lycus. A husband plunged in Hades gives thee strength?
460   *Megara.* He went to hell that he might compass heaven.
    Lycus. The burden of the earth's mass weighs him down.
    Megara. No weight can weigh down him who bore the skies.
    Lycus. I will compel thee.
    Megara. Whom thou canst compel,
Has not yet learned to die.
    Lycus. What princely gift
465 Can equal the new bridal I would give?
    Megara. Thy death or mine.
    Lycus. Then die, demented one.
    Megara. I haste to meet my husband.
    Lycus. Is a slave
Preferred by thee before our royal throne?
    Megara. How many kings that slave has brought to death!
470 *Lycus.* Why serves he then a king? why bears the yoke?
    Megara. If tyranny were not, would valor be?
    Lycus. To conquer beasts and monsters then, thou think'st,
Is valorous?
    Megara. To conquer what all fear,
Is valorous.
    Lycus. The shades of Tartarus
475 Press heavy on the boaster.
    Megara. None have found
The path from earth to heav'n an easy road.

Lycus. What father makes him hope a home in heaven?
Amphitryon. Unhappy wife of Hercules, be still;
'Tis mine to name the father and the race
Of great Alcides. Since that mighty man's
Illustrious deeds, since by his hand he made
Peace in whatever land sees Titan's rise
Or setting, since the gods were kept from harm,
And Phlegra reddened by the giant's blood,
Is not his father yet made manifest?
We have pretended Jove? Believe the hate
Of Juno.
Lycus. Why dost thou profane great Jove?
The race of mortals cannot wed with gods.
Amphitryon. Yet such the origin of many gods.
Lycus. Had they been slaves before they grew to gods?
Amphitryon. The Delian shepherded Admetus' sheep.
Lycus. But wandered not an exile through all lands.
Amphitryon. Upon a wandering island was he born,
His mother's self a wandering fugitive.
Lycus. Did beasts or monsters make Apollo fear?
Amphitryon. The dragon stained Apollo's earliest shafts.
Lycus. Thou knowest not the ills Alcides bore
While yet an infant?
Amphitryon. From his mother's womb
By lightning torn, young Bacchus later stood
Beside his father, thunder-bearing Jove;
And did not he who guides the moving stars
And makes the clouds to tremble lie concealed,
A child, within a cave on Ida's cliff?
Such high nativity costs heavy price,
And to be born of gods brings countless ills.
Lycus. Know, whom thou seest wretched is but man.
Amphitryon. Call not him wretched whom thou seest brave.
Lycus. And can we call him brave who put aside
His lion's skin and club to please a girl?
Who shone in vestments of Sidonian dye?
Shall we call brave the man whose bristling hair
Dripped nard, whose hands so famed for warlike deeds
Struck gentle music from the tambourine?
Who wreathed his warlike forehead with strange crowns?
Amphitryon. Young Bacchus did not blush to let his hair
Flow loose and in disorder, did not blush
To move with step unsteady, while his robe,
Bright with barbaric gold, behind him trailed.
The brave refresh themselves from heavy toil.
Lycus. Eurytus' ruined house gives proof of this,
And bands of maidens sacrificed like sheep—
No Juno, no Eurystheus ordered this,

These labors are his own.
    Amphitryon. Thou knowest not all:
It was indeed his work that Eryx fell,
525 By his own gauntlets slain, and that to him
The Libyan Antæus soon was joined;
That altars dripping blood of slaughtered guests
Drank, too, Busiris' blood so justly due;
These are Alcides' labors, 'twas his work
530 That Cycnus, whom no sword might wound or slay,
Was forced though free from wounds to suffer death:
The triple monster, Geryon, by his hand
Was conquered; thou shalt share the fate of these,
Though they ne'er sinned against the marriage bed.
535   *Lycus.* Whate'er for Jove is lawful is for kings
As lawful; thou hast given Jove a wife,
Thou shalt give to the king. This truth, not new,
With thee for teacher, let thy son's wife learn:
Her husband willing even, she may take
540 A better husband. But if she refuse
With steadfastness the proffered marriage torch,
She shall be forced to bear me noble seed.
    Megara. O shades of Creon, O ye household gods
Of Labdacus, O impious marriage torch
545 Of Œdipus, give ye the wonted fate
To such a marriage! O ye bloody wives
Of King Ægyptus' sons, be present now!
Of the Danaïdes one failed to act,
Let me fill up the measure of their crimes,
550   *Lycus.* Since still unbendingly thou dost refuse
Our offered marriage, threatenest thy king,
Thou shalt be made to feel a scepter's power.
Embrace the altars—no divinity
Shall snatch thee from me, not if Hercules
555 Could come, a victor, through the riven earth.
[*To his followers*] Heap wood and let the temples burn and fall
On those who suppliant seek them, let one pyre
Consume both wife and children with its flames.
    Amphitryon. The father of Alcides asks of thee
560 One favor which beseems me well to ask:
Let me be first to die.
    Lycus. The king who bids
That all should suffer punishment of death
Has yet to learn to tyrannize; seek out
Another vengeance, let the wretched live,
565 The happy die. While grow the funeral pyres
With high-heaped wood, I will, with votive gifts,
Go honor him who rules the angry seas.
    Amphitryon. O thou of gods most strong, of heavenly powers

Ruler and king, whose thunder makes men fear,
570 Restrain the cruel king's ungodly hand.
Why thus in vain entreat the gods? O son,
Hear me in whatsoever place thou art!
Why groans the earth? Why tremble suddenly
The temples? We are heard. It is, it is
575 The sounding step of Hercules.

Scene III

Chorus.

O Fortune, envious ever of the brave,
How ill thou meetest recompense to deed!
Eurystheus rules in rest and quietness;—
Alcmena's son, whose hand sustained the skies,
580 Must war with many monsters: he cut off
The Hydra's fruitful neck; and, when to sleep
The dragon guardian of the precious fruit
Had yielded up his ever-watchful eyes,
He bore from the beguiled Hesperides
585 The golden apples; he has visited
The wandering Scythians in their changing homes,
And peoples, dwellers in their native lands;
His foot has trod the frozen straits and seas
Silent on silent shores—there waves rise not
590 On the hard waters, for where ships have moved
With all sail set, a solid path is trod
By dwellers in Sarmatia, and the sea
That changes with the ever-changing year
Bears lightly sometimes horses, sometimes ships.
595 He overcame the maiden queen who leads
The virgin clans to war, who girds her loins
With golden baldrick; from her body took
Rich spoil, the armor of her snowy breast;—
She paid him honor on her bended knee.
600 By what hope driven headlong down to hell,
Daring to tread the way without return,
Saw'st thou Sicilian Proserpina's realm
There neither northern blasts nor western winds
Blow up the waters into swelling waves;
605 The shining of the twin Tyndarides
Brings there to timorous sailors no relief;
The sea lies languid there with gloomy depths,
And when with hungry teeth pale death bears down
The countless people to the land of shades,
610 One rower for so many is enough.
Would thou mightst bind the laws of the harsh Styx,

The distaff of the fates that turns not back!
When thou on Nestor's Pylos madest war,
The king who rules those many peoples fought
₆₁₅ With thee, against thee in his baleful hand
Advanced his triple-pointed spear—he fled
At but a wound, death's ruler feared to die.
Seize with strong hand thy fate, let in the light
To Hades' mournful depths, to upper day
₆₂₀ Through pathless stretches force an easy road.
With songs and supplications, Orpheus once
Prevailed upon the cruel king of shades:
He sought his wife Eurydice, the art
That moved birds, woods, and rocks, delayed the streams,
₆₂₅ And caused the beasts to listen, calmed hell's self
With unaccustomed music, and sweet sound
Reechoed clearly through the silent land.
The Thracian women mourned Eurydice,
And churlish gods wept unaccustomed tears,
₆₃₀ The stern-browed judges, who relentlessly
Arraign the criminal and bring to light
Old crimes, sat weeping for Eurydice,
Until at length the arbiter of death
Said: 'We are conquered, rise to upper day,
₆₃₅ I make but one condition; thou, O wife,
Follow thy husband; look not thou behind
To see thy wife, O husband, till thou seest
The sky and day, and gates of Tænarus
Are reached.' But true love cannot brook delay,
₆₄₀ By hasting to possess, he lost the gift.
The castle that was conquered by a song,
That castle strength can conquer.

ACT III

Scene I

Hercules, Theseus.

Hercules. O thou who governest the gracious light,
Heaven's ornament; who in thy flying car,
₆₄₅ Running alternate courses, liftest up
Thy brilliant head above the world, forgive,
Phœbus, forgive, if aught thou seest amiss;
Commanded so to do, I bring to light
The secrets of the world. Thou, heaven's judge
₆₅₀ And father, hide behind thy thunderbolt
Thy face. O thou whose scepter rules the sea,
Seek now its depths. Ye gods who from the skies

Look down on earth, avert your glances now.
Fearing pollution from the vision strange,
655 Look heavenward, shun so ominous a sight;
These two alone may look upon the crime:
She who commanded, he who brought to pass.
Earth offers space too small for Juno's hate
To find my labor and my chastisement.
660 I saw the kingdom to the sun unknown,
And inaccessible to all, the realm
Obscure, where Pluto reigns; and, so fate willed,
Subdued it. Chaos of eternal night,
And whatsoe'er is worse than night, I saw,—
665 The melancholy gods and death itself.
Death scorned, I come again, what more remains?
Hell I have seen and shown; if aught is left,
Give other labors. Long thou leavest my hands
Idle. What wouldst thou should be overcome?
670 But why does hostile soldiery surround
The temple? Why does fear of arms beset
The sacred portals?

Scene II

Hercules, Theseus, Amphitryon, Megara, The Children.

Amphitryon. Does hope deceive my sight, or does he come
Earth's vanquisher, the glory of the Greeks?
675 Leaves he the gloomy, sad, and silent realm?
Is this my son? My limbs are numb with joy!
O son, the sure though tardy help of Thebes,
Do I indeed embrace thee, once again
Come forth to upper air? Or does a shade
680 Beguile me? Is it thou? I recognize
Thy breast, thy shoulders, and thy noble hands,
Thy heavy club!
Hercules. My father, whence this woe?
These mourning garments of my wife? Whence comes
This doleful raiment of my sons? What loss
Weighs down our house?
685 *Amphitryon.* The father of thy wife
Is dead, and Lycus now usurps the throne,
Death seeks thy sons, thy father, and thy wife.
Hercules. Ungrateful land, did no one come to aid
The house of Hercules? The world I saved
690 Looked on at such a crime? Why waste the day
In mourning? Slay the foe! I can endure
This stain—Alcides' latest foe shall be
This Lycus! Theseus, friend, I go to drink

His hostile blood; remain thou here with these,
695 Lest sudden violence should threaten them.
The battle calls me; father, wife, defer
Your loved embraces; Lycus shall announce
To Dis that I have safely come again.

Scene III

Theseus, Amphitryon, Megara, The Children.

Theseus. Put by thy grief, O queen, and thou who seest
700 Thy son returned, restrain thy falling tears;
Lycus shall pay the debt to Creon due—
Shall pay? Nay pays.—Too slow the words, has paid!
  Amphitryon. Whatever favoring god will hear our prayer,
Bring now assistance to our fallen house.
705 O great-souled comrade of my mighty son,
His deeds of valor tell; what weary path
Led downward to the gloomy land of shades,
And how the Tartarean dog has borne
His heavy chains.
  Theseus. Thou bidst me call to mind
710 Those deeds that make me, though secure, afraid.
I hardly yet feel certain of my life;
Light blinds my sight, my weakened eyes scarce bear
The unaccustomed day.
  Amphitryon. O Theseus, quench
Whate'er of fear still lingers in thy heart,
715 Rob not thyself of labor's richest fruit;
Most sweet it is to call to mind those things
Most hardly suffered. Tell me thy dread fate.
  Theseus. Ye, I invoke, ye gods who rule the world,
And thee, the ruler of the realm of shades,
720 And thee whom, snatched from Enna, all in vain
Thy mother sought. O grant that I may speak
Truly of hidden things concealed in earth.
A well-known mountain lifts from Sparta's plains.
Its summits, where the heavy-wooded heights
725 Of Tænarus stretch downward to the sea;
Here lies the entrance to the hated home
Of Dis, the great cliff yawns, and open lies
With gaping jaws, the terrible abyss;
Through caverns limitless it shows to all
730 A pathway broad. At first not dark with shade—
A slender gleam from sunlight left behind,
A doubtful brightness from the troubled day,
Falls gently inward and deceives the eye—
So shines the light of dawn or failing day

735 With night commingled; here the boundless fields
Of empty space begin to open out,
Toward which haste ever all the human race.
Nor is the journey hard, the path itself
Leads on. As many times the tide impels
740 Unwilling ships, so here the flying air
And greedy chaos urge advance; retreat
Scarce ever do the constant shades permit.
Within the bosom of the vast abyss
Unruffled Lethe glides with placid shoals
745 And banishes all care; the languid stream
Winds ever as Meander's sluggish waves
Flow onward, or recede, or stand in doubt
Whether to seek their source or seek the sea.
Here lies the slow Cocytus' ugly fen,
750 Here the sad owl laments, the vulture here,
Here sounds the horned owl's ill-fated cry,
The gloomy foliage bristles with dark leaves;
Under the overhanging yew dull Sleep
Dwells, and sad Hunger lies with sickly jaws,
755 And tardy Shame hides here her conscious face;
Alarm, and Fear, and dark and crushing Grief,
Black Sorrow, trembling Sickness, steel-girt War,
Follow, and, hidden at the end of all,
Age with his staff assists his trembling steps.
760   *Amphitryon.* And is no fruitful land of Ceres there, or Bacchus?
    Theseus. There no happy fields grow green,
No ripe grain trembles in the gentle breeze,
No trees stretch out their boughs weighed down with fruit,
The sterile wastes of those sad depths are drear,
765 Eternally untilled that loathsome land;
The air is moveless, black night ever broods
Above a moveless world; the whole is dark
With mourning, and the land of Death is worse
Than Death himself.
    Amphitryon. And what of him who reigns
770 Within the gloomy place? Upon what seat
Sits he enthroned to give his people laws?
    Theseus. In an obscure recess of Tartarus
There lies a plain, dense vapors shut it in
With heavy gloom; here flow from single source
775 Two rivers; one is calm, its silent flood
Bears down the sacred waters of the Styx,
By this the gods make oath; but Acheron
Is hurried on with tumult wild and loud,
And in its course it carries rocks away,
780 Here is no path for backward-turning boats.
This double stream surrounds the royal seat

Of Dis, a darksome wood conceals his home.
The tyrant's threshold is a mighty cave;
Here lies the path the shades must take, and here
His kingdom's gates. An open place is here,
Where Pluto sits in cruel majesty
And to the new-come souls points out the way;
His brow is dark, but shows a kingliness
Like that of Jove, his brother, and declares
His noble race; his face is that of Jove,
But when he thunders. Of the fearful realm
The ruler is himself the greater part,
His glance gives fear to those whom others fear.
    Amphitryon. And is it true that in the lower world
A tardy justice shall be measured out,
That guilty men shall pay the penalty
They owe for crimes forgotten by themselves?
Who is this judge of truth, this arbiter
Of justice?
    Theseus. One inquisitor alone
Sits not to measure from that lofty seat
Late justice to the trembling criminal.
Minos of Gnosus sits in judgment there,
And Rhadamanthus, and that one whose son
Was Thetis' husband. Whatsoever wrong
A man has done he suffers; here the crime
Finds out its author, and the criminal
Is overtaken by his own ill deeds.
I saw fierce kings in prison, saw the backs
Of helpless tyrants by plebeians torn.
Who greatly governs, and, though lord of life,
Preserves his hands unstained, and mildly holds
A bloodless empire, nor puts men to death,
He, having lived a long and blessed life,
Seeks heaven, or, happy in the happy groves
Of fair Elysium, shall again be judge.
Ye who are kings abstain from human blood,
Your crimes, but greater, shall return on you.
    Amphitryon. And is a place ordained where guilty men
Are prisoned, where, as rumor says, keen pain
Of ceaseless fetters punishes base souls?
    Theseus. Ixion turns upon his flying wheel;
A stone weighs down the neck of Sisyphus;
In mid stream Tantalus, dry-lipped, pursues
The waves—the river reaches to his chin
And gives him hope, although so oft deceived,—
Upon his lips the water perishes,
Fruit fails him; Tityos affords a feast
Forever to the vultures, and in vain

The sad Danaïdes lift up full urns;
830 The impious Cadmean women raging roam,
And Phineas ever from his food must keep
The eager Harpies.
    Amphitryon. Of my son's brave fight
Tell me. Does he bring back a willing gift,
Or spoils of war?
    Theseus. A savage cliff o'erhangs
835 The stagnant shallows, where the waves move not,
And where the lazy waters ever sleep;
An old man hideous in mien and dress
Waits here and ferries o'er the silent stream
The trembling shades; his unkempt beard hangs low,
840 His filthy robe is gathered in a knot,
His hollow cheeks are soiled; the ferryman
With his long pole himself propels the boat;
Steering the vessel emptied of its freight
Shoreward, he seeks again the waiting shades;
845 The throng receding, Hercules demands
A way; hard Charon cries: 'Where goest thou,
Bold one? Thy swift feet stay.' Alcmena's son
Staid not, he seized the pole, and overcame
The ferryman, and stepped into the boat;
850 The skiff, for many ample, under one
Succumbed and settling heavily, each side
The reeling vessel drank the Lethe's waves.
Then conquered monsters fear, the Centaur grim,
The Lapithæ, inflamed with war and wine;
855 And Lerna's Hydra hides its fruitful heads
And seeks the Stygian fen's remotest part.
Then came to view the home of hungry Dis,
The Stygian dog affrights the manes here,
Lifts up with dreadful noise his threefold neck,
860 And guards the realm; snakes lick his head, his hair
Is bristling vipers, and a hissing snake
Forms his long tail, his rage is as his form.
He hears the sound of steps, his shaggy hair
Of waving adders stands erect, with ears
865 Lifted, he listens to the sound, no steps
But those of shades his ears are wont to catch.
As Jove's son nearer comes, within the cave
The dog sits doubtful and not unafraid,
Then with his baying wild he terrifies
870 The silent place, the threatening serpents hiss,
The dreadful clangor of his awful voice
Sent forth from triple mouths makes happy shades
To tremble. From his shoulder taking then
The lion's skin, the hero shields himself

875   With this protection from the hissing mouths;
     In his victorious hand his mighty club
     He lifts, now here, now there, with ceaseless blows
     He whirls it, strikes again; the conquered dog
     Gives o'er his threats and, wearied, hangs his heads,
880   And leaves the whole wide cavern free. Each lord
     Sitting upon his throne is filled with fear,
     And bids Alcides lead away the dog.
     Me, too, at his request they give to him.
     Then patting with his hand the monster's necks,
885   He binds him with an adamantine chain.
     The dog, that dark realm's watchful guard, forgets
     His wonted fierceness, droops his timorous ears,
     And owns a master, quietly endures
     To be led forth, and with submissive mien
890   Obeys, and strikes his flanks with serpent tail.
     But when he reached the mouth of Tænarus
     And the strange glow of unaccustomed light
     Upon his eyelids shone, the conquered one
     Resumed his former wrath and shook his chains
895   Raging; he almost dragged his victor back,
     And drew him down, and forced him to the ground.
     Alcides sought my aid, with doubled strength
     We two bore up to earth the angry dog,
     That struggled in an unavailing war.
900   But when he saw the day, and gazed upon
     The sunlight's clear expanse, he closed his eyes,
     Shut out the hated sun, and backward turned,
     Bent earthward his three necks, then hid his head
     Within Alcides' shadow. But there comes,
905   With many shouts, a throng of citizens,
     They wear the laurel on their brows and sing
     The praises of most glorious Hercules.

Scene IV

Chorus of Thebans.

     Eurystheus, born too soon into the world,
     Commanded Hercules to pierce earth's depths—
910   The number of his labors lacked alone
     This deed: to spoil the dark realm's king. He dared
     To enter those black portals where the path
     Leads downward to the distant land of shades,
     A gloomy way with dreadful forests dark,
915   But filled with thronging people. As the crowd
     Pass through the city eager for the games
     At the new theater; as they rush to see

Elean Jove when the fifth summer brings
The sacred feast; as when the time returns
₉₂₀ Of lengthening nights, and, coveting sweet sleep,
The balance holds the sun's car in the sea,
The people haste to Ceres' sacred rites,
And priests of Athens from the city pass
To render to the goddess of the night
₉₂₅ Worship and honor, so the silent throng
Move onward through the plain; some slow with age,
And sad and sated with their length of days;
Some, younger, seem to hither come in haste,
Virgins who have not known the marriage yoke,
₉₃₀ And youths with flowing hair, and little ones
Who scarcely yet can lisp their mother's name,—
To these is given to carry through the gloom
Light, that they less may fear; all others walk
In darkness, sadly. How then feels the soul
₉₃₅ When light is gone and one must know himself
Buried beneath the world's weight? Chaos harsh,
Base shadows, the dun color of the night,
Reign there, the leisure of a silent world,
And empty gloom.
₉₄₀ May old age bear us late to that dark land,
Too late none ever found the place from whence,
When found, none ever may return again.
What profit then to hasten cruel fate?
The wide earth's restless throngs shall seek the shades
₉₄₅ And sail the still Cocytus; all things move,
O Death, from east and west toward thee alone;
Oh, come not! Let us be prepared for thee!
Though late thou comest, yet ourselves we haste,
The very hour of birth begin to die.
₉₅₀   Thebes' happy day has come; O grateful ones,
Before the altars kneel, slay victims meet,
Ye men and maids the happy chorus join,
And let the rich earth from the ploughshare rest.
Peace by the hand of Hercules is made
₉₅₅ Between Aurora's land and Hesperus'
And that where shadows are not, where the sun
Moves ever in the zenith.
Alcides' hand has conquered every land
That Thetis waters with her wide waves' sweep.
₉₆₀ The streams of Tartarus are overpassed,
The lower world subdued, and he returns.
No fear remains, nought lies beyond that land.
Priests, crown your heads with holy poplar wreaths.

ACT IV

Scene I

Hercules, Theseus, Amphitryon, Megara, The Children.

    Hercules. [*Coming from the palace of Lycus.*]
Felled by my conquering hand lies Lycus, dead;
965 Whatever comrades have in life been his
Shall be the tyrant's comrades still in death.
Victorious now, I pay the sacred rites
To thee, my father, and the holy gods,
And heap the altars with the victims slain.
970 To thee, my help and stay, I make my prayers,
O warlike Pallas, in whose stern left hand
The ægis threatens, turning men to stone.
Lord of Lycurgus and the crimson sea,
Be present, bearing in thy hand the spear
975 Wound with green vines! And ye, twin deities,
Phœbus and Phœbus' sister,—she more skilled
In archery, as he in melody!
And thou my brother, whatsoever one
Inhabits heaven, not of Juno born!
980 Drive hither well-fed herds; the Indian spice
And odorous woods from Araby heap high
Upon the altars, let rich perfumes rise.
The poplar binds our hair, crown thou thyself,
O Theseus, with thy country's olive leaves.
985 O Thunderer, we lift our hands to thee!
Thebes' builders, and grim Zethus' wooded caves,
And Dirce's noble fountain, and the home
Of Tyre's king who came as pilgrim here,
Protect. [*To the servants.*] Put incense now upon the flame.
990   *Amphitryon.* First, son, make clean thy hands that drip with blood
Of slaughtered foes.
    Hercules. O would that I might pour
Libations to the gods of that loathed blood!
No liquor more acceptable could wet
The altars; hardly might one sacrifice
995 To Jove a worthier victim or more rich
Than this, an evil king.
    Amphitryon. Lift up thy voice
And pray thy father that he end at last
Thy labors, to the wearied give repose.
    Hercules. Prayers worthy of myself and Jove I make.
1000 The sky and earth and ocean keep their place,
Unhindered in their course th' eternal stars

Move onward, peace profound be over all;
For tillage only be the iron used,
The sword be sheathed, no storm disturb the sea,
1005 No lightning from an angry Jove flash forth,
No river swollen with the winter's snows
Lay bare the fields. All poisons die, no plant
With noxious juice be swelled, no tyrant harsh
Rule. If there yet lurk anywhere a crime,
1010 Let it make haste; if any monster wait,
Let it be mine. But what has come to pass?
The morn is darkened, Phœbus moves obscured,
Although the sky is cloudless; who is this
Who makes the day flee backward to its rise?
1015 Whence comes it night's black head is lifted up,
And stars are shining in the midday sky?
See where in heaven our earliest labor shines,
He flames with wrath, is ready to attack—
Some constellation he will seize, he stands
1020 Threatening and from his mouth he belches flame.
Whatever stars the melancholy fall
Or frozen winter in her chilly course
Brings back, he covers in a single bound,
Seeking the bull, the bringer of the spring,
Whose neck he breaks.
1025   *Amphitryon.* What sudden ill is this?
My son, why wanders so thy angry glance?
Why scan with troubled eyes the faithless heavens?
     Hercules. The conquered earth and swelling floods give place,
Th' infernal realms have felt our force, the sky
1030 Is free—a labor worthy Hercules.
To the high spaces of the heavenly world
I fly, my father promises a star.—
What if he now refuse? Earth has not room
For Hercules and gives him back at length
1035 To the celestial ones. Behold, in vain
The entire number of the gods invites
And opens wide the doors of heaven, if one
Refuse me entrance. Wilt thou then unbar
The gates of heaven for me? Or shall I drag
1040 The portals of the stubborn world away?
Why hesitate? Resistless, I will loose
The chains of Saturn and against the might
Of an unduteous father will set free
That father's father; I will lead to war
1045 The raging Titans, rocks and trees I'll bring,
The Centaur's mountain in my right hand seize,
By hill on hill will make a path to heaven;
Already on his Pelion Chiron sees

Great Ossa piled, Olympus placed above
1050 Shall make a third step and shall reach the sky,
Or I will hurl it there.
    Amphitryon. Be far the thought!
A little calm thy great heart's forceful rage.
    Hercules. Behold the dreaded giants come in arms,
And Tityos leaves the shades; how near the stars
1055 He stands with empty, lacerated breast;
Cithæron totters, high Pallene shakes,
And Tempe fails, One tears up Pindus' ridge,
One seizes Œta, horribly he threats.
The flaming furies smite with sounding lash,
1060 More near, more near they press their burning torch
Into my face, and wild Tisiphone,
Her head encircled with its serpent crown,
Fills up with torch opposed the empty door
Behind the ravished dog. [*He sees his children.*]
    But see where lurk
1065 The offspring of the hostile king, base seed
Of Lycus; to your hated father now
This right hand gives you back; swift shaft, fly forth,
So are Herculean weapons fitly used.
    Amphitryon. Where blindly strikes his rage? His mighty bow
1070 Is bent, the quiver opened, and the shaft
Flies singing forth, it passes through the neck
And leaves the wound. [*Megara flies with the other child.*]
    Hercules. From every hiding place
I'll search the other out. Why make delay?
A greater war is mine: to overthrow
1075 Mycene, that by my hand smitten down
The Cyclops' rocks may fall. Thither I go,
To break the doors and tear away the posts,
The stricken house shall fall. It open lies,
I see the wicked father's son concealed.
1080   *Amphitryon.* Lo, stretching toward his knees beseeching hands,
The child with piteous voice entreats,—base crime,
Of aspect sad and awful. His right hand
Seizes the kneeling child and whirls him round
Six times, then hurls him far, the child's head strikes,
1085 The roof is moistened with the scattered brains.
Ill-fated Megara, like one insane,
To hiding flies, protecting on her breast
Her youngest born.
    Hercules. Though thou shouldst fly to seek
The bosom of the Thunderer, this hand
Would bear thee thence.
1090   *Amphitryon.* [*To Megara.*] Oh whither, wretched one?
What hiding dost thou seek? No place is safe

From angry Hercules. Embrace his knees,
With soft entreaty strive to soothe his wrath.
    Megara. Spare, husband, spare, I pray thee! Recognize
1095 Thy Megara! This child reflects thy form
And features, see his little hands stretched forth?
    Hercules. I have thee, stepdame; give me my revenge!
From thy loathed yoke free troubled Jove; but first,
Before the mother, slay the wretched child.
1100   *Megara.* What wouldst thou, wilt thou slay thy son?
    Amphitryon. The child
Before his father's glance is terrified,
Fear slays him and he dies without a wound;
Now 'gainst the wife the heavy club is raised,
Her bones are crushed, nor does her headless trunk exist.
1105 None live. Oh gray-beard, too long lived,
Dost dare see this? If mourning irks, death's near.
Sink in my heart thy dart, and wet thy club
With my blood; him whom falsely they proclaim
Thy father, slay; remove this shameful thing
1110 That stains thy fame, lest longer it should dim thy glory.
    Chorus. Wouldst thou fling thyself, old man,
Across the path of death? Insane with grief,
Where goest thou? Fly, hide thyself afar,
And spare the hand of Hercules this crime.
1115 *Hercules.* 'Tis well, the base king's brood are all cut off.
Those vowed to thee, O wife of mighty Jove,
Are slain. A free gift, worthy thee, is brought,
And other victims still shall Argives give.
    Amphitryon. My son, a worthy gift is not yet made,
1120 Complete the sacrifice, the victim kneels
Before the altar, see he waits thy hand
With lowered head. I freely give myself,
Slay me. But what is this? His eyes' fierce glance
Wanders, and drowsiness makes dim his sight.
1125 Do I behold the hand of Hercules
Tremble? His eyelids droop with sleep, his head
Sinks wearied on his breast, his knees give way,
He falls upon the earth like some great tree,
The glory of the woods, or mighty crag
1130 That sinks into the sea. Dost thou still live
Or does the rage that hurled thine own to death
Give thee as well to Lethe? It is sleep,
He breathes—may calm be granted him a space,
That vigor, conquered by disease, return
1135 In dreamless sleep to soothe his troubled breast.
Slaves, take his weapons, lest he wake and rave.

Scene II

Chorus.

The heavens mourn, and heaven's great father mourns,
The fertile earth, and the unstable sea's
Unstable waves; thou mournest most of all
1140 Who floodest earth and ocean with thy rays
And with thy brightness puttest night to flight,
Alcides saw with thee thy rise, he saw
Thy setting, Titan, knew thy two abodes.
Ye heaven-dwellers, from these tumults wild
1145 Set free his spirit, turn his darkened mind
To better things. Thou vanquisher of ills,
Sweet sleep, the soul's repose, the better part
Of human life, Astraea's winged child,
Mild brother of harsh Death, confusing oft
1150 The true and false, at once the best and worst
Foreteller of events, the wanderer's peace,
Rest after day, companion of the night,
Who comest to the slave as to the king,
Who teachest man, afraid of death, to learn
1155 By slow degrees to know death's last long night,
O gently, softly soothe the wearied one,
Let heavy languor on the vanquished lie;
By slumber let his dauntless limbs be bound,
Leave not his savage breast before he finds
1160 Again his former mind.
    See, on the ground he lies, his wild heart filled
With dreadful dreams, his trouble not yet eased;
Accustomed on his heavy club to lean
His wearied head, he throws his arms about
1165 And with his empty right hand seeks in vain
Its weight. The fever's tide has not yet ebbed,
But surges as the waves by storm wind vexed
Surge to and fro and their long anger keep,
Tumultuous even when the wind has ceased.
1170 Depart, tempestuous madness, from his soul;
Return, O valor, gentleness, and health.
Better, perhaps, a mind by madness stirred,
Insanity alone can prove him free
From guilty stain. Most nearly pure is he
1175 Who sins and knows it not.
    Now, smitten by Herculean palms, his breast
Resounds, and blows from his all-conquering hand
Fall upon shoulders that once bore the world.
The heavens hear his heavy groans, the queen

1180 Of the dark realm, and tameless Cerberus,
Who lurks within his cave's depths, bound in chains;
Chaos re-echoes with the mournful cries
And the great deeps that now uncovered lie.
Not lightly does he smite his mighty breast
1185 By such calamity weighed down, three realms
Echo the blows. Now give him cruel wounds,
Thou weapon, ornament long hung about
His neck,—thou quiver strong, and gallant shaft;
Thou club, strong oak, with thy hard knots oppress
1190 His breast, O serve him now, ye well-known arms,
In this his bitter need.
O boys, O children of a luckless race,
By the sad path thy father knew go hence;
Ye have not, sharer of your father's fame,
1195 Wrecked vengeance on hard kings with harsher war,
Nor, brave with hand and cæstus, learned to bend
Your supple members in the Argive games;
Ye have but dared to balance the light shafts
From Scythian quivers, and with certain aim
1200 To send them, and to shoot the flying stag.
Go, shadows, to the Stygian portals go,
Ye innocents who on life's threshold fall,
By crime and by a father's madness slain!
Go, seek the wrathful monarch!

ACT V

Scene I

Hercules, Amphitryon, Theseus.

    Hercules. [*Awaking and looking around in wonder.*]
1205 What place is this? What realm? What clime of earth?
Where am I? Underneath the eastern sky,
Or the cold constellation of the bear,
Or where the waters of the western seas
Wash up against the limits of the land?
1210 What air is this I breathe? on what soil rest
My wearied limbs? 'Tis true, I have returned!
Why prostrate lie those bloody bodies there?
Has not my mind put by the shapes of hell?
Although returned does hell's sad throng still move
1215 Before my eyes? It shames me to confess:—
I fear! I know not what my soul forebodes
Of heavy ill. My father, where art thou?
Where are my sons, my wife? Why is my side
Bare of the lion's spoil? Whither has fled

1220 My lion's skin that served as cloak and couch?
Where are my bow and arrows? Who could take
My weapons from me and I still alive?
What man could bear away such spoil nor fear
The sleeping Hercules? May I but see
1225 That man! Thou strong one, come; my father Jove,
Leaving his heaven, has begotten thee
At whose creation longer than at mine
The night endured. But what is this I see?
My sons lie bathed in blood, my wife is dead!
1230 Does Lycus reign and Hercules returned?
Ye who beside Ismenus' waters dwell,
Or in Athenian meadows, or the realm
Of Trojan Pelops by two oceans wet,
Help; show the author of these savage deeds;
1235 My anger else will kindle against all,
I count him foe who shows me not my foe.
Alcides' vanquisher, wouldst thou be hid?
Come forth; though thou seekst vengeance for the steeds
Of bloody Thrace, or Geryon's slaughtered flocks,
1240 Or Libya's lord, I do not shun the fight.
I stand defenceless, with my weapons armed
Thou mayest fall upon me weaponless.
But why do Theseus and my father shun
My glance? Why hide their faces? Stay your tears,
1245 Speak, who has slain my all? What, father, dumb?
Yet speak thou, Theseus, Theseus, faithful friend.
Each, silent, hides his face and weeps; what shame
Is mine? Has Argos tyrant, has the line
Of Lycus overwhelmed us with such woe?
1250 By thine own self and by thy honored name,
To me propitious ever, by the fame
Of my great deeds, speak, who o'erthrew my house?
Whose prey am I?
    Amphitryon. Unspoken be these ills.
    Hercules. Shall I lack vengeance?
    Amphitryon. Vengeance oft recoils.
1255   *Hercules.* Who ever bore unmoved such wrongs as mine?
    Amphitryon. Who stood in fear of heavier wrongs than these.
    Hercules. O father, can aught worse than this be found?
    Amphitryon. Thou knowest but a part of all thy woe.
    Hercules. Have pity, father; supplicating hands
1260 I stretch—but what is this? He turns away;
Here surely crime lies hid. Whence comes this blood?
What shaft is that with children's murder wet?
Alas! My own, in Hydra's venom dipped!
I need not ask what hand could bend that bow,
1265 Or draw the bowstring that reluctant yields

To me. My father, speak, is mine the crime?
He speaks not, it is mine.
    Amphitryon. The grief is thine, .
The crime thy stepdame's, thou art free from fault.
    Hercules. Now send thy thunders from all parts of heaven,
1270 O great progenitor; forgetting me,
Avenge thy grandsons, though with tardy hand.
The starry heavens roar, the sky shoots flame.
To Caspian cliffs bound fast, let eager birds
Upon my body feed. Why now lies bare
1275 Prometheus' rock, the steep and woodless height
Of Caucasus, where birds and beasts of prey
Are fed? Let the Symplegades which close
The Scythian waters stretch across the deep
Each way my fast bound hands, and when recurs
1280 Th' alternate change, when the two rocks unite
And at the blow the sea in foam is flung
To heaven, I shall lie between the rocks!
Why, building high a pile of heaped-up wood,
Should not this blood-stained form be burned with fire?
1285 Thus, thus, it must be done; to realms below
I will give back Alcides.
    Amphitryon. Ah, not yet
Does madness leave him or his raving cease,
But all his raging burns against himself.
    Hercules. Grim country of the Furies, prison house
1290 Of hell-abiders, long decreed abode
Of guilty throngs, if place of banishment
Lies hid beyond the shades of Erebus
Unknown to Cerberus and me, O earth,
There hide me. I will lurk beyond the bounds
1295 Of Tartarus. O heart, too fiercely tried!
Who worthily might mourn for you, my sons,
Scattered through all the house? My tearless eyes
Have not the power to weep these heavy ills.
Give back my bow, my arrows; give my club.
1300 For thee, my sons, I break my shaft, for thee
Destroy my bow; this heavy club shall burn
An offering to thy shades; this quiver, full
Of Hydra-poisoned arrows, shall be laid
Upon thy funeral pile; the arms that slew
1305 Shall pay the penalty. You, too, shall burn,
O most unfortunate and cruel hands.
    Amphitryon. Who ever called an act of madness crime?
    Hercules. Great madness often gains the height of crime.
    Amphitryon. Now, Hercules, thou needest all thy strength;
1310 Bear patiently this heavy weight of woe.
    Hercules. Frenzy has not so quenched my sense of shame

That I can see all peoples flee my face.
My weapons, Theseus! Give me back, I pray,
In haste my stolen arms; if I am sane,
1315 Give back my spear; if madness holds me yet,
Fly, father, for I take the road to death.
  Amphitryon. I pray thee by the sacred bond of blood,
And by the holy name that binds us twain—
Father or foster-father as you will—
1320 By these gray hairs that call for reverence,
Spare a bereft old man, weighed down with years.
Thou only pillar of a falling house,
One star of the afflicted, live for me.
I never yet have reaped thy labor's fruit,
1325 But ever have I feared unfriendly seas,
Or savage monsters, or some cruel king,
Or one proved faithless to the holy gods.
Ever the father of an absent son,
I long to see thee, touch thee, know thee mine.
1330   *Hercules.* Why longer should my spirit see the light?
Nought now remains, my hand has banished all:
Intelligence and weapons, wife and sons,
My glory and my strength, my madness too.
There is no healing for a soul defiled,
1335 The criminal must be by death made whole.
  Amphitryon. Thou'lt slay thy father.
  Hercules. Nay, but, lest I should, I slay myself.
  Amphitryon. Before thy father's eyes?
  Hercules. Through me such crime is even now well known.
  Amphitryon. Remember rather deeds that all must praise,
1340 And seek forgiveness for a single crime.
  Hercules. Shall he give pardon to himself, who found
Pardon for none? I did my much-praised deeds
Obedient to command, this deed is mine.
Have pity, father, whether thou art moved
1345 By fatherly compassion, my sad fate,
Or by my loss of innocence: give back
My weapons, let my hand avenge my fate.
  Theseus. Thy father's prayers have surely force enough,
Yet be by my entreaties also moved.
1350 Rise, meet this new attack and overcome.
As thou art wont. Take courage, never yet
By evil was thy great heart put to shame.
Thou needest all thy valor, Hercules;
Prevent the anger of great Hercules.
1355   *Hercules.* If yet I live, I have done grievous wrong;
But if I die, I have endured such wrong.
I haste to cleanse the land; before my eyes,
But now, a monster hovered, harsh and wild,

Unholy, cruel; up, my hand, begin
This heavy labor, greater than them all.
Dost stand inactive, brave in thy attack
On boys alone and trembling motherhood?
Unless my arms are given back to me,
The woods of Thracian Pindus I will fell,
And burn Cithæron's ridge and Bacchus' grove,
My funeral pyre; or all the Theban homes,
The citizens, the temples of the gods,
Above my body I will heap, will lie
Entombed beneath a city overthrown;
And if the ruined walls should prove too light
For my strong shoulders, and the seven gates
Too lightly rest, in the world's heart, I'll hide,
Pressed down beneath the burden of the earth.
    Amphitryon. I give the weapons back.
    Hercules. Those words become
The father of Alcides. Lo, this lad
Was smitten by this arrow.
    Amphitryon. Juno sent
That arrow by thy hand.
    Hercules. I see it now!
    Amphitryon. Behold, his heart, o'erwhelmed with misery,
Swells in his troubled breast.
    Hercules. The shaft is meet!
    Amphitryon. Lo, now of thine own will thou doest sin
And consciously.
    Hercules. What then wouldst thou command?
    Amphitryon. We ask for nothing, all our grief is full.
Thou only canst preserve my son for me;
Thou canst not take him from me. Fear is gone,
Thou canst not make me wretched, glad thou mayest.
Whatever thou shouldst do, resolve to act
As knowing that thy fate and glory stand
At parting of the ways: live thou or die,
This spirit, wearied both by time and fate,
Trembles upon my lips to quickly pass.—
So slowly does one give a father life?
I will not longer bear delay, but thrust
The fatal iron in my breast—this crime
Will be the crime of no mad Hercules.
    Hercules. O father, spare me, spare, call back thy hand.
Succumb, my valor, hear a father's words;
Add to thy other labors this one more,
Herculean,—let me live! O Theseus, friend,
Lift up my stricken father from the ground,
My guilty hands must shun that sacred head.
    Amphitryon. I clasp thy hands most gladly; I will go

Leaning on this; embracing this, my heart
Will put away its sorrows.
    Hercules. Whither fly?
Where hide myself? In what land lie concealed?
1405 What Nile, or Tanais, or Persian flood,
Or fiercely flowing Tigris, or wild Rhine,
Or Tagus, or Iberis' turgid stream,
That flows with wealth, can wash this right hand clean?
Might cold Mæotis, pour its icy flood
1410 Upon me, or the ocean through my hands
Plow ever, still they'ld show the stain of blood.
O murderer, whither flee? To east or west?
There is no place of exile, earth rejects
And all the stars flee from me; Titan saw
1415 With milder face the hell dog Cerberus.
O Theseus, faithful friend, seek out for me
Some secret, far-remote abiding place;
Since, looking on another's guilt, thou still
Canst love the guilty, show me now, I pray,
1420 The gratitude thou owest: take me back
To hell's dark shades, endue me in thy chains,
That place will hide me. But that knows me, too!
    Theseus. One land awaits thee, there will Mars restore
The weapons to thy hands made clean from blood.
1425 That land, Alcides, calls thee which is wont
To make unspotted the immortal gods.

THE DAUGHTERS OF TROY

DRAMATIS PERSONÆ

Agamemnon.
Ulysses.
Pyrrhus.
Calchas.
Talthybius.
Astyanax.
Hecuba.
Andromache.
Helen.
Polyxena.
An Old Man.
Messenger.
Chorus of Trojan Women.

Scene: *Troy.*

THE DAUGHTERS OF TROY

ACT I

Scene I

Hecuba. Let him who puts his trust in kingly crown,
Who rules in prince's court with power supreme
Who, credulous of heart, dreads not the gods,
But in his happy lot confides, behold
5   My fate and Troy's. Never by clearer proof
Was shown how frail a thing is human pride.
Strong Asia's capital, the work of gods,
Is fallen; and she beneath whose banners fought
The men who drink the Tanais' cold stream
10 That flows by sevenfold outlet to the sea,
And those who see the new-born day where blends
Tigris' warm waters with the blushing strait,
Is fallen; her walls and towers, to ashes burned,
Lie low amid her ruined palaces.
15 The royal courts take fire; far and near
Smolders the home of King Assaracus.
But flames stay not the eager conqueror's hand
From plundering Troy. The sky is hid with smoke;
And day, as though enveloped in black cloud,
20 Is dark with ashes. Eager for revenge,
The victor stands and measures her slow fall;

Forgets the long ten years; deplores her fate;
Nor yet believes that he has vanquished her,
Although he sees her conquered in the dust.
25 The pillagers are busy with the spoil;
A thousand ships will hardly bear it hence.
    Witness, ye adverse deities; and ye,
My country's ashes, and thou, Phrygia's king,
Buried beneath the ruins of thy realm;
30 Thou, too, great shade, whose life was all in all
To Troy; my numerous offspring, lesser shades;—
Whatever ills have happened; whatsoe'er
Apollo's raving priestess, to whose word
The god denied belief, has prophesied,
35 I first foresaw, ere yet my fated child
Was born, nor hid my fear, but prophesied
Vainly, before Cassandra spoke in vain.
Alas, 'twas not the crafty Ithacan,
Nor the companions of his night attack,
40 Nor Sinon false, who flung into your midst
Devouring flame; the glowing torch was mine!
Aged, and sick of life, why weep for Troy?
Unhappy one, recall more recent woes;
The fall of Troy is now an ancient grief!
45 I've seen the murder of a king—base crime!
And, at the altar's foot incurred, I've seen
A baser crime, when Æacus' fierce son,
His left hand in the twisted locks, bent back
That royal head, and drove the iron home
50 In the deep wound; freely it was received,
And buried deep, and yet drawn forth unstained,
So sluggish is the blood of frozen age.
This old man's cruel death at the last mete
Of human life, and the immortal gods
55 Witnesses of the deed, and fallen Troy's
Fair altars, cannot stay the savage hand.
Priam, the father of so many kings,
Has found no grave, and in the flames of Troy
No funeral pyre, and yet the wrathful gods
60 Are not appeased; behold, the lot is cast
That gives to Priam's daughters and his sons
A master; and I go to servitude.
One would have Hector's wife, one Helenus',
And one Antenor's; nor are wanting those
65 Who long for thee, Cassandra; me alone
They shun, and I alone affright the Greeks.
    Why rest from lamentations, captive ones?
Make moan, and smite your breasts, pay funeral rites;
Let fatal Ida, home of doom-fraught judge,

70 Reëcho now your sorrowful lament.

Scene II

Hecuba, Chorus of Trojan Women.

 Chorus. You bid those weep who are not new to grief;
Our lamentations have not ceased to rise
From that day when the Phrygian stranger sought
Grecian Amyclæ, and the sacred pine
75 Of Mother Cybele, through Grecian seas
A pathway cut. Ten times the winter snows
Have whitened Ida—Ida stripped of trees
To furnish Trojan dead with funeral pyres—
Ten times the trembling reaper has gone forth
80 To cut the bearded grain from Ilium's fields,
Since any day has seen us free from tears.
New sorrows ask new mourning. Hasten now
Your lamentations, beat upon your breasts;
We, the ignoble crowd, will follow still
85 Our mistress, we are not untaught in tears.
 Hecuba. O faithful ones,
Companions of my grief, unbind your hair;
About your shoulders let it flow defiled
With Troy's hot ashes; fill your hands with these,
90 This much of Troy you are allowed to take.
Come with bare breasts, loose robes, and naked limbs;
Why veil your modest bosoms, captive ones?
Gird up your flowing tunics, free your hands
For fierce and frequent beating of your breasts.
95 So I am satisfied, I recognize
My Trojan followers; again I hear
Their wonted lamentations. Weep indeed;
We weep for Hector.
 Chorus. We unbind our hair,
So often torn in wild laments, and strew
100 Troy's glowing ashes on our heads; permit
Our loosened robe to drop from shoulders bare;
Our naked bosoms now invite our blows.
O sorrow, show thy power; let Ilium's shores
Give back the blows, nor from her hollow hills
105 Faint Echo sound the closing words alone,
But let her voice repeat each bitter groan,
And air and ocean hear. With cruel blows
Smite, smite, nor be content with faint laments:
We weep for Hector.
110 *Hecuba.* For thee our hands have torn our naked arms
And bleeding shoulders; Hector, 'tis for thee

We beat our brows and lacerate our breasts;
The wounds inflicted in thy funeral rites
Shall gape and flow with blood once more. Thou wast
115 The pillar of thy land, her fates' delay,
The prop of wearied Phrygians, and the wall
Of Troy; by thee supported, firm she stood,
Ten years upheld. With thee thy country fell,
Her day of doom and Hector's were the same.
120 Weep now for Priam, smite for him your breasts;
Hector has tears enough.
    Chorus. Ruler of Phrygia, twice a captive made,
Receive our tears, receive our wild laments.
Whilst thou wast king, Troy suffered many woes;
125 Twice by Greek weapons were her walls assailed;
Twice were they made a target for the darts
Of Hercules; and when that kingly band,
Hecuba's offspring, had been offered up,
With thee, their sire, the funeral rites were stayed;
130 An offering to great Jove, thy headless trunk
Lies on Sigeum's plain.
    Hecuba. Women of Troy,
For others shed your tears; not Priam's death
I weep; say rather all, thrice happy he!
Free he descended to the land of shades,
135 Nor will he ever bear on conquered neck
The Grecian yoke; nor the Atridæ see;
Nor look on shrewd Ulysses; nor, a slave,
Carry the trophies on his neck to grace
A Grecian triumph; feel his sceptered hands
140 Bound at his back; nor add a further pomp
To proud Mycenæ, forced in golden chains
To follow Agamemnon's royal car.
    Chorus. Thrice happy Priam! as a king he went
Into the land of spirits; wanders now
145 Through the safe shadows of Elysian Fields,
In happiness among the peaceful shades,
And seeks for Hector. Happy Priam say!
Thrice happy he, who, dying in the fight,
Bears with him to destruction all his land.

ACT II

Scene I

Talthybius, Chorus of Trojan Women.

150   *Talthybius.* O long delay, that holds the Greeks in port
Whether they seek for war or for their homes.
    Chorus. Say what the reason of the long delay,
What god forbids the Greeks the homeward road?
    Talthybius. I tremble, and my spirit shrinks with fear;
155 Such prodigies will hardly find belief.
I saw them, I myself; Titan had touched
The mountain summits, dayspring conquered night,
When, on a sudden, with a muttered groan,
Earth trembled, and laid bare her lowest depths;
160 The forests, the high wood and sacred grove
Thundered with mighty ruin; Ida's cliffs
Fell from her summit; nor did earth alone
Tremble, the ocean also recognized
Her own Achilles, and laid bare her depths;
165 In the torn earth a gloomy cavern yawned;
A way was opened up from Erebus
To upper day; the tomb gave up its dead;
The towering shade of the Thessalian chief
Leaped forth as when, preparing for thy fate,
170 O Troy, he put to flight the Thracian host,
And struck down Neptune's shining, fair-haired son;
Or as when, breathing battle 'mid the host,
He choked the rivers with the fallen dead,
And Xanthus wandered over bloody shoals
175 Seeking slow channels; or as when he stood
In his proud car, a victor, while he dragged
Hector and Troy behind him in the dust.
   His wrathful voice rang out along the shore:
Ye cravens, go, refuse the honors due
180 My manes. Let the thankless ships set sail
Upon my seas. Not lightly Greece has felt
Achilles' wrath; that wrath shall heavier fall.
Polyxena, betrothed to me in death,
Must die a sacrifice at Pyrrhus' hand,
185 And moisten with her blood my tomb. He spake,
Exchanged the day for night, and sought again
The realm of Dis. He took the riven path;
Earth closed above him, and the tranquil sea
Lay undisturbed, the raging wind was still,
190 Softly the ocean murmured, Tritons sang

From the blue deep their hymeneal chant.

Scene II

Agamemnon, Pyrrhus.

Pyrrhus. When, homeward turning, you fain have spread
Your happy sails, Achilles was forgot.
By him alone struck down, Troy fell; her fall,
195 Ev'n at his death, was but so long delayed
As she stood doubtful whither she should fall;
Haste as you will to give him what he asks,
You give too late. Already all the chiefs would
Have carried off their prizes; what reward
200 Of lesser price have you to offer him
For so great valor? Does he merit less?
He, bidden shun the battle and enjoy
A long and peaceful age, outnumbering
The many years of Pylos' aged king,
205 Put off the false disguise of woman's dress
His mother gave, and stood confessed a man
Electing war. When haughty Telephus
Refused him entrance to the rugged coast
Of rocky Mysia, with his royal blood
210 He stained Achilles' hand, but found that hand
Gentle as strong. When Thebes was overcome
Eëtion, its conquered ruler, saw
His realm made captive. With like slaughter fell
Little Lyrnessus, built at Ida's foot;
215 Brisëis' land was captured; Chryse, too,
The cause of royal strife, was overthrown;
And well-known Tenedos, and Sciro's isle
That, rich with fertile pastures, nourishes
The Thracian herd, and Lesbos that divides
220 The Ægean straits, Cilla to Phœbus dear,
Yes, and whatever land Caïcus laves
Swollen by rains of spring. Such overthrow
Of nations, such distress, so many towns
O'erwhelmed in such a whirlpool would have been
225 To any other, glory, honor, fame,—
Achilles is but on the march; so sped
My father, and so great the war he waged
While he made ready for his great campaign.
Though I were silent of his other deeds,
230 Would it not be enough that Hector died?
My father conquered Ilium; as for you,
You have but torn it down. I joy to speak
The noble deeds of my illustrious sire:

How Hector's father saw him prostrate fall;
235 How Memnon in his uncle's sight was slain,
Whose mother shuns the light, with pallid cheek
Mourning his fate; and at his own great deeds
Achilles trembles, and, a victor, learns
That death may touch the children of a god.
240 The Amazons' harsh queen, thy final fear,
Last yielded. Wouldst thou honor worthily
His mighty arms, then yield him what he will,
Though he should ask a virgin from the land
Of Argos or Mycenae. Dost thou doubt;
245 Changing so soon, art loth to offer up
A maiden, Priam's child, to Peleus' son?
Thy child to Helen was a sacrifice,
'Tis not an unaccustomed gift I ask.

Agamemnon. To have no power to check the passions' glow
250 Is ever found a fault of youthful blood;
That which in others is the zeal of youth,
In Pyrrhus is his father's fiery heart.
Thus mildly once I stood the savage threats
Of Æacus' fierce son; most patiently
255 He bears, who is most strong. With slaughter harsh
Why sprinkle our illustrious leader's shade?
Learn first how much the conqueror may do,
The conquered suffer. 'Tis the mild endure,
But he who harshly rules, rules not for long.
260 The higher Fortune doth exalt a man,
Increasing human power, so much the more—
Fearing the gods who too much favor him,
And not unmindful of uncertain fate—
He should be meek. In conquering, I have learned
265 How in a moment greatness is o'erthrown.
Has triumph over Troy too soon made proud?
We stand, we Greeks, in that place whence Troy fell.
Imperious I have been, and borne myself
At times too proudly; Fortune's gifts correct
270 In me the pride they oft in others rouse.
Priam, thou mak'st me proud, but mak'st me fear.
What can I deem my scepter, but a name
Made bright with idle glitter; or my crown,
But empty ornament? A sudden chance
275 May rob me of them, needing not, perhaps,
A thousand ships nor ten years' war. I own
(May I do this, O Argive land, nor wound
Thy honor?) I have troubled Phrygia
And wished her conquered; but I would have stayed
280 The hand that crushed and laid her in the dust.
A foe enraged and victory gained by night

Will never check their raging, at command;
Whatever cruel or unworthy deed
Appeared in any, anger was the cause—
285 Anger and darkness and the savage sword
Made glad with blood and seeking still for more.
    All that yet stands of ruined Troy shall stand,
Enough of punishment—more than enough—
Has been exacted, that a royal maid
290 Should fall, and, offered as a sacrifice
Upon a tomb, should crimson with her blood
The ashes, and this hateful crime be called
A marriage—I will never suffer it.
Upon my head would rest the guilt of all;
295 He who forbids not crime when he has power,
Commands it.
    Pyrrhus. Shall Achilles' shade receive no prize?
    Agamemnon. Ah yes, for all shall tell his praise,
And unknown lands shall sing his glorious name;
And if his shade would take delight in blood
300 Poured forth upon his ashes, let us slay
Rich sacrifice of Phrygian sheep. No blood
Shall flow to cause a sorrowing mother's tears.
What fashion this, by which a living soul
Is sacrificed to one gone down to hell?
305 Think not to soil thy father's memory
With such revenge, commanding us to pay
Him reverence with blood.
    Pyrrhus. Harsh king of kings!
So arrogant while favoring fortune smiles,
So timid when aught threatens! Is thy heart
310 So soon inflamed with love and new desire;
And wilt thou always bear from us the spoil?
I'll give Achilles back, with this right hand,
His victim, and, if thou withholdest her,
I'll give a greater, one more meet to be
315 The gift of Pyrrhus. All too long our hand
Has ceased from slaughter, Priam seeks his peer.
    Agamemnon. That was, indeed, the worthiest warlike act
Of Pyrrhus: with relentless hand he slew
Priam, whose suppliant prayer Achilles heard.
320   *Pyrrhus.* We know our father's foes were suppliants,
But Priam made his prayer himself, whilst thou,
Not brave to ask, and overcome with fear,
Lurked trembling in thy tent, and sought as aid
The intercessions of the Ithacan
And Ajax.
325   *Agamemnon.* That thy father did not fear,
I own; amid the slaughter of the Greeks

And burning of the fleet, forgetting war,
He idly lay, and with his plectrum touched
Lightly his lyre.
　　Pyrrhus. Mighty Hector then
330 Laughed at thy arms but feared Achilles' song;
Amid the universal fear, deep peace
Reigned through Thessalia's fleet.
　　Agamemnon. There was in truth
Deep peace for Hector's father in that fleet.
　　Pyrrhus. To grant kings life is kingly.
　　Agamemnon. Why didst thou
335 With thy right hand cut short a royal life?
　　Pyrrhus. Mercy gives often death instead of life.
　　Agamemnon. Mercy seeks now a virgin for the tomb?
　　Pyrrhus. Thou deemst it crime to sacrifice a maid?
　　Agamemnon. More than their children, kings should love their land.
340 　　*Pyrrhus.* No law spares captives or denies revenge.
　　Agamemnon. What law forbids not, honor's self forbids.
　　Pyrrhus. To victors is permitted what they will.
　　Agamemnon. He least should wish to whom is granted most.
　　Pyrrhus. And this thou say'st to us, who ten long years
345 Have borne thy heavy yoke, whom Pyrrhus freed?
　　Agamemnon. Does Scyros breed such pride?
　　Pyrrhus. No guilty stain
Of brother's blood is there.
　　Agamemnon. Shut in by waves—
　　Pyrrhus. Nay, but the seas are kin. I know thy house—
Yea, Atreus' and Thyestes' noble line!
350 　　*Agamemnon.* Son of Achilles ere he was a man,
And of the maid he ravished secretly—
　　Pyrrhus. Of that Achilles, who, by right of race,
Through all the world holds sway, possesses still
The ocean through his mother, and the shades
355 Through Æacus, through Jupiter the sky.
　　Agamemnon. Achilles, who by Paris' hand was slain.
　　Pyrrhus. One whom not even the gods fought openly.
　　Agamemnon. To curb thy insolence and daring words
I well were able, but my sword can spare
The conquered.

　　　　　[*To some of the soldiers, who surround him.*]

360 Call the gods' interpreter,
We'll rule us by his council.

　　　　　[*A few of the soldiers go out, Calchas comes in.*]

Scene III

Agamemnon, Pyrrhus, Calchas.

    Agamemnon. [*To Calchas.*] Thou, who hast freed the anchors of the fleet,
Ended the war's delay, and by thy arts
Canst open heaven, to whom the secret things
365 Revealed in sacrifice, in shaken earth,
And star that draws through heaven its flaming length.
Are messengers of fate, whose words have been
To me the words of doom, speak, Calchas, tell
What thing the god commands, and govern us
By thy wise counsels.
370   *Calchas.* Fate a pathway grants
To Grecians only at the wonted price.
A virgin must be slain upon the tomb
Of the Thessalian leader, and adorned
In robes like those Thessalian virgins wear
375 To grace their bridals, or Ionian maids,
Or daughters of Mycene; and the bride
Shall be by Pyrrhus to his father brought—
So is she rightly wed. Yet not alone
Is this the cause that holds our ships in port,
380 But blood must flow, and nobler blood than thine,
Polyxena. Whom cruel fate demands—
Grandchild of Priam, Hector's only son—
Hurled headlong from Troy's wall must meet his death;
Then shall our thousand sails make white the strait.

Scene IV

Chorus of Trojan Women.

385 Is it true, or does an idle story
Make the timid dream that after death,
When the loved one shuts the wearied eyelids,
When the last day's sun has come and gone,
And the funeral urn has hid the ashes,
390 He shall still live on among the shades?
Does it not avail to bear the dear one
To the grave? Must misery still endure
Longer life beyond? Does not all perish
When the fleeting spirit fades in air
395 Cloudlike? When the funeral fire is lighted
'Neath the body, does no part remain?
    Whatsoe'er the rising sun or setting
Sees; whatever ebbing tide or flood

Of the ocean with blue waters washes,
400 Time with Pegasean flight destroys.
As the sweep of whirling constellations,
As the circling of their king the sun
Speed the ages, as, obliquely turning,
Hecate hastes, so all must seek their fate;
405 He who touches once the gloomy water
Sacred to the gods, exists no more.
   As the sordid smoke from smoldering embers
Swiftly dies, or as a heavy cloud,
That the north wind scatters, ends its being
410 So the soul that rules us slips away;
After death is nothing; death is nothing
But the last mete of a swift-run race,
Then let eager souls their hopes relinquish,
Fearful find the end of fear. Believe
415 Eager time and the abyss engulf us;
Death is fatal to the flesh, nor spares
Spirit even; Tænarus, the kingdom
Of the gloomy monarch, and the door
Where sits Cerberus and guards the portal,
420 Are but empty rumors, senseless names,
Fables vain, like dreams that trouble sleep.
Ask you whither go we after death?
Where they lie who never have been born.

ACT III

Scene I

Andromache, An Old Man.

   Andromache. Why tear your hair, my Phrygian followers,
425 Why beat your breasts and mar your cheeks with tears?
The grief is light that has the power to weep.
Troy fell for you but now, for me long since
When fierce Achilles urged at speed his car,
And dragged behind his wheel my very self;
430 The axle, made of wood from Pelion's groves,
Groaned heavily, and under Hector's weight
Trembled. O'erwhelmed and crushed, I bear unmoved
Whate'er befalls, for I am stunned with grief.
I would have followed Hector long ago,
435 And freed me from the Greeks, but this my son
Held me, subdued my heart, forbade my death,
Compelled me still to ask the gods a boon,
Added a longer life to misery.
He took away my sorrow's richest fruit—

440 To know no fear. All chance of better things
Is snatched away, and worse are yet to come;
'Tis wretchedness to fear where hope is lost.
   Old Man. What sudden fear assails thee, troubled one?
   Andromache. From great misfortunes, greater ever spring;
445 Troy needs must fill the measure of her woes.
   Old Man. Though he should wish, what can the god do more?
   Andromache. The entrance of the bottomless abyss
Of gloomy Styx lies open; lest defeat
Should lack enough of fear, the buried foe
450 Comes forth from Dis. Can Greeks alone return?
Death certainly is equal; Phrygians feel
This common fear; but me alone a dream
Of dreadful night has terrified.
   Old Man. What dream
   Andromache. The sweet night's second watch was hardly passed,
455 The Seven Stars were turning from the height;
At length there came an unaccustomed calm
To me afflicted; on my eyes there stole
Brief sleep, if that dull lethargy be sleep
That comes to grief-worn souls; when, suddenly,
460 Before my eyes stood Hector, not as when
He bore against the Greeks avenging fire,
Seeking the Argive fleet with Trojan torch;
Nor as he raged with slaughter 'gainst the Greeks,
And bore away Achilles' arms—true spoil,
465 From him who played Achilles' part, nor was
A true Achilles. Not with flame-bright face
He came, but marred with tears, dejected, sad,
Like me, and all unkempt his loosened hair;
Yet I rejoiced to see him. Then he said,
470 Shaking his head: 'O faithful wife, awake!
Bear hence thy son and hide him, this alone
Is safety. Weep not! Do you weep for Troy?
Would all were fallen! Hasten, seek some place
Of safety for the child.' Then I awoke,
475 Cold horror and a trembling broke my sleep.
Fearful, I turned my eyes now here, now there.
Me miserable, careless of my son,
I sought for Hector, but the fleeting shade
Slipped from my arms, eluded my embrace.
480 O child, true son of an illustrious sire;
Troy's only hope; last of a stricken race;
O offspring of an all too noble house,
Too like thy father! Such my Hector's face,
Such was his gait, his manner, so he held
485 His mighty hands, and so his shoulders broad,
So threatened with bold brow when shaking back

His heavy hair! Oh, born too late for Troy,
Too soon for me, will ever come that time,
That happy day, when thou shalt build again
₄₉₀ Troy's walls, lead back again her scattered hosts,
Avenging and defending mightily,
And give again a name to Troy's fair land?
But, mindful of my fate, I dare not wish;
Let us but live, for life is all that slaves
₄₉₅ Can hope. Alas, what safety can I find,
Where hide thee? That high citadel, god-built,
World-famous, to the envious exposed,
Is dust, her streets flame-swept, and naught remains
Of all the mighty city, not so much
₅₀₀ As where to hide an infant. Oh, what place
Of safety can I find? The mighty tomb,
Reared to my husband—this the foe must fear.
His father, Priam, in his sorrow built,
With no ungenerous hand, great Hector's tomb;
₅₀₅ I trust him to his father. Yet I fear
The baleful omen of the place of tombs,
And a cold sweat my trembling members bathes.
    Old Man. The safe may choose, but we must seize defence.
    Andromache. We may not hide him without heavy fear
Lest some betray him.
₅₁₀   *Old Man.* Cover up the trace
Of our device.
    Andromache. And if the foe should ask?
    Old Man. In the destruction of the land he died,—
It oft has saved a man that he was deemed already dead.
₅₁₅   *Andromache.* No other hope is left.
He bears the heavy burden of his name;
If he must come once more into their power
What profits it to hide him?
    Old Man. Victors oft
Are savage only in the first attack.
    Andromache. [*To Astyanax.*] What distant, pathless land will keep thee safe,
₅₂₀ Or who protect thee, give thee aid in fear?
O Hector, now as ever guard thine own,
Preserve the secret of thy faithful wife,
And to thy trusted ashes take thy child!
My son, go thou into thy father's tomb.
₅₂₅ What, do you turn and shun the safe retreat?
I recognize thy father's strength of soul,
Ashamed of fear. Put by thy inborn pride,
Thy courage; take what fortune has to give.
See what is left of all the Trojan host:
₅₃₀ A tomb, a child, a captive! We must yield
To our misfortunes. Dare to enter now

Thy buried father's sacred resting-place;
If fate is kind thou hast a safe retreat,
If fate refuse thee aid, thou hast a grave.
535   *Old Man.* The sepulcher will safely hide thy son;
Go, lest thy fears betray thee and so him,
    Andromache. One's fear is lightlier borne when near at hand,
But elsewhere will I go, since that seems best.
    Old Man. Restrain thy words, speak not, but curb thy fear,
540 This way the Grecian leader bends his steps.

Scene II

Andromache, Ulysses with a retinue of warriors. [The old man withdraws.]

    Ulysses. Coming a messenger of cruel fate,
I pray you deem not mine the bitter words
I speak, for this is but the general voice
Of all the Greeks, too long from home detained
545 By Hector's child: him do the fates demand.
The Greeks can hope for but a doubtful peace,
Fear will compel them still to look behind
Nor lay aside their armor, while thy child,
Andromache, gives strength to fallen Troy.
550 So prophesies the god's interpreter;
And had the prophet Calchas held his peace,
Hector had spoken; Hector and his son
I greatly fear: those sprung of noble race
Must needs grow great. With proudly lifted head
555 And haughty neck, the young and hornless bull
Leads the paternal herd and rules the flock;
And when the tree is cut, the tender stalk
Soon rears itself above the parent trunk,
Shadows the earth, and lifts its boughs to heaven;
560 The spark mischance has left from some great fire
Renews its strength; like these is Hector's son.
If well you weigh our act, you will forgive,
Though grief is harsh of judgment. We have spent
Ten weary winters, ten long harvests spent
565 In war; and now, grown old, our soldiers fear,
Even from fallen Troy, some new defeat.
'Tis not a trifling thing that moves the Greeks,
But a young Hector; free them from this fear;
This cause alone holds back our waiting fleet,
570 This stops the ships. Too cruel think me not,
By lot commanded Hector's son to seek;
I would have sought Orestes, equally,
Suffer with patience what your conqueror bore.
    Andromache. Alas, my son,

Would that thou wert within thy mother's arms!
575 Would that I knew what fate encompassed thee,
What region holds thee, torn from my embrace!
Although my breast were pierced with hostile spears,
My hands bound fast with wounding chains, my sides
By biting flame were girdled, not for this
580 Would I put off my mother-guardianship!
What spot, what fortune holds thee now, my son?
Art thou a wanderer in an unknown land,
Or have the flames of Troy devoured thee?
Or does the conqueror in thy blood rejoice?
585 Or, slain by some wild beast, perhaps thou liest
On Ida's summit, food for Ida's birds?
    Ulysses. No more pretend. Thou mayst not so deceive
Ulysses; I have ere this overcome
The wiles of mothers, though of blood divine.
590 Put by thy empty plots; where is thy son?
    Andromache. Where is my Hector? Where the Trojan host?
Where Priam? Thou seek'st one, I seek them all.
    Ulysses. What thou refusest willingly to tell,
Thou shalt be forced to say.
    Andromache. She rests secure
595 Who can, who ought, nay, who desires to die.
    Ulysses. Near death may put an end to such proud boast.
    Andromache. Ulysses, if thou hop'st through fear to force
Andromache to speak, threat longer life;
Death is to me a wished-for messenger.
600   *Ulysses.* With fire, scourge, torment, even death itself,
I will drag forth thy heart's deep-hidden thought;
Necessity is stronger far than love.
    Andromache. Threat flames, wounds, hunger, thirst, the bitter stings
Of cruel grief, all torments, sword plunged deep
605 Within this bosom, or the dungeon's gloom—
Whatever angry, fearful victors may;
Learn that a mother's courage casts out fear.
    Ulysses. And yet this love, in which thou standst entrenched
So stubbornly, admonishes the Greeks
610 To think of their own children. Even now,
After these long ten years, this weary war,
I should fear less the danger Calchas threats,
If for myself I feared—but thou prepar'st
War for Telemachus.
    Andromache. Unwillingly
615 I give the Grecians joy, but I must give.
Ulysses, anguish must confess its pain;
Rejoice, O sons of Atreus; carry back
As thou art wont, Ulysses, to the host
The joyous news: great Hector's son is dead.

Ulysses. How prove it to the Greeks?
620   *Andromache.* Fall on me else
The greatest ill the victor can inflict:
Fate free me by an easy, timely death,
And hide me underneath my native soil,
Lightly on Hector lie his country's earth
625 As it is true that, hidden from the light,
Deep in the tomb, among the shades he rests.
    Ulysses. Accomplished then the fate of Hector's race;
A joyous message of established peace
I take the Greeks. [*He turns to go, then hesitates.*]
    Ulysses, wouldst thou so?
630 The Greeks will trust thee, for thou trustest—whom?
A mother. Would a mother tell this lie
Nor fear the augury of dreaded death?
They fear the auguries, who fear naught else.
She swears it with an oath—yet, falsely sworn,
635 What has she worse to fear? Now call to aid
All that thou hast of cunning, stratagem,
And guile, the whole Ulysses; truth dies not.
Watch well the mother; see—she mourns, she weeps,
She groans, turns every way her anxious steps,
640 Listens with ear attentive; more she fears
Than sorrows; thou hast need of utmost care.
[*To Andromache.*] For other mothers' loss 'tis right to grieve;
Thee, wretched one, we must congratulate
That thou hast lost a son whose fate had been
645 To die, hurled headlong from the one high tower
Remaining of the ruined walls of Troy.
    Andromache. [*Aside.*] Life fails, I faint, I fall, an icy fear
Freezes my blood.
    Ulysses. [*Aside.*] She trembles; here the place
For my attack; she is betrayed by fear;
650 I'll add worse fear. [*To his followers.*]
    Go quickly; somewhere lies,
By mother's guile concealed, the hidden foe—
The last remaining foe of our Greek race.
Go, seek him, drag him hither. [*After a pause as though the child were found.*] It is well;
The child is taken; hasten, bring him me.
655 [*To Andromache.*] Why do you look around and seem to fear?
The boy is dead.
    Andromache. Would fear were possible!
Long have I feared. The mind must oft unlearn
The lesson learned.
    Ulysses. Since by a happier fate
Snatched hence, the lad forestalls the sacrifice,
660 The lustral offering from the walls of Troy

And may not now obey the seer's command,
Thus saith the prophet: this may be atoned,
And Grecian ships at last may find return,
If Hector's tomb be leveled with the ground,
His ashes scattered on the sea; the tomb
Must feel my hand, since Hector's child escapes
His destined death.
    Andromache. [*Aside.*] Alas, what shall I do?
A double fear distracts me; here my son,
And there my husband's sacred sepulcher,
Which conquers? O inexorable gods,
O manes of my husband—my true gods,
Bear witness; in my son 'tis thee I love,
My Hector, O that he may live to bear
His father's image!—Shall the sacred dust
Be cast upon the waves? Nay, better death.—
Canst thou, a mother, bear to see him die,—
To see him from Troy's tower downward hurled?
I can and will, that Hector, after death,
Be not the victor's sport. The boy can feel
The pain, where death has made the father safe.
Decide, which one to give to punishment.
Ungrateful, why in doubt? Thy Hector's here!
'Tis false, each one is Hector; this one lives,
Perchance th' avenger of his father's death.
I cannot save them both, what shall I do?
Oh, save the one whom most the Grecians fear!
    Ulysses. I will fulfil the oracle, will raze
The tomb to its foundations.
    Andromache. What you sold to us?
    Ulysses. I'll do it, level with the dust the sepulcher.
    Andromache. I call the faith of heaven,
Achilles' faith, to aid; come, Pyrrhus, save thy father's gift.
    Ulysses. The tomb shall instantly
Be leveled with the plain.
    Andromache. This crime alone
The Greeks had shunned; ye've sacked the holy fanes
Even of favoring gods, but spared the tomb.
I will not suffer it, unarmed I'll stand
Against your armored host; rage gives me strength,
And as the savage Amazon opposed
The Grecian army, or the Mænad wild,
Armed with the thyrsus, by the god possessed,
Wounds herself in her madness, feeling not
The pain, and scatters terror through the grove,
So will I rush into your midst and die
Defending the dear ashes of my dead. [*She places herself before the grave.*]
    Ulysses. [*Angrily to the shrinking soldiers.*]

705   Why pause? A woman's wrath and feeble noise
Alarms you so? Do quickly my command.
[*The soldiers go toward the grave, Andromache throws herself upon them.*]
    Andromache. The sword must first slay me.—Ah, woe is me,
They drive me back. Hector, come forth the tomb;
Break through the fate's delay, and overwhelm
710 The Grecian chief—thy shade would be enough!
He shakes the weapon, hurls the fire-brand;
Greeks, see you Hector? Or do I alone
Perceive him?
    Ulysses. I will lay it in the dust.
    Andromache. [*Aside.*] What have I done? To ruin I have brought
715 Father and son together; yet, perchance,
With supplications I may move the Greeks.
The tomb's vast weight will presently destroy
Its hidden treasure; O my wretched child,
Die anywhere the Fates decree but here.
720 Oh, may the father not o'erwhelm the son,
The son fall not upon his father's dust!
[*She casts herself at the feet of Ulysses.*]
Ulysses, at thy feet a suppliant
I fall, and with my right hand clasp thy knees;
Never before a suppliant, here I ask
725 Thy pity on a mother; hear my prayer
With patience; on the fallen lightly press,
Since thee the gods lift up to greater heights!
The gifts thou grant'st the wretched are to fate
A hostage; so again thou mayst behold
730 Thy wife; and old Laertes' years endure
Until once more he see thee; so thy son
Receive thee home, outrun thy fairest hopes
In his good fortune, and his age exceed
Laertes', and his gifts outnumber thine.
735 Have pity on a mother to whose grief
Naught else remains of comfort.
    Ulysses. Bring forth the boy, then thou mayst ask for grace.
    Andromache. Come hither from thy hiding-place, my son,
Thy wretched mother's lamentable theft.

Scene III

Ulysses, Andromache, Astyanax.

740   *Andromache.* Ulysses, this is he who terrifies
The thousand keels, behold him. Fall, my son,
A suppliant at the feet of this thy lord,
And do him reverence; nor think it base,
Since Fortune bids the wretched to submit.

⁷⁴⁵ Forget thy royal race, the power of one
Renowned through all the world; Hector forget;
Act the sad captive on thy bended knee,
And imitate thy mother's tears, if yet
Thou feelest not thy woes. [*To Ulysses.*] Troy saw long since
⁷⁵⁰ The weeping of a royal child: the tears
Of youthful Priam turned aside the threats
Of stern Alcides; he, the warrior fierce
Who tamed wild beasts, who broke the gates of Dis,
And opened up the dark way back to earth,
⁷⁵⁵ Was conquered by his youthful foeman's tears.
'Take back,' he said, 'the reins of government,
Receive thy father's kingdom, but maintain
Thy scepter with a better faith than he;'
So fared the captives of this conqueror;
⁷⁶⁰ Study the gentle wrath of Hercules!
Or do the arms alone of Hercules
Seem pleasing to thee? Of as noble race
As Priam's, at thy feet a suppliant lies,
And asks of thee his life; let fortune give
⁷⁶⁵ To whom she will Troy's kingdom.
    Ulysses. Indeed the mother's sorrow moves me much!
Our Grecian mothers' sorrow moves me more,
To cause whose bane this child would grow a man.
    Andromache. These ruins of a land to ashes burned
⁷⁷⁰ Could he arouse? Or could these hands build Troy?
Troy has no hope, if such is all remains.
We Trojans can no longer cause thee fear.
Does recollection of his father rouse
Pride? In the dust that father's form was dragged.
⁷⁷⁵ With Troy in ruins, even his father's self
Had lost that courage which great ills o'ercome.
If vengeance is your wish, what worse revenge
Than to this noble neck to fit the yoke?
Make him a slave. Who ever yet denied
This bounty to a king?
⁷⁸⁰   *Ulysses.* The seer forbids,
'Tis not Ulysses who denies the boon.
    Andromache. Artificer of fraud, plotter of guile,
Whose warlike valor never felled a foe;
By the deceit and guile of whose false heart
⁷⁸⁵ E'en Greeks have fallen, dost thou make pretence
Of blameless god or prophet? 'Tis the work
Of thine own heart. Thou, who by night mak'st war,
Now dar'st at last one deed in open day—
A brave boy's death.
    Ulysses. My valor to the Greeks
⁷⁹⁰ Is known, and to the Phrygians too well known.

We may not waste the day in idle talk—
Our ships weigh anchor.
    Andromache. Grant a brief delay,
While I, a mother, for my son perform
The last sad office, satiate my grief,
My mother's sorrow, with a last embrace.
    Ulysses. I would that I might pity! What I may,
Time and delay, I grant thee; let thy tears
Fall freely; weeping ever softens grief.
    Andromache. O pledge of love, light of a fallen house,
Last of the Trojan dead, fear of the Greeks,
Thy mother's empty hope, for whom I prayed—
Fool that I was—that thou mightst have the years
Of Priam, and thy father's warlike soul,
The gods despise my vows; thou ne'er shalt wield
A scepter in the kingly halls of Troy,
Mete justice to thy people, nor shalt send
Thy foes beneath thy yoke, nor put to flight
The Greeks, drag Pyrrhus at thy chariot wheels,
Nor ever in thy slender hands bear arms;
Nor wilt thou hunt the dwellers in the wood,
Nor on high festival, in Trojan games,
Lead swiftly on a band of noble youth,
Nor round the altars with swift-moving steps,
That the reechoing of the twisted horn
Makes swifter, honor with accustomed dance
The Phrygian temples. Oh, most bitter death!
    Ulysses. Great sorrow knows no limit, cease thy moans!
    Andromache. How narrow is the time we seek for tears!
Grant me a short delay: that with these hands
His living eyes be bound. My little one,
Thou diest, but feared already by thy foes;
Thy Troy awaits thee; go, in freedom go,
To meet free Trojans.
    Astyanax. Mother, pity me!
    Andromache. Why hold thy mother's hands and clasp her neck,
And seek in vain a refuge? The young bull,
Thus fearful, seeks his mother when he hears
The roaring of the lion; from her side
By the fierce lion driv'n, the tender prey
Is seized, and crushed, and dragged away; so thee
Thy foeman snatches from thy mother's breast.
Child, take my tears, my kisses, my torn locks;
Thus laden with remembrances of me
Go to thy father, bear him these few words
Of my complaint: 'If still thy spirit keeps
Its former cares, if died not on the flames
Thy former love, why leave Andromache

To serve the Grecians? Hector, cruel one,
Dost thou lie cold and vanquished in the grave?
Achilles came again.' Take then these tears,
840 These locks, for these are all that now remain
Since Hector's death, and take thy mother's kiss
To give thy father; leave thy robe for me,
Since it has touched his tomb and his dear dust;
I'll search it well so any ashes lurk
Within its folds.
845   *Ulysses.* Weep no more; bear him hence;
Too long he stays the sailing of the fleet.

Scene IV

Chorus of Trojan Women.

What country calls the captives? Tempe dark?
Or the Thessalian hills? or Phthia's land
Famous for warriors? Trachin's stony plains,
850 Breeders of cattle? or the great sea's queen,
Iolchos? or the spacious land of Crete
Boasting its hundred towns? Gortyna small?
Or sterile Tricca? or Mothone crossed
By swift and frequent rivers? She who lies
855 Beneath the shadow of the Œtean woods,
Who sent the hostile bow not once alone
Against the walls of Troy?
Or Olenos whose homes lie far apart?
Or Pleuron, hateful to the virgin god?
860 Or Trœzen on the ocean's curving shore?
Or Pelion, mounting heavenward, the realm
Of haughty Prothous? There in a vast cave
Great Chiron, teacher of the savage child,
Struck with his plectrum from the soundings strings
865 Wild music, stirred the boy with songs of war.
Perchance Carystus, for its marbles famed,
Calls us; or Chalcis, lying on the coast
Of the unquiet sea whose hastening tide
Beats up the strait; Calydna's wave-swept shore;
870 Or stormy Gonoëssa; or the isle
Of Peparethus, near the seaward line
Of Attica; Enispe, smitten oft
By Boreas; or Eleusis, reverenced
For Ceres' holy, secret mysteries?
875 Or shall we seek great Ajax' Salamis?
Or Calydon, the home of savage beasts?
Or countries that the Titaressus laves
With its slow waters? Scarphe, Pylos old,

Or Bessas, Pharis, Pisa, Elis famed
For the Olympian games?
It matters not what tempest drives us hence,
Or to what land it bears us, so we shun
Sparta, the curse alike of Greece and Troy;
Nor Argos seek, nor cruel Pelop's home,
Mycenae, and Neritus hemmed within
Narrower limits than Zacynthus small,
Nor treacherous cliffs of rocky Ithaca.
O Hecuba, what fate, what land, what lord
Remains for thee? In whose realm meetst thou death?

ACT IV

Scene I

Helen, Hecuba, Andromache, Polyxena.

Helen [soliloquizing]. Whatever sad and joyless marriage bond
Holds slaughter, lamentations, bloody war,
Is worthy Helen. Even to fallen Troy
I bring misfortune, bidden to declare
The bridal that Achilles' son prepares
For his dead father, and to lend my robe
And Grecian ornaments. By me betrayed,
And by my fraud, must Paris' sister die.
So be it, this were happier lot for her;
A fearless death must be a longed-for death.
Why shrink to do his bidding? On the head
Of him who plots the crime remains the guilt.
[*Aloud to Polyxena.*]
Thou noble daughter of Troy's kingly house,
A milder god on thy misfortune looks
Prepares for thee a happy marriage day.
Not Priam nor unfallen Troy could give
Such bridal, for the brightest ornament
Of the Pelasgian race, the man who holds
The kingdom of the wide Thessalian land,
Would make thee his by lawful marriage bonds.
Great Tethys, and the ocean goddesses,
And Thetis, gentle nymph of swelling seas,
Will call thee theirs; when thou art Pyrrhus' bride
Peleus will call thee kin, as Nereus will.
Put off thy robe of mourning, deck thyself
In gay attire; unlearn the captive's mien,
And suffer skilful hands to smooth thy hair
Now so unkempt. Perchance fate cast thee down
From thy high place to seat thee higher still;

To their great profit some have been enslaved.
920   *Andromache.* This one ill only lacked to fallen Troy:
Pleasure, while Pergamus still smoking lies!
Fit hour for marriage! Dare one then refuse?
When Helen would persuade, who doubtful weds?
Thou curse! Two nations owe to thee their fall!
925   Seest thou the royal tomb, these bones that lie
Unburied, scattered over all the field?
Thy bridal is the cause. All Asia's blood,
All Europe's flows for thee, whilst thou, unstirred,
Canst see two husbands fighting, nor decide
930   Which one to wish the victor! Go, prepare
The marriage bed; what need of wedding torch
Or nuptial lights, when burning Troy provides
The fires for these new bridals? Celebrate,
O Trojan women, honor worthily
The marriage feast of Pyrrhus. Smite your breasts,
935   And weep aloud.
       Helen. Soft comfort is refused
By deep despair, which loses reason, hates
The very sharers of its grief. My cause
I yet may plead before this hostile judge,
940   Since I have suffered heavier ills than she.
Andromache mourns Hector openly,
Hecuba weeps for Priam, I, alone,
In secret, weep for Paris. Is it hard,
Grievous, and hateful to bear servitude?
945   For ten long years I bore the captive's yoke.
Is Ilium laid low, her household gods
Cast down? To lose one's land is hard indeed—
To fear it worse. Your sorrow friendship cheers,
Me conquerors and conquered hate alike.
950   For thee there long was doubt whom thou shouldst serve,
My master drags me hence without the chance
Of lot. Was I the bringer of the war?
Of so great Teucrian carnage? Think this true
If first a Spartan keel thy waters cut;
955   But if of Phrygian oars I was the prey,
By the victorious goddess as a prize
Given for Paris' judgment, pardon me!
An angry judge awaits me, and my cause
Is left to Menelaus. Weep no more,
960   Andromache, put by thy grief. Alas,
Hardly can I myself restrain my tears.
       Andromache. How great the ill that even Helen weeps!
Why does she weep? What trickery or crime
Plots now the Ithacan? From Ida's top,
965   Or Troy's high tower, will he cast the maid

Upon the rocks? Or hurl her to the deep
From the great cliff which, from its riven side,
Out of the shallow bay, Sigeon lifts?
What wouldst thou cover with deceitful face?
970 No ill were heavier than this: to see
Pyrrhus the son-in-law of Hecuba
And Priam. Tell the penalty thou bringst.
Take from defeat at least this evil,—fraud.
Thou seest thou dost not find us loth to die.
975   *Helen.* Would that Apollo's prophet bade me take
The long delay of my so hated life;
Or that, upon Achilles' sepulcher,
I might be slain by Pyrrhus' cruel hand,
The sharer of thy fate, Polyxena,
980 Whom harsh Achilles bids them give to him—
To offer to his manes, as his bride
In the Elysian Fields.
[*Polyxena shows great joy, Hecuba sinks fainting to the ground.*]
    Andromache. See with what joy a noble woman meets
Death-sentence, bids them bring the royal robe,
985 And fitly deck her hair. She deemed it death
To be the bride of Pyrrhus, but this death
A bridal seems. The wretched mother faints,
Her sinking spirit fails; unhappy one,
Arise, lift up thy heart, be strong of soul!
990 Her life hangs by a thread—how slight a chance
Would make her happy!—But she breathes, she lives,
Death flies the wretched.
    Hecuba. Lives Achilles still
To vex the Trojans? Still pursues his foes?
Light was the hand of Paris; but the tomb
995 And ashes of Achilles drink our blood.
Once I was circled by a happy throng
Of children, by their kisses weary made,
Parted my mother love amongst them all.
She, now, alone is left; for her I pray,
1000 Companion, solace, healer of my grief,
The only child of Hecuba, her voice
Alone may call me mother! Bitter life,
Pass from me, slip away, spare this last blow!
Tears overflow my cheeks—a storm of tears
Falls from my eyes!
1005   *Andromache.* We are the ones should weep,
We, Hecuba, whom, scattered here and there,
The Grecian ships shall carry far away.
The maid will find at least a sepulcher
In the dear soil of her loved native land.
1010   *Helen.* Thy own lot known, yet more thou'lt envy hers.

Andromache. Is any portion of my lot unknown?
Helen. The fatal urn has given thee a lord.
Andromache. Whom call I master? Speak, who bears me hence a slave?
Helen. Lot gave thee to the Scyrian king.
1015 *Andromache.* Happy Cassandra, madness spared thee this,
Madness and great Apollo's aid.
Helen. The prince
Of kings claims her.
Hecuba. Rejoice, rejoice, my child;
Cassandra envies thee thy bridals, thine
Andromache desires. Is there one
Seeks Hecuba for bride?
1020 *Helen.* Thou fall'st a prey
To the unwilling Ithacan.
Hecuba. Alas, what raging, cruel, unrelenting god
Gives kings by lot to be the prey of kings?
What god unfriendly thus divides the spoil?
1025 What cruel arbiter forbids us choose
Our masters? With Achilles' arms unites
Great Hector's mother? To Ulysses' lot!
Conquered and captive am I now indeed,
Beset by all misfortunes! 'Tis my lord
1030 Puts me to shame, and not my servitude!
Isle small and sterile, by rough seas enclosed,
Thou wilt not hold my grave! Lead on, lead on,
Ulysses, I delay not, I will go—
Will follow thee; my fate will follow me.
1035 No tranquil calm will rest upon the sea;
Wind, war, and flame shall rage upon the deep,
My woes and Priam's! When these things shall come,
Respite from punishment shall come to Troy.
Mine is the lot, from thee I snatch the prize!
1040 But see where Pyrrhus comes with hasty steps
And savage mien. Why pause? On, Pyrrhus, on!
Into this troubled bosom drive the sword,
And join to thy Achilles his new kin!
Slayer of aged men, come, here is blood,
1045 Blood worthy of thy sword; drag off thy spoil,
And with thy hideous slaughter stain the gods—
The gods who rule in heaven and those in hell!
What can I pray for thee? I pray for seas
Worthy these rites; I pray the thousand ships,
1050 The fleet of the Pelasgians, may meet
Such fate as that I fain would whelm the ship
That bears me hence a captive.

Scene II

Chorus. Sweet is a nation's grief to one who grieves—
Sweet are the lamentations of a land!
1055 The sting of tears and grief is less when shared
By many; sorrow, cruel in its pain,
Is glad to see its lot by others shared,
To know that not alone it suffers loss.
None shuns the hapless fate that many bear;
1060 None deems himself forlorn, though truly so,
If none are happy near him. Take away
His riches from the wealthy, take away
The hundred cattle that enrich his soil,
The poor will lift again his lowered head;
1065 'Tis only by comparison man's poor.
O'erwhelmed in hopeless ruin, it is sweet
To see none happy. He deplores his fate
Who, shipwrecked, naked, finds the longed-for port
Alone. He bears with calmer mien his fate
1070 Who sees, with his, a thousand vessels wrecked
By the fierce tempest, and upon a plank
Escaping safe, returns to shore, the while
The northwest wind, collecting all the waves,
Drives them from shore: and when the radiant ram,
1075 The gold-fleeced leader of the flock, bore forth
Phryxus and Helle, Phryxus mourned the fall
Of Helle dropped into the Grecian sea.
Pyrrha, Deucalion's wife, restrained her tears,
As he did, when they saw the sea, naught else,
1080 And they alone of living men remained.
The fleet shall soon far scatter this sad band,
Soon shall the trumpet sound to spread the sail,
Soon dip the laboring oars, and Troy's shores flee,
When shall the land grow faint and far, the sea
1085 Expand before, Mount Ida fade behind?
Then grows our sorrow; then what way Troy lies
Mother and son shall gaze. The son shall say,
Pointing the while, 'There where the curving line
Of smoke floats, there is Ilium.' By that sign
1090 Shall Trojans know their country.

ACT V

Scene I

Hecuba, Andromache, Messenger.

Messenger. O bitter, cruel, lamentable fate!
In these ten years of war what crime so hard,
So sad, has Mars encountered? What decree
Of fate shall I lament? Thy bitter lot, Andromache?
Or thine, thou aged one?
    Hecuba. Whatever woe thou mournst is Hecuba's;
Their own griefs only others have to bear,
I bear the woes of all, all die for me,
And sorrow follows all who call me friend.
    Andromache. Tell of the deaths—the tale of double crime;
Suffering ever loves to hear its woes;
Speak, tell us all.
    Messenger. One mighty tower remains
Of Troy, no more is left; from this high seat
Priam, the arbiter of war, was wont
To view his troops; and in this tower he sat
And, in caressing arms, embraced the son
Of Hector, when that hero put to flight
With fire and sword the trembling, conquered Greeks.
From thence he showed the child its father's deeds.
This tower, the former glory of our walls,
Is now a lonely, ruined mass of rock
Thither the throng of chiefs and people flock;
From the deserted ships the Grecian host
Come pouring; on the hills some find a place,
Some on the rising cliffs, upon whose top
They stand tiptoe; some climb the pines, and beech,
And laurel, till beneath the gathered crowd
The whole wood trembles; some have found the peaks
Of broken crags; some climb a ruined roof,
Or toppling turret of the falling wall;
And some, rude lookers-on, mount Hector's tomb.
Through all the crowded space, with haughty mien,
Passes the Ithacan, and by the hand
Leads Priam's grandson; nor with tardy step
Does the young hero mount the lofty wall.
Standing upon the top, with fearless heart
He turns his eagle glance from side to side.
As the young, tender cub of some wild beast,
Not able yet to raven with its teeth,
Bites harmlessly, and proudly feels himself

A lion; so this brave and fearless child,
Holding the right hand of his enemy,
Moves host and leaders and Ulysses' self.
He only does not weep for whom all weep,
1135 But while the Ithacan begins the words
Of the prophetic message and the prayers
To the stern gods, he leaps into the midst
Of Priam's kingdom, of his own accord.
    Andromache. Was ever such a deed by Colchians done,
1140 Or wandering Scythians, or the lawless race
That dwells beside the Caspian? Never yet
Has children's blood Busiris' altars stained,
Nor Diomedes feasted his fierce steeds
On children's limbs! Who'll take thy body up,
1145 My son, and bear it to the sepulcher?
    Messenger. What would that headlong leap have left? His bones
Lie dashed in pieces by the heavy fall,
His face and noble form, inheritance
From his illustrious father, are with earth
1150 Commingled; on the cruel rocks his neck
Is broken, and his head is crushed, his brains
Dashed out; his body lies devoid of form.
    Andromache. This, too, is like his father.
    Messenger. When headlong from the wall the boy was cast,
1155 And the Achaians wept the crime they did,
Then turned these same Achaians to new crimes,
And to Achilles' tomb. With quiet flow
The Rhœtean waters beat the further side,
And on the other side the level plain
1160 Slopes gently upward, and surrounds the place
Like a wide amphitheater; here the strand
Is thronged with lookers-on, who think to end
With this last death their vessels' long delay,
And glad themselves to think the foeman's seed
1165 At last cut off. The fickle, common crowd
Condemn the crime, but feast their eyes on it.
The Trojans haste with no less eagerness
To their own funeral rites, and, pale with fear,
Behold the final fall of ruined Troy.
1170 As at a marriage, suddenly advance
The bridal torches, Helen goes before,
Attendant to the bride, with sad head bent.
'So may Hermione,' the Phrygians pray,
'Be wed, and so base Helen find again
1175 Her husband.' Sudden terror seizes both
The awe-struck peoples. With her glance cast down,
Modestly comes the victim; but her cheeks
Glow, and her beauty shines unwontedly;

So shines the light of Phœbus gloriously
1180 Before his setting, when the stars return
And day is darkened by approaching night.
The throng is silenced; all men praise the maid
Who now must die: some praise her lovely form,
Her tender age moves some, and some lament
1185 The fickleness of fortune; everyone
Is touched at heart by her courageous soul,
Her scorn of death. She comes, by Pyrrhus led;
All wonder, tremble, pity; when the hill
Is reached, and on his father's grave advanced,
1190 The young king stands, the fearless maid shrinks not,
But waits unflinchingly the fatal blow.
Her unquelled spirit moves the hearts of all;
And—a new prodigy—Pyrrhus is slow
At slaughter; but at length, with steady hand,
1195 He buries to the hilt the gleaming sword
Within her breast; the life-blood gushes forth
From the deep wound; in death as heretofore
Her soul is strong; with angry thud she falls
As she would make the earth a heavy load
1200 Upon Achilles' breast. Both armies weep;
The Trojans venture only feeble moans;
The victors weep aloud: and thus was made
The sacrifice. Her blood, upon the ground
Once spilt, flowed not away, but eagerly
1205 The tomb absorbed and greedily sucked in
Each crimson drop.
    Hecuba. Go, conquering Greeks,
Securely seek your homes; with all sail set,
Your fleet may safely skim the longed-for sea.
The lad and maid are dead, the war is done!
1210 Where can I hide my woe, where lay aside
The long delay of the slow-passing years?
Whom shall I weep? my husband, grandson, child,
Or country? Mourn the living or the dead?
O longed-for death, with violence dost thou come
1215 To babes and maidens, but thou fleest from me!
Through long night sought, mid fire, and swords, and spears,
Why fly me? Not the foe, nor ruined home,
Nor flame could slay me, though so near I stood
To Priam!
    Messenger. [*Talthybius, coming from the Greek camp.*]
        Captive women, seek with speed
The sea; the sails are set, the vessels move.

THE PHŒNICIAN WOMEN

DRAMATIS PERSONÆ

Œdipus.
Eteocles.
Polynices.
Antigone.
Jocasta.
A Theban Guard.

Scene: *Thebes*.

THE PHŒNICIAN WOMEN

ACT I

Scene I

Œdipus, Antigone.

Œdipus. O guide of thy blind father, only cheer
To one sore wearied, daughter well-beloved
Though got at such a heavy price, forsake
Thy wretched parent, wherefore shouldst thou lead
His wandering steps? O let him stumble on!
'Tis better I should find the way I seek,
Alone—the path that takes me out of life
And frees from sight of this crime-laden head
The earth and sky. How little have I done!
The daylight, conscious of my evil deeds,
I do not see, indeed; but I am seen!
O child, unclasp the hand that clings to mine,
Where'er my blind steps lead me let me roam.
I go, I go, where high Cithæron lifts
Its rugged summit, where Actæon swift,
Roaming among the rocks, was made a prey
By his own dogs; where through the shadowy groves
And dusky woodlands of the bosky vales
The mother, god-inspired, led forth her band,
And on her waving thyrsus lifted up
That head transfixed, rejoicing in ill deeds;
Where Zethus' bullock ran and dragged along
The shattered body—on the bristling thorns
Blood marked the course of the swift bullock's flight;
Or where with lofty summit Ino's cliff
Rises beside the sea, where fleeing crime

But finding crime the mother sought to drown
Herself, her son, and leaped into the waves.
Thrice happy he whose better fortune gave
30 So good a mother! In these woods of ours
There lies another place that calls to me,
My footstep shall not falter, I will go
Thither without a guide, why hesitate
To take my rightful place? O give me death,
35 Cithæron, give me back my former lodge,
That where in infancy I should have died,
There in my age I may breathe out my life.
O ever savage, ruthless, cruel, fell,
Whether thou slay or spare, long, long ago
40 This lifeless trunk was due thee, now at last
Fulfil my father's mandate, mother's will.
My spirit longs to see accomplished now
The deed so long delayed. Why hold me clasped
With fatal love, my child? Why hold me so?
45 My father calls, I follow! Follow thee!
Yet spare! Behold where angry Laius comes,
Bearing the bloodstained standard of the realm
Snatched from him. With his hands he seeks to tear
My eyeballs' empty sockets. Dost thou see
50 My father, child? I see him! Now at last
Spew out thy baneful life, O coward soul,
Brave to destroy thy eyesight, not thyself!
Leave off thy long atonements, weak delays!
Why longer drag along thy life's slow length?
55 Why live? No crime remains for thee to do.
Ah, wretch! I here proclaim I still may sin!—
Go virgin, leave thy father; for her sake—
Thy mother's—fear I all.
    Antigone. No power on earth,
O father, can unknit my hand from thine,
60 And none shall ever snatch me from thy side.
My brothers may with drawn sword seek to gain
The opulent realm and th' illustrious home
Of Labdacus, but mine the better part
Of all my father's realm—my father's self.
65 That brother who now holds in captured Thebes
The Theban scepter cannot take from me
This share, nor can that other who now leads
Argolic hosts; though Jupiter should speak
With thunderous voice out of the riven sky,
70 Although his bolt should fall to break our bond,
I will not let thee go. Though thou forbid,
Yet will I guide thee; though thou wish it not,
I will against thy will direct thy steps.

Seekst thou the plain? I go. The rugged heights?
75 I do not bar the way, but go before.
Whatever path thou treadst, make me thy guide,
We choose the selfsame road. Thou canst not die
Without me, with me thou mayst find thy death.
Here rises with steep sides the lofty cliff,
80 And views wide reaches of the sea that lies
Below, wilt thou go thither? There o'erhangs
The barren rock, there yawns the gaping jaws
Of the rent earth, shall I direct thee there?
There fall the hungry torrents, rolling down
85 The sundered rocks from off the broken hills,
Shall we rush headlong in? Lo, I go first,
I go where'er thou wilt, I do not urge,
I would not hinder. Father, wouldst thou cut
Thy thread of life? Is death thy dearest wish?
90 I go before thee if thou seekest death,
I follow if thou live. Yet change thy mind,
Call to thy aid thy will, so strong of old,
With force heroic master thy distress,
To die is to be conquered by thy woes,
Oh, be courageous still.
95   *Œdipus.* From so base home
Whence comes such noble growth? Whence comes this maid
So different from her race? Canst thou believe,
O fate, that this is true? Has any good
Been born of me? It never yet has been
100 That fortune smiled on me except to harm.
Nature obeys new laws; the streams, reversed,
Bear back swift waters to their fountain-head,
The torch of Phœbus ushers in the night,
And Hesperus brings the day; that I may find
105 Some increase of my woe, I, even I,
Shall have a loyal child. In death alone
Can Œdipus be safe. I may avenge
My father, unavenged till now; why cease
To mete out punishment, inert right hand?
110 Whatever hitherto was measured out
Was given for a mother. Dauntless maid,
Let go thy father's hand, thou dost prolong
My death; thy living father's funeral rites,
Already all too long, thou lengthenest,
115 Cover the hateful body with the earth.
Thou errest, though with nobleness of aim,
And deemst it loyalty to drag about
A father who lacks yet his burial rites.
Who hinders one in haste to find his death
120 Equals in guilt the one who forces death

On one unwilling. Yet he equals not!
The first I deem, indeed, the greater sin,
I rather would be hurried to my end
Than be from death's jaws snatched away. My child,
125 No longer strive, in my own hands I hold
The right to live or die: I laid aside
Freely my sovereign power, but still retain
Sovereignty o'er myself. If thou indeed
Art loyal, give again thy father's sword,
130 The sword with parent's slaughter infamous.
Thou giv'st it? Do my children also hold
This with the realm? Wherever there is need
Of crime, there that should be; I give it up,
My sons shall have it, yea both sons. Prepare
135 The torches rather and a heap of wood;
On the high funeral pyre I'll cast myself,
Embrace the flames and 'neath the desolate pile
Will hide this too firm heart; set free at last,
Will give to ashes all that lives in me.
140 Where is the pitiless sea? Where jutting crags
O'erhang, where swift Ismenus' savage shoals
Roll downward, lead me, if thou leader art.
Where on the high cliff sat the Sphinx, half brute,
Proposing riddles, there I'll go to die,
145 Thither direct my steps, oh, place me there!
Not empty should that baleful seat be left,
Let it be by the greater monster filled.
There sitting on the rocks I will propose
The riddle of our fortune none can solve.
150 Whoe'er thou art who plow'st th' Assyrian fields,
Whoe'er, a suppliant, offerest up thy prayers
Where dwelt the far-famed dragon, ye who drink
Eurotas or inhabit Sparta, famed
For the twin brothers, husbandmen who reap
155 Elis, Parnassus, and the fertile fields
Of rich Boeotia, listen; what like this
Could she propose—Thebes' savage curse who wove
Dark, baneful riddles? What so hard to loose?
His father's father's son-in-law, yet found
160 His father's rival, brother to his sons,
And father of his brothers; at one birth
The father's mother bore the husband sons,
And grandsons to herself. Who can search out
This prodigy? I, even I, who bore
165 The trophies from the conquered Sphinx, perplexed,
Am slow to read my riddle. Why waste words?
Why strive with prayers to soften my hard heart?
Fixed is my purpose to pour out this life,

　　　　　Too long with death contending, and to seek
170　The land of shadows, for the blackest night
　　　　Is all too little for this crime of mine.
　　　　Hide me in Tartarus, or if beyond
　　　　Aught lies, there hide me; what I should have done
　　　　Long since, I now will do. It cannot be
175　Death is forbidden. Wilt thou keep the sword?
　　　　Wilt thou close up the way that leads to death,
　　　　Nor grant a halter? Wilt thou take away
　　　　Poisonous herbs? What profits all thy care?
　　　　In every place is death, most graciously
180　God ordered this; one may destroy man's life,
　　　　But none can snatch death from him, countless gates
　　　　To this lie open. I have need of nought,
　　　　Wont am I to employ my brave right hand.
　　　　Come, hand, with all thy force, with all thy guile,
185　With all thy strength; I purpose not to wound
　　　　One place alone, I am all black with sin,
　　　　Deal death in whatsoever part thou wilt.
　　　　Lay wide the bosom, tear away the heart
　　　　So filled with crime, the inmost parts lay bare,
190　Let my weak throat sound with redoubled blows,
　　　　And let my veins, by wounding nails torn through,
　　　　Bleed; or where thou art wont direct thy wrath:
　　　　Open again these wounds, with putrid gore
　　　　Wet them, and drag this unsubdued, hard heart
195　By this gate forth. O father, wheresoe'er
　　　　Thou mayst be found, judge of my penalty,
　　　　I have not thought by any punishment
　　　　Ever to fully expiate my sin;
　　　　I was not satisfied with death alone,
200　I have not paid my ransom with my eyes,
　　　　I wished to perish for thee limb by limb,
　　　　At length exact the penalty I owe.
　　　　Now I atone, 'twas then but sacrifice
　　　　I offered; oh, be present, inward urge
205　My feeble hand; oh, plunge it deeper still!
　　　　A timid, slight libation then I poured,
　　　　Hardly drew forth the eyes that eagerly
　　　　Followed my hand. My spirit even now
　　　　Falters, is loth with trembling hand to tear
210　These sockets. Œdipus, be brave indeed,
　　　　Less bold than thou hast purposed thou hast been,
　　　　In plucking out thine eyes; deep in thy brain
　　　　Bury thy hand, and perfect thou the death
　　　　Where I began to die.
　　　　　　　Antigone. I pray thee show
215　Some pity, great-souled father; calmly hear

Thy daughter's words. I would not lead thee back
To the old home, nor to the kingly throne
With all its splendor, would not have thee bear
With weak, untroubled breast the wrath of God
220 Which time has not yet softened, but 'tis meet
So strong a man should not be crushed by grief,
Or fly, o'ercome by manifold distress.
It is not, father, as thou deemst it, brave
To be afraid of life; 'tis brave to face
225 The greatest ills, nor flinch, nor turn the back.
He who has trampled on his destiny,
He who has rent life's good and cast it by,
And made his own life heavier, who has need
No more of God, why should he wish to die?
230 Why seek his death? Either were cowardly.
No one who longs for death despises it.
The man whose evil fate is at its worst
Is safe. Although he would, what god could make
Thy trouble heavier? Nor canst thou thyself
235 Unless in deeming thou art worthy death.
Thou art not, for no sin has touched thy heart.
Thou canst more surely call thyself guilt free,
Since thou art innocent although the gods
Willed otherwise. What maddens thee? What adds
240 New stings to misery? What urges thee
Into the land of death? What drives thee hence?
Wouldst thou shun day? Thou hast. Or wouldst thou flee
Thy lofty palace and thy native land?
For thee, although thou livest, native land
245 Is dead. Or wouldst thou fly thy mother, sons?
Fate has removed thee from the sight of these.
What death from others takes, life takes from thee.
The tumult of the throne? At thy command
The press of crowding fortune fell away.
What wouldst thou fly, my father?
250   *Œdipus.* Ah! Myself!
I flee a bosom conscious of all crimes,
I flee this hand, this sky, I flee the gods.
Do I yet touch the earth where Ceres grows
Fruitful and fair? With noxious life still breathe
255 The vital air? or satisfy my thirst
With water? or enjoy in any way
The gifts of mother Nature? Base, defiled,
Detestable, do I yet feel the touch
Of thy pure hand? or can I yet perceive
260 Voices which speak the names of father, son?
Oh, could I with destroying hand throw wide
Those paths where enter sound! Might I destroy

These narrow pathways for the human voice!
O child, thy wretched father would have fled
265 Long, long ago, the knowledge that thou art,
Thou, part of my great sin. My crimes stick fast,
Repeated o'er and o'er. O eyes and ears,
Let all ye gave me pass away from me!
O'erwhelmed with blackest shadows, why not go
270 Into the everlasting shades of Dis?
Why keep my spirit here? Why weight the world?
Why wander yet among the souls that live?
What crime is left? Realm, parents, children, all,
Valor, the glory of sagacious mind,
275 Have perished; fate has taken from me all.
Tears still were left, these from myself I snatched.
Go, for my soul will listen to no prayers,
New penalties and equal to my crimes
I seek. Yet what can ever equal those?
280 I was condemned to death in infancy,
Who ever drew so bad a lot? ere yet
I saw the light, ere from my mother's womb
I was set free, already I was feared!
Night seizes many, just when they are born,
285 And carries them away from the new day;
Death found me even ere I saw the light.
Some meet an early death within the womb,
But have they also sinned? Still hidden close,
Secreted in the womb, not knowing yet
290 That I should be the doer of great crimes,
A god impelled; my father at his word
Condemned me, pierced with steel my tender feet,
And left me in the forest, food for beasts
And savage birds (oft wet with blood of kings)
295 Which dark Cithæron breeds. Yet whom the gods
Sentenced, and whom a father cast away,
Death also fled. I have fulfilled the word
Spoken at Delphos: I attacked and slew
My father. This might be by love made good.
300 My father I have slain, but I have loved
My mother—of our marriage torch to speak
Is loathsome, yet against my will I'll pay
This penalty, will tell the beastly crime,
Unheard-of, strange, at thought of which men shrink,
305 The crime which makes ashamed the man who slew
His father. This right hand, with father's blood
Made wet, even to my father's marriage bed
I took, and found sin's wages—greater sin.
My father's murder was a slight offence
310 Compared with this. Lest all too small should be

My guilt, my mother in my marriage bed
Was made a mother. Nature cannot yield
A greater crime than this, but should there be
A greater, those to whom 'twere possible
₃₁₅ Have been by me created. From my hand
I cast aside the patricide's reward,
The scepter, with it armed another hand.
I knew right well my kingdom's destiny,
Without the sacrifice of sacred blood
₃₂₀ No man can hold it. Nameless ills to come
My father heart presages. Seeds are sown
Of future slaughter. He who holds the realm
Will not resign it, he who wishes it
Calls upon justice and the gods who see
₃₂₅ The violated pact; exiled, he moves
Argos and all the cities of the Greeks
To arms; destruction comes to wretched Thebes;
The flying spear, flames, slaughter 'gainst her rise,
And greater ills, if greater ills there be,
₃₃₀ That none may doubt I have begotten sons.

  Antigone. If thou no other reason hadst to live,
This were enough: that thou shouldst fatherlike
Control thy maddened sons, thou canst avert,
And thou alone, the threats of impious war,
₃₃₅ Thou only canst restrain those youths insane,
Give to the people peace, to Thebes repose,
And, to the broken compact, faith renewed.
If thou thyself shouldst to thyself refuse
The right to live, thou tak'st from many more
The right of life.

₃₄₀   *Œdipus.* For empire and for blood.
For war and treachery athirst, base, vile,
In short my own, can these or can their like
Feel filial love? They joy in doing ill,
And deem nought sacred when rage drives them forth.
₃₄₅ Those base born ones consider nothing base,
Their wretched father's shame affects them not,
Nor does their native country, they are mad
For sovereignty; whither they tend I know,
How much they strive to do; therefore I seek
₃₅₀ A speedy way of death, make haste to die
While none is guiltier in my house than I.
Why, daughter, dost thou weep and clasp my knees?
Why strive with prayers to guide my untamed heart?
Elsewhere invulnerable, here alone
₃₅₅ Can fortune wound me, thou alone canst warm
My frozen love, in all our house but thou
Canst teach me goodness. Nought to me is hard

Or grievous if I know it is thy wish.
If thou shouldst bid him, Œdipus would cross
360 Th' Ægean straits, would take between his lips
The flame earth belches from Sicilia's mount,
Would cast himself before the fiery snake
That rages for the fruit that Hercules
Stole from the grove, at thy command he'd bare
365 His bosom to the birds, at thy command
Would live.

ACT II

Œdipus, Antigone, Messenger.

Messenger. O noble scion of a royal stock,
Thebes, trembling at the brothers' hostile arms,
Invokes thee, prays that thou wouldst turn aside
370 The torch of war that threats thy father's land.
Nor threats alone, the danger nearer comes.
A brother claims the promised interchange
Of royal power, into war would force
The Grecian cities, seven camps invest
375 The walls of Thebes. Make haste to bring her aid,
Prevent at once impiety and war.
Œdipus. Am I the man should put an end to crime,
Or teach the hand to keep itself unstained
With blood of kindred? Have I learned the laws
380 Of justice and of duteous love? They seek
To follow the example of my crimes,
Gladly I recognize and praise their deed,
Exhort them do some action worthy me.
Dear offspring, forward! prove your noble birth
385 By deeds, surpass my glory and my fame,
Do something that shall make thy father glad
That he has lived till now! I know you will,
Your ancestry assures me that you will,
Such greatness cannot with poor, common crimes
390 Content itself. Bring weapons, cast the torch
Into the sacred temples of the gods,
Mow down with flames thy native country's grain,
Throw all into disorder, ruin all,
Destroy the city walls, and to the dust
395 Level the city, with their shrines destroy
The great divinities, and bring to nought
The household gods become so infamous,
Burn up the city, lay thy whole house low,
And to my marriage bed put first the torch.
400   *Antigone.* Thy passionate, wild sorrow put aside;

The public sorrow urges thee to be
The bringer of sweet peace between thy sons.
    Œdipus. Thinkst thou thou seest here a meek old man,
And that thou callest to aid thee one who loves
₄₀₅ Sweet peace? This heart of mine with wrath is swelled,
Rage burns within me, greater war I seek
Than aught that destiny or youth desires.
I am not satisfied with cruel war,
Brother with brother wars—'tis not enough.
₄₁₀ Crimes that are due, crimes that are like my own,
Crimes that become our bed,—let these be done.
Give weapons to the mother. From the woods
No one shall drag me, in the hollow cliffs
I'll lurk, or in dense thickets hide myself,
₄₁₅ There will I wait on wandering Rumor's words,
And hear whate'er I can of brothers' war.

ACT III

Scene I

Jocasta.

Happy Agave! The wild crime she did,
She herself bore; a blood-stained bacchanal,
She carried forth the dreadful spoil, her son
₄₂₀ Dismembered; guilt was hers, yet nought of crime
Beyond her own great sin was brought to pass.
'Tis light to bear the burdens of the crimes
Myself have done. I have made others sin;
This also, even this is light to bear.
₄₂₅ I have brought forth the guilty, to my woes
This bitterness still lacked—that I should love
An enemy. Three times the winter snows
Have fallen and three times the summer grain
Before the bending sickle been laid low,
₄₃₀ Since, of his land deprived, my son has roamed
An exile, and, a fugitive, has craved
Aid from the Grecian kings. He has become
Adrastes' son-in-law—that king who rules
The waters the Corinthian Isthmus cuts,
₄₃₅ Who now to aid his son-in-law leads forth
His hosts, and with him seven other kings.
I know not what I ought to wish or think;
He claims the kingdom, reason good he has
For claiming, yet he seeks it by ill means.
₄₄₀ Alas, whose part shall I, the mother, take?
Each is my son, I cannot safely show

My love for either. If I wish one well
I wish the other ill. With equal love
I love them both, and yet my spirit yearns,
445 Favoring still the weakest, toward the son
Whose lot is heaviest though his cause is just.
His evil fortune binds me to his side.

Scene II

Antigone, Jocasta, A Theban Guard.

    Theban Guard. Queen, while in weeping and in wild lament
Thou wastest time, the battle line is here,
450 Drawn up in open war, the trumpet calls
To arms, th' advancing eagle calls to war.
Drawn up in serried ranks the kings prepare
Seven battle fields, and Cadmus' sons go forth
With equal courage, swiftly here and there
455 The soldiers rush; see how black clouds of dust
Obscure the day, there rises from the field
Clouds dark as smoke, raised by the hurrying feet
Of horsemen and, if those who fear see true,
The hostile standards shine, the foe's first ranks
460 Are present, and the golden banners bear
Illustrious names of well-known generals.
Go, to the brothers bring fraternal love,
Give peace to all and with a mother's voice
Forbid the war.
    Antigone. Haste, mother, haste, fly fast,
465 Hold back the weapons, from the brothers' hands
Strike down the sword, between the hostile spears
Set thy brave breast, O mother, stop the war,
Or perish first.
    Jocasta. I go, I go, my head
I'll offer to their swords, between the swords
470 I'll stand, and he who would his brother slay
Must slay his mother first. At my request
The duteous son will lay his weapon down,
The son who is not duteous shall begin
His war with me; though old, I may restrain
475 The fiery youths, no impious crime shall be
While I am witness, or if impious crime
Can be committed and I witness it,
One crime were not enough.
    Antigone. The fight is on,
The neighboring banners gleam, the noise of war
480 Resounds, O mother, now employ thy prayers.
But see, as though prevailed on by thy tears,

Slowly, with spears at rest, the line draws near.
    Theban Guard. The line moves slowly, but the leaders haste.
    Jocasta. What winged wind will sweep me through the air,
485 With the mad rushing of the tempest driven?
Would that the Sphinx or the Stymphalian birds
That darken like a heavy cloud the day
Would bear me swiftly on their eager wings!
Or that the harpies, seeing the fierce rage
490 Of the two cruel kings, would snatch me hence
And cast me down between the battle lines.
    Theban Guard. Like one insane she moves, she's mad, indeed!
As the swift Parthian arrow from the bow
Is driven, as the raft is swept along
495 By the wild winds, or as a falling star
Drops from the skies, when with swift fires it breaks
A path unswerving, so her maddened flight
She takes, and stands between the hostile lines.
The fight a moment fails, compelled to yield
500 Before a mother's prayers, on either side
The warriors, eager to begin the work
Of mutual slaughter, in their right hands hold
The weapons poised, but motionless as yet
Both armies stand, at peace. The swords of all
505 Are sunk to earth, or hidden in the sheath,
Only the brothers' hands still brandish them.
The mother shows her loose hair, white and torn;
She supplicates, but they deny; she wets
Their knees with tears—who hesitates so long
510 Can in the end deny a mother's prayers.

ACT IV

Scene I

Polynices, Eteocles, Jocasta, The Two Armies.

    Jocasta. Against me turn your weapons and your fires,
Attack me only, valorous youths who come
From Argive cities; and ye warriors fierce,
Who from the Theban citadel descend,
515 Fall upon me alone. Let friend and foe
Alike attack this womb, which bore these sons—
My husband's brothers. Tear these limbs apart,
Scatter them far and wide. I bore you both.
Do you more quickly lay aside the sword?
520 And shall I say who fathered you, my sons?
Give me your hands, give them while yet unstained;
Till now ye have unwittingly done wrong,

Each crime was fortune's that against us sinned,
This is the first base act brought forth between
525 Those conscious of their guilt. In my hand lies
Whate'er you will: if holy piety
Be pleasing to you, give your mother peace;
If crime be pleasing, greater is prepared,
A mother stands between you, make an end
530 Of war or of the hinderer of war.
Whom with alternate prayers and anxious words
Shall I first strive to touch, whom first embrace?
With equal love am I to each one drawn.
One was far off—but if the brother's pact
535 Should hold, the other soon would be far off.
Shall I then never see the two at once
Except as now? Embrace me first, my son,
Who hast endured misfortunes manifold
And labors manifold, and now, foredone
540 By a long exile, dost at last behold
Thy mother. Nearer draw, within its sheath
Put up thy impious sword, and in the earth
Bury thy spear that trembles, poised to slay.
Thy shield prevents thy breast from meeting mine,
545 Lay it aside; loose from thy brow the bands
And from its warlike covering free thy head,
That I may see thy face. Where dost thou look?
Dost thou observe thy brother's battle line
With timid glance? I'll hide thee in my arms,
550 Through me must be the pathway to thy blood.
Why hesitate? Art thou afraid to trust
Thy mother?
    Polynices. Yea, I am afraid. No more
Do nature's laws avail. Since I have known
A mother's precedent, I cannot trust
Even a mother's promise.
555   *Jocasta.* Put again
Thy hand upon thy sword, bind on once more
Thy helmet, take thy shield, retain thy arms
Until thy brother shall have been disarmed.
Thou who first used the sword, put by the sword.
560 If peace is odious, if thou seekest war
Thy mother asks thee for a short delay
That she may kiss the son from flight returned,
Whether it be the first kiss or the last.
Listen unarmed while I entreat for peace.
565 Thou fearest him, he thee? I fear thee both,
But for the sake of each. Why willst thou not
Lay by the sword? Be glad at these delays:
You seek to wage a war in which 'twere best

To be o'ercome. Thy hostile brother's guile
570 Fearst thou? 'tis often needful to deceive
Or be oneself deceived, yet is it best
To suffer rather than commit a crime.
Fear not, a treacherous thrust from either side
Thy mother will receive. Do I prevail?
575 Shall I be envious of thy father's fate?
Have I come hither to prevent a crime,
Or see it nearer? See, he sheathes his sword,
He drops his spear, he lays aside his arms;
And now to thee thy mother turns with prayers
580 And tears, I see again thy face, long sought.
Thee, from thy native land a fugitive,
A foreign king's penates long kept safe.
By divers seas and by a changeful fate
Thou hast been driven. Followed by her train,
585 Thy mother did not to thy marriage bed
Conduct thee, nor adorn the festal halls
Herself, nor with the sacred fillets bind
The happy torches, thy bride's father gave
No gift of gold, a treasure for a king,
590 Nor fields, nor towns; thy bridal gift is war.
Thou of a foe art made the son-in-law,
Far from thy land, the guest of alien laws,
Sought by a stranger, driven from thine own,
An exile through no crime that thou hast done.
595 Lest thou shouldst taste not all thy parents' fate,
This too thou hadst from them: to wed amiss.
O son, sent back to me from many lands;
O son, thy anxious mother's hope and fear;
For whose return I often prayed the gods,
600 Though thy return would snatch away as much
As it would give; how long, I asked, how long,
Before I cease to fear on his account?
The mocking god replied, till thou shalt fear
Himself. Thou hadst been far, but for this war;
605 Hadst thou been far I should have known no war.
The sight of thee is given at a price
Heavy to pay, but to thy mother's eyes
The sight is welcome. Now, ere cruel Mars
Dares some dread crime, let the two hosts withdraw;
610 Great sin it is that they have come so near.
I am amazed, I shudder, when I see
Two brothers stand so near the edge of crime.
My limbs are weak, how nearly had I seen
A crime of greater infamy than aught
615 Thy wretched father ever looked upon.
I am set free from fear of such a crime,

Such now I shall not see; and yet I feel
Unhappy that so nearly I have seen.
Oh! by the ten months' labor of my womb,
620 And by thy noble sister's piety,
And by thy father's eyes which he dragged forth,
Enraged against himself and from himself
Exacting the hard penalty of crime,
Though innocent of any guilt; I pray:
625 Save from the cursed torch thy country's walls,
Turn back the standards of the hostile lines;
Though thou turnst back, great portion of thy crime
Already is complete—thy land has seen
Its open plains o'errun by hordes of foes,
630 Has seen afar the shining troops, has seen
The Cadmean meadows trampled by the horse,
And princes in their chariots of war
Advancing, and the blaze of lighted beams
Prepared to burn our homes, and—even for Thebes
635 An unaccustomed crime—two brothers roused
To war against each other. All the host
Saw, the whole people saw, thy sister saw,
And I, thy mother. That he saw it not,
Thy father to his mangled eyeballs owes.
640 Ah, what if Œdipus should see thee now,
That judge who even for error would exact
The penalty? O waste not with the sword
Thy country and thy home, nor overthrow
The Thebes thou so desirest to rule.
645 What madness has possession of thy mind?
Wilt thou by wild assault destroy the land?
That it may be thine own wouldst make it nought?
Thou dost but to thine own cause injury,
When thou inflam'st thy land with hostile arms,
650 Layest the ripe grain low, and far and wide
Spreadst terror. None thus devastate their own.
Thou must believe it but an alien land,
Which thou commandest to be seized by fire
And taken by the sword. Decide which one
655 Shall be the king, but let the kingdom stand.
Wilt thou with fire and spear destroy these roofs?
Or canst thou shake Amphion's mighty work?
Wouldst shake these walls, not built by man's hand
That lifts with noisy crane the slow moved weight,
660 But called together by the cither's sound
And singing—of themselves the stones moved up
Into the highest turrets—wouldst thou break
These walls in pieces? Wouldst thou bear away
A victor's spoil, thy father's vanquished peers

665 Lead hence, and shall the cruel soldiers drag
　　 Mothers in chains, snatched from their husband's arms?
　　 Shall Theban maidens, mingled with the herd
　　 Of captives, go as gifts to Argive maids?
　　 Shall I myself, with hands behind me bound,
670 The plunder of fraternal triumph be?
　　 Canst thou behold thy fellow citizens
　　 On all sides given o'er to death and flight?
　　 Canst thou against these dear walls lead the foe?
　　 Hast thou a heart so savage and so wild,
675 So cruel in its wrath? Thou art not yet
　　 A king, what will thy sceptered hand perform?
　　 I do beseech thee, put aside thy rage
　　 And swelling anger, give to duteous love
　　 Again thy heart.
　　　　　Polynices. That I a fugitive
680 May wander? That I may afar from Thebes
　　 Be kept? May ever as a guest desire
　　 The aid of strangers? Had I broken faith,
　　 Had I foresworn myself, what had I borne?
　　 Shall I to aliens pay the penalty
685 Of treachery, and he alone enjoy
　　 The profit of the crime? Thou bidst me go,
　　 I would indeed obey a mother's word;
　　 Where shall I go? My royal halls would be
　　 My haughty brother's dwelling, a poor hut
690 Would cover me: give to the exiled that,
　　 Let me exchange a realm for that poor home.
　　 But shall I, given to my wife, a slave,
　　 Bear the harsh judgments of a wealthy bride
　　 And as a mean and humble follower
695 Obey the royal parents of my wife?
　　 'Tis hard to fall from power to servitude.
　　　　　Jocasta. If thou desirest to be a king
　　 Nor canst from the harsh scepter free thy hand,
　　 Many there are in the world's circle wide
700 That thou canst seize. Where Tmolus lifts its heights
　　 Sacred to Bacchus, where wide stretches lie
　　 Of fruitful soil, where rich Pactolus flows
　　 And inundates the country with its gold.
　　 Nor does Mæander with its wandering stream
705 Through meadowlands less happy wind its way;
　　 Swift Hermus rolls through fertile fields; there lies
　　 Gargara, loved by Ceres, and the land
　　 Which Zanthus, swoll'n with Ida's snows, makes wet;
　　 There lies the shore where the Ionian sea
710 Changes its name, across the narrow strait,
　　 Opposite to Abydos, Sestos stands;

Or, farther east, with safe and frequent ports,
Lies Lycia: seek these kingdoms with the sword,
Let thy bride's father bear his hostile arms
715 Against these peoples, and betray these lands,
And give them to thee to be ruled by thee.
Think that thy father hitherto has held
This kingdom. Better far for thee would be
Exile than this return. Exiled thou art
720 Through guilt not thine; through crime thyself must do
Thou wilt return. 'Twere better thou shouldst seek
With these thy warriors a new realm, unstained
By any crime. The sharer of thy war,
Thy brother, will himself then fight for thee
725 Go wage a war where we may wish thee well.
A kingdom won by crime is heavier far
Than any exile. Weigh the ills of war,
Think on uncertain Mars' vicissitudes.
Though thou shouldst lead with thee the flower of Greece,
730 Though far and wide thy countless hosts should spread,
Yet doubtful were the fortune of the war—
'Tis as Mars wills, he makes of equal strength
Two swords, although they were before ill matched,
Blind chance brings hope or fear. Though all the gods
735 Favored thy vows, they have withdrawn from thee
And, put to flight, have sought the Theban side,
The soldiery, in awful overthrow
Lying, are scattered over all the field.
Say thou wage war, from thy slain brother bear
740 A victor's spoils, thy palms would soon be crushed;
Thinkst thou such war can bring the conqueror joy
When he commits in it accursed crime?
Him whom thou seekest now to overthrow,
Him, conquered, wretched one, thou wilt bewail.
745 Go, put an end to this disastrous war,
From terror free thy native land, from grief
Set free thy parents.
    Polynices. Shall no punishment
For all his crime and treachery be borne
By my base brother?
    Jocasta. Fear not. He shall pay
750 Hard penalty indeed, for he shall reign,
This is his penalty. And shouldst thou doubt,
Look on his father's, his grandfather's fate;
Cadmus and Cadmus' offspring tell thee this:
Never unpunished did a Theban hold
755 The scepter, none shall hold it who break faith,
And even now among such sinful ones
Thou numberest a brother.

Eteocles. Be it so!
'Tis worth so much to be among Thebes' kings.
Thee, place I mid the throng of exiled ones.
    Jocasta. Reign hated by the people.
    Eteocles. He who fears
Hatred can never wish to be a king.
God, the creator of the universe,
Has bound together hate and kingly power.
A great king, I believe, will overcome
Hatred itself. Their peoples' love prevents
Many from ruling; most is possible
Where hate abides. Who wishes to be loved
Rules with a languid hand.
    Jocasta. Not long maintained
Will be unwelcome empire.
    Eteocles. Kings may give
The laws of empire with a better grace,
Speak thou of exiles. For my realm I wish—
    Jocasta. To give thy native land, thy household gods,
Thy wife, to the destroying flames?
    Eteocles. Hard price
Is ever for imperial power paid.

MEDEA

DRAMATIS PERSONÆ

Jason.
Creon.
Medea.
Nurse.
Messenger.
Chorus of Corinthian Women.

Scene: *Corinth.*

MEDEA

ACT I

Scene I

    Medea. [*Alone.*] Ye gods of marriage;
Lucina, guardian of the genial bed;
Pallas, who taught the tamer of the seas
To steer the Argo; stormy ocean's lord;
Titan, dividing bright day to the world;
And thou three-formed Hecate, who dost shed

Thy conscious splendor on the hidden rites!
Ye by whom Jason plighted me his troth;
And ye Medea rather should invoke:
10   Chaos of night eternal; realm opposed
To the celestial powers; abandoned souls;
King of the dusky realm; Persephone,
By better faith betrayed; you I invoke,
But with no happy voice. Approach, approach,
15   Avenging goddesses with snaky hair,
Holding in blood-stained hands your sulphurous torch!
Come now as horrible as when of yore
Ye stood beside my marriage-bed; bring death
To the new bride, and to the royal seed,
20   And Creon; worse for Jason I would ask—
Life! Let him roam in fear through unknown lands,
An exile, hated, poor, without a home;
A guest now too well known, let him, in vain,
Seek alien doors, and long for me, his wife!
25   And, yet a last revenge, let him beget
Sons like their father, daughters like their mother!
'Tis done; revenge is even now brought forth—
I have borne sons to Jason. I complain
Vainly, and cry aloud with useless words,
30   Why do I not attack mine enemies?
I will strike down the torches from their hands,
The light from heaven. Does the sun see this,
The author of our race, and still give light?
And, sitting in his chariot, does he still
35   Run through the accustomed spaces of the sky,
Nor turn again to seek his rising place,
And measure back the day? Give me the reins;
Father, let me in thy paternal car
Be borne aloft the winds, and let me curb
40   With glowing bridle those thy fiery steeds!
Burn Corinth; let the parted seas be joined!
This still remains—for me to carry up
The marriage torches to the bridal room,
And, after sacrificial prayers, to slay
45   The victims on their altars. Seek, my soul—
If thou still livest, or if aught endures
Of ancient vigor—seek to find revenge
Through thine own bowels; throw off woman's fears,
Intrench thyself in snowy Caucasus.
50   All impious deeds Phasis or Pontus saw,
Corinth shall see. Evils unknown and wild,
Hideous, frightful both to earth and heaven,
Disturb my soul,—wounds, and the scattered corpse,
And murder. I remember gentle deeds,

55 A maid did these; let heavier anguish come,
Since sterner crimes befit me now, a wife!
Gird thee with wrath, prepare thine utmost rage,
That fame of thy divorce may spread as far
As of thy marriage! Make no long delay.
60 How dost thou leave thy husband? As thou cam'st.
Homes crime built up, by crime must be dissolved.

Scene II

Enter Chorus of Corinthian women, singing the marriage song of Jason and Creusa.

Chorus. Be present at the royal marriage feast,
Ye gods who sway the scepter of the deep,
And ye who hold dominion in the heavens;
65 With the glad people come, ye smiling gods!
First to the scepter-bearing thunderers
The white-backed bull shall stoop his lofty head;
The snowy heifer, knowing not the yoke,
Is due to fair Lucina; and to her
70 Who stays the bloody hand of Mars, and gives
To warring nations peace, who in her horn
Holds plenty, sacrifice a victim mild.
Thou who at lawful bridals dost preside,
Scattering darkness with thy happy torch,
75 Come hither with slow step, dizzy with wine,
Binding thy temples with a rosy crown.
Thou star that bringest in the day and night,
Slow-rising on the lover, ardently
For thy clear shining maids and matrons long.
80   In comeliness the virgin bride excels
The Athenian women and the strong-limbed maids
Of Sparta's unwalled town, who on the top
Of high Taÿgetus try youthful sports;
Or those who in the clear Aonian stream,
85 Or in Alpheus' sacred waters bathe.
The child of the wild thunder, he who tames
And fits the yoke to tigers, is less fair
Than the Ausonian prince. The glorious god
Who moves the tripod, Dian's brother mild;
90 The skilful boxer Pollux; Castor, too,
Must yield the palm to Jason. O ye gods
Who dwell in heaven, ever may the bride
Surpass all women, he excel all men!
   Before her beauty in the women's choir
95 The beauty of the other maids grows dim;
So with the sunrise pales the light of stars,

    So when the moon with brightness not her own
Fills out her crescent horns, the Pleiads fade.
Her cheeks blush like white cloth 'neath Tyrian dyes,
100 Or as the shepherd sees the light of stars
Grow rosy with the dawn. O happy one,
Accustomed once to clasp unwillingly
A wife unloved and reckless, snatched away
From that dread Colchian marriage, take thy bride,
105 The Æolian virgin—'tis her father's will.
    Bright offspring of the thyrsus-bearing god,
The time has come to light the torch of pine;
With fingers dripping wine flash out the fires,
Sound the gay music of the marriage song,
110 Let the crowd pass their jests; 'tis only she
Who fled her home to wed a stranger guest,
Need steal away into the silent dark.

ACT II

Scene I

Medea, Nurse.

    Medea. Alas, the wedding chorus strikes my ears;
Woe, woe to me! I could not hitherto
115 Believe—can hardly yet believe such wrong.
And this is Jason's deed? Of father, home,
And kingdom reft, can he desert me now,
Alone and in a foreign land? Can he
Despise my worth who saw the flames and seas
120 By my art conquered? thinks, perchance, all crime
Exhausted! Tossed by every wave of doubt,
I am distracted, seeking some revenge.
Had he a brother! Ah, he has a bride;
Through her be thrust the steel! Is this enough?
125 If Grecian or barbarian cities know
Crime that this hand knows not, that crime be done!
Thy sins return to mind exhorting thee:
The stolen treasure of a kingdom, too;
Thy little comrade, wicked maid, destroyed,
130 Torn limb from limb and scattered on the sea
An offering to his father; Pelias old
Killed in the boiling cauldron. I have shed
Blood basely, but not yet, not yet have shown
The power of wrath; unhappy love did all.
135   Had Jason any choice, by foreign law
And foreign power constrained? He should have bared
His breast to feel the sword. O bitter grief,

Speak milder, milder words. Let Jason live;
Mine as he was, if this be possible,
140 But, if not mine, still let him live secure,
To spare me still the memory of my gift!
The fault is Creon's; he abuses power
To annul our marriage, sever strongest ties,
And tear the children from their mother's breast;
145 Let Creon pay the penalty he owes.
I'll heap his home in ashes, the dark flame
Shall reach Malea's dreaded cape, where ships
Find passage only after long delay.
    Nurse. Be silent, I implore thee, hide thy pain
150 Deep in thy bosom. He who silently
Bears grievous wounds, with patience, and a mind
Unshaken, may find vengeance. Hidden wrath
Finds strength, when open hatred loses hope
Of vengeance.
    Medea. Light is grief that hides itself,
155 And can take counsel. Great wrongs lie not hid.
I am resolved on action.
    Nurse. Foster-child,
Restrain thy fury; hardly art thou safe though silent.
    Medea. Fortune tramples on the meek, but fears the brave.
    Nurse. When courage is in place it wins approval.
160   *Medea.* It can never be that courage should be out of place.
    Nurse. To thee,
In thy misfortune, hope points out no way.
    Medea. The man who cannot hope should naught despair.
    Nurse. Colchis is far away, thy husband lost;
165 Of all thy riches nothing now remains.
    Medea. Medea now remains! Land, sea, sword, fire,
God and the thunderbolt, are found in me.
    Nurse. The king is to be feared.
    Medea. I claim a king for father.
    Nurse. Hast thou then no fear of arms?
    Medea. I, who saw warriors spring from earth?
170   *Nurse.* Thou'lt die!
    Medea. I wish it.
    Nurse. Flee!
    Medea. Nay, I repent of flight.
    Nurse. Thou art a mother.
    Medea. And thou seest by whom.
    Nurse. Wilt thou not fly?
    Medea. I fly, but first revenge.
    Nurse. Vengeance may follow thee.
    Medea. I may, perchance, find means to hinder it.
175   *Nurse.* Restrain thyself
And cease to threaten madly; it is well

That thou adjust thyself to fortune's change.
    Medea. My riches, not my spirit, fortune takes.
The hinge creaks,—who is this? Creon himself,
180 Swelling with Grecian pride.

Scene II

Creon with Attendants, Medea.

    Creon. What, is Medea of the hated race
Of Colchian Æëtes, not yet gone?
Still she is plotting evil; well I know
Her guile, and well I know her cruel hand.
185 Whom does she spare, or whom let rest secure?
Verily I had thought to cut her off
With the swift sword, but Jason's prayers availed
To spare her life. She may go forth unharmed
If she will set our city free from fear.
190 Threatening and fierce, she seeks to speak with us;
Attendants, keep her off, bid her be still,
And let her learn at last, a king's commands
Must be obeyed. Go, haste, and take her hence.
    Medea. What fault is punished by my banishment?
195   *Creon.* A woman, innocent, doth ask, 'What fault?'
    Medea. If thou wilt judge, examine; or if king, command.
    Creon. Unjust or just, a king must be obeyed.
    Medea. An unjust king not long endures.
    Creon. Go! 'Plain to Colchis!
    Medea. Willingly I go;
200 Let him who brought me hither take me hence.
    Creon. Thy words come late, my edict has gone forth.
    Medea. The man who judges, one side still unheard,
Were hardly a just judge, though he judge justly.
    Creon. Pelias for listening to thee died, but speak,
205 Let me give time to hear so fair a plea.
    Medea. How hard it is to calm a wrathful soul,
How he who takes the scepter in proud hands
Deems his own will sufficient, I have learned;
Have learned it in my father's royal house.
210 For though the sport of fortune, suppliant,
Banished, alone, forsaken, on all sides
Distressed, my father was a noble king.
I am descended from the glorious sun.
What lands the Phasis in its winding course
215 Bathes, or the Euxine touches where the sea
Is freshened by the water from the lakes,
Or where armed maiden cohorts try their skill
Beside Thermodon, all these lands are held

        Within my father's kingdom, where I dwelt
220   Noble and favored, and with princely power.
        He whom kings seek, sought then to wed with me.
        Swift, fickle fortune cast me headlong forth
        And gave me exile. Put thy trust in thrones—
        Such trust as thou mayst put in what light chance
225   Flings here and there at will! Kings have one power,
        A matchless honor time can never take:
        To help the wretched, and to him who asks
        To give a safe retreat. This I have brought
        From Colchis, this at least I still can claim:
230   I saved the flower of Grecian chivalry,
        Achaian chiefs, the offspring of the gods;
        It is to me they owe their Orpheus
        Whose singing melted rocks and drew the trees;
        Castor and Pollux are my twofold gift;
235   Boreas' sons, and Lynceus whose sharp eye
        Could pierce beyond the Euxine, are my gift,
        And all the Argonauts. Of one alone,
        The chief of chiefs, I do not speak; for him
        Thou owest me naught; those have I saved for thee,
240   This one is mine. Rehearse, now, all my crime;
        Accuse me; I confess; this is my fault—
        I saved the Argo! Had I heard the voice
        Of maiden modesty or filial love,
        Greece and her leaders had regretted it,
245   And he, thy son-in-law, had fallen first
        A victim to the fire-belching bull.
        Let fortune trample on me as she will,
        My hand has succored princes, I am glad!
        Thou hast the recompense for all my crimes.
250   Condemn me, but give back the cause of crime.
        Creon, I own my guilt—guilt known to thee
        When first a suppliant I touched thy knees,
        And asked with outstretched hands protecting aid.
        Again I ask a refuge, some-poor spot
255   For misery to hide in; grant a place
        Withdrawn, a safe asylum in thy realm,
        If I must leave the city.
            Creon. I am no prince who rules with cruel sway,
        Or tramples on the wretched with proud foot.
260   Have I not shown this true by choosing him
        To be my son-in-law who is a man
        Exiled, without resource, in fear of foes?
        One whom Acastus, king of Thessaly,
        Seeks to destroy, that so he may avenge
265   A father weak with age, bowed down with years,
        Whose limbs were torn asunder? That foul crime

His pious sisters impiously dared,
Tempted by thee; if thou wilt go away,
Jason can then maintain his innocence;
270 No guiltless blood has stained him, and his hands
Touched not the sword, are yet unstained by thee.
Foul instigator of all evil deeds,
With woman's wantonness in daring aught,
And man's courageous heart—and void of shame,
275 Go, purge our kingdom; take thy deadly herbs,
Free us from fear; dwelling in other lands
Afar, invoke the gods.
    Medea. Thou bidst me go?
Give back the ship and comrade of my flight.
Why bid me go alone? Not so I came.
280 If thou fear war, both should go forth, nor choice
Be made between two equally at fault:
That old man fell for Jason's sake; impute
To Jason flight, rapine, a brother slain,
And a deserted father; not all mine
285 The crimes to which a husband tempted me;
'Tis true I sinned, but never for myself.
    Creon. Thou shouldst be gone, why waste the time with words?
    Medea. I go, but going make one last request:
Let not a mother's guilt drag down her sons.
290   *Creon.* Go, as a father I will succor them,
And with a father's care.
    Medea. By future hopes,
By the king's happy marriage, by the strength
Of thrones, which fickle fortune sometimes shakes,
I pray thee grant the exile some delay
295 That she, perchance about to die, may press
A last kiss on her children's lips.
    Creon. Thou seekst time to commit new crime.
    Medea. In so brief time what crime were possible?
    Creon. No time too short for him who would do ill.
300   *Medea.* Dost thou deny to misery short space for tears?
    Creon. Deep dread warns me against thy prayer; yet I will grant
One day in which thou mayst prepare for flight.
    Medea. Too great the favor! Of the time allowed,
Something withdraw. I would depart in haste.
305   *Creon.* Before the coming day is ushered in
By Phœbus, leave the city or thou diest.
The bridal calls me, and I go to pay
My vows to Hymen.

Scene III

Chorus. He rashly ventured who was first to make
In his frail boat a pathway through the deep;
Who saw his native land behind him fade
In distance blue; who to the raging winds
Trusted his life, his slender keel between
The paths of life and death. Our fathers dwelt
In an unspotted age, and on the shore
Where each was born he lived in quietness,
Grew old upon his father's farm content;
With little rich, he knew no other wealth
Than his own land afforded. None knew yet
The changing constellations, nor could use
As guides the stars that paint the ether; none
Had learned to shun the rainy Hyades;
None had as yet to Goat, or Northern Wain
That follows slow by old Boötes driven,
Or Boreas, or Zephyr, given names.
Rash Tiphys was the first to tempt the deep
With spreading canvas; for the winds to write
New laws; to furl the sail; or spread it wide
When sailors longed to fly before the gale,
And the red topsail fluttered in the breeze.
The world so wisely severed by the seas
The pine of Thessaly united, bade
The ocean suffer scourgings at our hands,
And distant waters bring us unknown fears.
The ill-starred ship paid heavy penalty
When the two cliffs, the gateway of the sea,
Moved as though smitten by the thunderbolt,
And the imprisoned waters smote the stars.
Bold Tiphys paled, and from his trembling hand
Let fall the rudder; Orpheus' music died,
His lyre untouched; the Argo lost her voice.
When, belted by her girdle of wild dogs,
The maid of the Sicilian straits gave voice
From all her mouths, who feared not at her bark?
Who did not tremble at the witching song
With which the Sirens charmed the Ausonian sea?
The Thracian Orpheus' lyre had almost forced
Those hinderers of ships to follow him!
What was the journey's prize? The golden fleece,
Medea, fiercer than the raging flood,—
Worthy reward for those first mariners!
 The sea forgets its former wrath; submits
To the new laws; and not alone the ship

Minerva builded, manned by sons of kings,
355 Finds rowers; other ships may sail the deep.
Old metes are moved, new city walls spring up
On distant soil, and nothing now remains
As it has been in the much-traveled world.
The cold Araxes' stream the Indian drinks;
360 The Persian quaffs the Rhine; a time shall come
With the slow years, when ocean shall strike off
The chains from earth, and a great world shall then
Lie opened; Tiphys shall win other lands—
Another Tiphys—Thule cease to be
365 Earth's utmost bound.

ACT III

Scene I

Medea, Nurse.

   Nurse. Stay, foster-child, why fly so swiftly hence?
Restrain thy wrath! curb thy impetuous haste!
As a Bacchante, frantic with the god
And filled with rage divine, uncertain walks
370 The top of snowy Pindus or the peak
Of Nysa, so Medea wildly goes
Hither and thither; on her face the mark
Of frenzied rage, her visage flushed, her breast
Shaken by sobs. She cries aloud, her eyes
375 Are drowned in scalding tears; again she laughs;
All passions surge within her angry heart.
Where will she fling the burden of her soul?
She hesitates, she threatens, storms, complains,
Where falls her vengeance? where will break this wave
380 Of fury? Passion overflows! she plans
No easy crime, no ordinary deed.
Herself she will surpass; I mark old signs
Of raging; something terrible she plans,
Some deed inhuman, devilish, and wild.
385 Ye gods, avert the horrors I foresee!
   Medea. Wretch, dost thou seek how far to show thy hate?
Imitate love! And must I then endure
Without revenge the royal marriage-torch?
Shall this day prove unfruitful, sought and gained
390 Only by earnest effort? While the earth
Hangs free within the heavens; while the vault
Of heaven sweeps round the earth with changeless change;
While the sands lie unnumbered; while the day
Follows the sun, the night brings up the stars;

395 Arcturus never wet in ocean's wave
   Rolls round the pole; while rivers seaward flow,
   My hate shall never cease to seek revenge.
   Did ever fierceness of a ravening beast;
   Or Scylla or Charybdis sucking down
400 The waters of the wild Ausonian
   And the Sicilian seas; or Ætna fierce,
   That holds imprisoned great Enceladus
   Breathing forth flame, so glow as I with threats?
   Not the swift rivers, nor the storm-tossed sea,
405 Nor wind-blown ocean, nor the force of flame
   By storm-wind fanned, can imitate my wrath.
   I will o'erthrow and bring to naught the world!
   Did Jason fear the king? Thessalian war?
   True love fears naught. Or was he forced to yield,
410 And gave consent unwillingly? But still
   He might have sought his wife for one farewell.
   This too he feared to do. He might have gained
   From Creon some delay of banishment.
   One day is granted for my two sons' sake!
415 I do not make complaint of too short time,
   It is enough for much; this day shall see
   What none shall ever hide. I will attack
   The very gods, and shake the universe!
      Nurse. Lady, thy spirit so disturbed by ills
420 Restrain, and let thy storm-tossed soul find rest.
      Medea. Rest I can never find until I see
   All dragged with me to ruin; all shall fall
   When I do;—so to share one's woe is joy.
      Nurse. Think what thou hast to fear if thou persist;
425 No one can safely fight with princely power.

Scene II

The Nurse withdraws; enter Jason.

   Jason. The lot is ever hard; bitter is fate,
Equally bitter if it slay or spare;
God gives us remedies worse than our ills.
Would I keep faith with her I deem my wife
430 I must expect to die; would I shun death
I must forswear myself. Not fear of death
Has conquered honor, but love full of fear
Knowing the father's death involves the sons.
O holy Justice, if thou dwell in heaven,
435 I call on thee to witness that the sons
Vanquish their father! Say the mother's love
Is fierce and spurns the yoke, she still will deem

Her children of more worth than marriage joys.
I fain would go to her with prayers, and lo,
440 She starts at sight of me, her look grows wild,
Hatred she shows and grief.
    Medea. Jason, I flee!
I flee, it is not new to change my home,
The cause of banishment alone is new;
I have been exiled hitherto for thee.
445 I go, as thou compellst me, from thy home,
But whither shall I go? Shall I, perhaps,
Seek Phasis, Colchis, and my father's realm
Whose soil is watered by a brother's blood?
What land dost thou command me seek? what sea?
450 The Euxine's jaws through which I led that band
Of noble princes when I followed thee,
Adulterer, through the Symplegades?
Little Iolchos? Tempe? Thessaly?
Whatever way I opened up for thee
455 I closed against myself. Where shall I go?
Thou drivest into exile, but hast given
No place of banishment. I will go hence.
The king, Creusa's father, bids me go,
And I will do his bidding. Heap on me
460 Most dreadful punishment, it is my due.
With cruel penalties let the king's wrath
Pursue thy mistress, load my hands with chains,
And in a dungeon of eternal night
Imprison me—'tis less than I deserve!
465 Ungrateful one, recall the fiery bull;
The earth-born soldiers, who at my command
Slew one another; and the longed-for spoils
Of Phrixus' ram, whose watchful guardian,
The sleepless dragon, at my bidding slept;
470 The brother slain; the many, many crimes
In one crime gathered. Think how, led by me,
By me deceived, that old man's daughters dared
To slay their aged father, dead for aye!
By thy hearth's safety, by thy children's weal,
475 By the slain dragon, by these blood-stained hands
I never spared from doing aught for thee,
By thy past fears, and by the sea and sky
Witnesses of our marriage, pity me!
Happy thyself, make me some recompense!
480 Of all the ravished gold the Scythians brought
From far, as far as India's burning plains,
Wealth our wide palace hardly could contain,
So that we hung our groves with gold, I took
Nothing. My brother only bore I thence,

⁴⁸⁵ And him for thee I sacrificed. I left
My country, father, brother, maiden shame:
This was my marriage portion; give her own
To her who goes an exile.
    Jason. When angry Creon thought to have thee slain,
⁴⁹⁰ Urged by my prayers, he gave thee banishment.
    Medea. I looked for a reward; the gift I see is exile.
    Jason. While thou mayst fly, fly in haste!
The wrath of kings is ever hard to bear.
    Medea. Thou giv'st me such advice because thou lov'st
⁴⁹⁵ Creusa, wouldst divorce a hated wife!
    Jason. And does Medea taunt me with my loves?
    Medea. More—treacheries and murders.
    Jason. Canst thou charge such sins to me?
    Medea. All I have ever done.
    Jason. It only needs that I should share the guilt of these thy crimes!
⁵⁰⁰   *Medea.* Thine are they, thine alone;
He is the criminal who reaps the fruit.
Though all should brand thy wife with infamy,
Thou shouldst defend and call her innocent:
She who has sinned for thee, toward thee hold pure.
⁵⁰⁵   *Jason.* To me my life is an unwelcome gift
Of which I am ashamed.
    Medea. Who is ashamed to owe his life to me can lay it down.
    Jason. For thy sons' sake control thy fiery heart.
    Medea. I will have none of them, I cast them off,
⁵¹⁰ Abjure them; shall Creusa to my sons give brothers?
    Jason. To an exile's wretched sons
A mighty queen will give them.
    Medea. Never come that evil day that mingles a great race
With race unworthy,—Phœbus' glorious sons with sons of Sisyphus.
⁵¹⁵   *Jason.* What, cruel one,
Wouldst thou drag both to banishment? Away!
    Medea. Creon has heard my prayer.
    Jason. What can I do?
    Medea. For me? Some crime perhaps.
    Jason. Two wrathful kings I fear.
    Medea. Medea's wrath is still more fierce!
⁵²⁰ Let us essay our power, the victor's prize be Jason.
    Jason. Passion-weary, I submit;
Thou too shouldst fear a lot so often tried.
    Medea. Fortune has ever served me faithfully.
    Jason. Acastus comes.
    Medea. Creon's a nearer foe,
⁵²⁵ Flee thou from both. Medea does not ask
That thou shouldst arm thyself against the king,
Or soil thy hands with murder of thy kin;
Flee with me innocent.

Jason. Who will oppose
If double war ensue, and the two kings join forces?
530   *Medea.* Add to them the Colchian troops
And King Æëtes, Scythian hosts and Greeks,
Medea conquers all!
    Jason. I greatly fear
A scepter's power.
    Medea. Do not covet it.
    Jason. We must cut short our converse, lest it breed suspicion.
535   *Medea.* Now from high Olympus send
Thy thunder, Jupiter; stretch forth thy hand,
Prepare thy lightning, from the riven clouds
Make the world tremble, nor with careful hand
Spare him or me; whichever of us dies
540 Dies guilty; thy avenging thunderbolt
Cannot mistake the victim.
    Jason. Try to speak
More sanely; calm thyself. If aught can aid
Thy flight from Creon's house, thou needst but ask.
    Medea. My soul is strong enough, and wont to scorn
545 The wealth of kings; this boon alone I crave,
To take my children with me when I go;
Into their bosoms I would shed my tears, new sons are thine.
    Jason. Would I might grant thy prayer;
Paternal love forbids me, Creon's self
550 Could not compel me to it. They alone
Lighten the sorrow of a grief-parched soul.
For them I live, I sooner would resign breath, members, light.
    Medea. [*Aside.*] 'Tis well! He loves his sons
This, then, the place where he may feel a wound!
555 [*To Jason.*] Before I go, thou wilt, at least, permit
That I should give my sons a last farewell,
A last embrace? But one thing more I ask:
If in my grief I've poured forth threatening words,
Retain them not in mind; let memory hold
560 Only my softer speech, my words of wrath obliterate.
    Jason. I have erased them all
From my remembrance. I would counsel thee
Be calm, act gently; calmness quiets pain.

              [*Exit Jason.*]

Scene III

Medea, Nurse.

Medea. He's gone! And can it be he leaves me so,
565 Forgetting me and all my guilt? Forgot?
Nay, never shall Medea be forgot!
Up! Act! Call all thy power to aid thee now;
This fruit of crime is thine, to shun no crime!
Deceit is useless, so they fear my guile.
570 Strike where they do not dream thou canst be feared.
Medea, haste, be bold to undertake
The possible—yea, that which is not so!
Thou, faithful nurse, companion of my griefs
And varying fortunes, aid my wretched plans.
575 I have a robe, gift of the heavenly powers,
An ornament of a king's palace, given
By Phœbus to my father as a pledge
Of sonship; and a necklace of wrought gold;
And a bright diadem, inlaid with gems,
580 With which they used to bind my hair. These gifts,
Endued with poison by my magic arts,
My sons shall carry for me to the bride.
Pay vows to Hecate, bring the sacrifice,
Set up the altars. Let the mounting flame
585 Envelop all the house.

Scene IV

Chorus. Fear not the power of flame, nor swelling gale,
Nor hurtling dart, nor cloudy wind that brings
The winter storms; fear not when Danube sweeps
Unchecked between his widely severed shores,
590 Nor when the Rhone hastes seaward, and the sun
Has broken up the snow upon the hills,
      And Hæmus flows in rivers.
A wife deserted, loving while she hates,
Fear greatly; blindly burns her anger's flame,
595 She cares not to be ruled, nor bears the curb,
Nor fears to die; she courts the hostile swords.
Ye gods, we ask your grace divine for him
Who safely crossed the seas; the ocean's lord
Is angry for his conquered kingdom's sake;
600   Spare Jason, we entreat!
Th' impetuous youth who dared to drive the car
Of Phœbus, keeping not the wonted course,
Died in the heavenly fires himself had lit.

Few are the evils of the well-known way;
605 Seek the old paths your fathers safely trod,
The sacred federations of the world
    Keep still inviolate.
The men who dipped the oars of that brave ship;
Who plundered of their shade the sacred groves
610 Of Pelion; passed between the unstable cliffs;
Endured so many hardships on the deep;
And cast their anchor on a savage coast,
Passing again with ravished foreign gold,
Atoned with fearful death for dire wrong
615   To Ocean's sacred laws.
The angry deep demanded punishment:
To an unskilful pilot Tiphys gave
The rudder. On a foreign coast he fell,
Far from his father's kingdom, and he lies
620 With nameless shades, under a lowly tomb.
Becalmed in her still harbor Aulis held
Th' impatient ships, remembering in wrath
    The king that she lost thence.
Sweet voiced Camena's son, who touched his lyre
625 So sweetly that the floods stood still, the winds
Were silent, and the birds forgot to sing,
And forests followed him, on Thracian fields
Lies dead, his head borne down by Hebrus' stream.
He touched again the Styx and Tartarus,
630   But not again returns.
Alcides overthrew the north wind's sons;
He slew that son of Neptune who could take
Unnumbered forms; but after he had made
Peace over land and sea, and opened wide
635 The realm of Dis, lying on Œta's top
He gave his body to the cruel fire,
Destroyed by his wife's gift—the fatal robe
    Poisoned with Centaur's blood.
Ancæus fell a victim to the boar
640 Of Caledonia; Meleager slew
His mother's brother, perished by the hand
Of his own mother. They have merited
Their lot, but what the crime that he atoned
Whom great Alcides sought so long in vain,
645 The tender Hylas drawn beneath safe waves?
Go now, brave soldiers, boldly plow the main,
    But fear the gentle streams.
Idmon the serpents buried in the sands
Of Libya, though he knew the future well.
650 Mopsus, to others true, false to himself,
Fell far from Thebes; and if the seer spoke true,

Peleus must wander exiled from his realm;
And Nauplius, seeking injury to the Greeks
By his deceitful beacon fires, shall fall
⁶⁵⁵ Into the ocean; Palamedes, too,
Shall suffer, dying for his father's sin.
Oïleus, smitten by the thunderbolt,
Shall perish on the sea; Admetus' wife
To save her husband's life shall give her own.
⁶⁶⁰ He who commanded that the golden spoil
Be carried in the ships had traveled far,
But, plunged in seething cauldron, Pelias died
In narrow limits. 'Tis enough, ye gods;
        Ye have avenged the sea!

ACT IV

Scene I

⁶⁶⁵   *Nurse.* I shrink with horror! Ruin threatens us!
How terribly her wrath inflames itself!
Her former force awakes, thus I have seen
Medea raging and attacking God,
Compelling heaven. Greater crime than then
⁶⁷⁰ She now prepares. No sooner had she sought
Wildly her fatal shrine than she put forth
Her every power, and what before she feared
She does; lets loose all ills, mysterious arts.
With her left hand the dismal sacrifice
⁶⁷⁵ Preparing, she invokes whatever ills
The Libyan sands with their fierce heat create,
Or frost-bound Taurus with perpetual snow
Encompasses. Drawn by her magic spell,
Come from their desert holes a scaly host.
⁶⁸⁰ The serpent drags his heavy length along,
Darts his forked tongue, and seeks his destined prey.
Hearing her incantation, he draws back
And knots his swelling body coiling it.—
'They are but feeble poisons earth brings forth,
⁶⁸⁵ And harmless darts,' she says, 'heaven's ills I seek.
Now is the time for deeper sorcery.
The dragon like a torrent shall descend,
Whose mighty folds the Great and Lesser Bear
Know well (the Great Bear o'er the Phrygians shines,
⁶⁹⁰ The Less o'er Tyre); Ophiuchus shall loose
His grasp, and poison flow. Come at my call,
Python, who dared to fight twin deities.
The Hydra once cut off by Hercules,
Accustomed from its wounds to gain fresh strength,

₆₉₅ Shall come. Thou ever watchful Colchian one,
Be present with the rest—thou, who first slept
Lulled by my incantations.' When the brood
Of serpents has been called she blends the juice
Of poisonous herbs; all Eryx' pathless heights
₇₀₀ Bear, or the snow-capped top of Caucasus
Wet with Prometheus' blood, where winter reigns;
All that the rich Arabians use to tip
Their poisoned shafts, or the light Parthians,
Or warlike Medes; all Suebian witches cull
₇₀₅ In the Hyrcanian forests in the north;
All poisons that the earth brings forth in spring
When birds are nesting; or when winter cold
Has torn away the beauty of the groves
And bound the world in icy manacles.
₇₁₀ Whatever herb gives flower the cause of death,
Or juice of twisted root, her hands have culled.
These on Thessalian Athos grew, and those
On mighty Pindus; on Pangæus' height
She cut the tender leaves with bloody scythe.
₇₁₅ These Tigris nurtured with its eddies deep,
The Danube those; Hydaspes rich in gems
Flowing with current warm through levels dry,
Bætis that gives its name to neighboring lands
And meets the western ocean languidly,
₇₂₀ Have nurtured these. The knife cut those at dawn;
These other herbs at dead of night were reaped;
And these were plucked with the enchanted nail.
Death-dealing plants she chooses, wrings the blood
Of serpents, and she takes ill-omened birds,
₇₂₅ The sad owl's heart, the quivering entrails cut
From the horned owl living;—sorts all these.
In some the eager force of flame is found,
In some the bitter cold of sluggish ice;
To these she adds the venom of her words
₇₃₀ As greatly to be feared. But lo, I hear
The sound of her mad footstep and her song.
Earth trembles when she hears.

Scene II

Medea, before the altar of Hecate.

Medea. Lo, I invoke you, all ye silent shades,
Infernal gods, blind Chaos, sunless home
₇₃₅ Of shadowy Dis, and squalid caves of Death
Bound by the banks of Tartarus. Lost souls,
For this new bridal leave your wonted toil.

      Stand still, thou whirling wheel, Ixion touch
      Again firm ground; come, Tantalus, and drink
740   Unchecked the wave of the Pirenian fount.
      Let heavier punishment on Creon wait:—
      Thou stone of Sisyphus, worn smooth, roll back;
      And ye Danaïdes who strive in vain
      To fill your leaking jars, I need your aid.
745   Come at my invocation, star of night,
      Endued with form most horrible, nor threat
      With single face, thou three-formed deity!
         For thee, according to my country's use,
      With hair unfilleted and naked feet
750   I've trod the lonely groves; called forth the rain
      From cloudless skies; have driven back the sea;
      And forced the ocean to withdraw its waves.
      Earth sees heaven's laws confused, the sun and stars
      Shining together, and the two Bears wet
755   In the forbidden ocean. I have changed
      The circle of the seasons:—at my word
      Earth flourishes with summer; Ceres sees
      A winter harvest; Phasis' rushing stream
      Flows to its source; and Danube that divides
760   Into so many mouths restrains its flood
      Of waters—hardly moving past its shores.
      The winds are silent; but the waters speak,
      The wild seas roar; the home of ancient groves
      Loses its leafy shade; and day returns
765   At my command; the sun stands still in heaven.
      My incantations move the Hyades.
      It is thy hour, Dian.
         For thee my bloody hands have wrought this crown
      Nine times by serpents girt; those knotted snakes
770   Rebellious Typhon bore, who made revolt
      Against Jove's kingdom; Nessus gave this blood
      When dying; Œta's funeral pyre provides
      These ashes which have drunk the poisoned blood
      Of dying Hercules; and here thou seest,
775   Althea's vengeful brand, she sacrificed
      A mother's to a sister's love. These quills
      The Harpies left within some trackless cave,
      Their refuge when they fled from Zetes' wrath;
      And these were dropped by the Stymphalian birds
780   That felt the wound of arrows dipped in blood
      Of the Lernæan Hydra.
         The altars find a voice, the tripod moves,
      Stirred by the favoring goddess. Her swift car
      I see approach—not the full-orbed that rolls
785   All night through heaven; but as, with darkened light,

Her orb contracted, with wan face she moves
Through night's dark skies, vexed by Thessalian charms.
So, pale one, from thy torch shed murky light,
Affright the nations that they clash for thee
₇₉₀ Corinthian cymbals. Here I pay to thee,
On altars made of turf and red with blood,
These solemn rites; have stolen from the tomb
This torch that gives its baleful funeral light;
To thee with bowed head I have made my prayer;
₇₉₅ And in accordance with funereal use,
Have filleted my loosened hair, have plucked
This branch that grows beside the Stygian wave;
Like a wild Mænad, laying bare my breast,
With sacred knife I cut for, thee my arm;
₈₀₀ My blood is on the altars! Hand, learn well
To use the knife and shed blood dear to thee.
See, from the wound, the sacred stream flows forth,
Daughter of Perses, have I asked too oft
Thine aid? Recall no more my former prayers.
₈₀₅ To-day as always I invoke thine aid
For Jason only! Ah, endue this robe
With such a baleful power that the bride
May feel at its first touch consuming fire
Of serpent's poison in her inmost veins;
₈₁₀ For fire flames hid in the bright gold, a gift
Prometheus gave and taught me how to store—
He now atones his daring theft from heaven
With tortured vitals. Mulciber has given
This flame, and I in sulphur nurtured it;
₈₁₅ I brought a spark from the destroying fire
Of Phaethon; I have the flame breathed forth
By the Chimæra, and the fire I snatched
From Colchis' savage bull; and mixed with these
Medusa's venom. I have bade all keep
₈₂₀ Their poison unrevealed; now, Hecate, add
The sting to poison, keep the seeds of flame
Hid in my gift; let them deceive the sight
Nor burn the touch; but let them penetrate
Her very heart and veins, melt all her limbs,
₈₂₅ Consume her bones in smoke. Her burning hair
Shall glow more brightly than the nuptial torch!
My vows are heard, and Hecate thrice has barked,
And shaken fire from her gleaming brand.
   'Tis finished! Call my sons. My royal gifts,
₈₃₀ Ye shall be borne by them to the new bride.
Go, go, my sons, a hapless mother's brood,
Placate with gifts and prayers your father's wife!
But come again with speed, that I may know

A last embrace!

Scene III

835   *Chorus.* Where hastes the blood-stained Mænad, headlong driven
By angry love? What mischief plots her rage?
With wrath her face grows rigid; her proud head
She fiercely shakes, and dares defiantly
Threaten the king.
840 Who would believe her exiled from the realm?
Her cheeks glow crimson, pallor puts to flight
The red, no color lingers on her face;
Her steps are driven to and fro as when
A tigress rages, of her young bereft,
845 Beside the Ganges in the gloomy woods.
Medea knows not how to curb her love
Or hate. Now love and hate together rage.
When will she leave the fair Pelasgian fields
The wicked Colchian one, and free from fear
850 Our king and kingdom? Drive with no slow rein
Thy car, Diana; let the sweet night hide
The sunlight. Hesperus, end the dreaded day.

ACT V

Scene I

Messenger, Chorus.

Messenger [*enters in haste*]. All are destroyed, the royal empire falls,
Father and child lie in one funeral pyre.
    Chorus. Destroyed by what deceit?
    Messenger. That which is wont to ruin princes—gifts.
855   *Chorus.* Could these work harm?
    Messenger. I myself wonder, and can hardly deem
The wrong accomplished, though I know it done.
    Chorus. How did it happen?
    Messenger. A destructive fire
860 Spreads everywhere as at command; even now
The city is in fear, the palace burned.
    Chorus. Let water quench the flames.
    Messenger. It will not these,
As by a miracle floods feed the fire.
The more we fight it so much more it glows.

Scene II

Medea, Nurse.

⁸⁶⁵   *Nurse.* Up ! up! Medea! Swiftly flee the land
Of Pelops; seek in haste a distant shore.
    Medea. Shall I fly? I? Were I already gone
I would return for this, that I might see
These new betrothals. Dost thou pause, my soul,
⁸⁷⁰ And shrink to follow up thy first success?
This joy's but the beginning of revenge.
Thou still dost love if thou art satisfied
To widow Jason. For this work prepare:
Honor begone and maiden modesty,—
⁸⁷⁵ It were a light revenge pure hands could yield.
Strengthen thy drooping spirit, stir up wrath,
Drain from thy heart its all of ancient force,
Thy deeds till now call love; awake, and act,
That they may see how light, how little worth,
⁸⁸⁰ All former crime—the prelude of revenge!
What was there great my novice hands could dare?
What was the madness of my girlhood days?
I am Medea now, through crime made strong.
Rejoice, because through thee thy brother died;
⁸⁸⁵ Rejoice, because through thee his limbs were torn;
Through thee thy father lost the golden fleece;
That, armed by thee, his daughters Pelias slew.
Find thou a way, revenge. No novice hand
Thou bring'st to crime; what wilt thou do; what dart
⁸⁹⁰ Let fly against thy treacherous enemy?
I know not what of crime my madness plots,
Nor yet dare I confess it to myself!
In folly I made haste—would that my foe
Had children by this other! Mine are his,
⁸⁹⁵ We'll say Creusa bore them! 'Tis enough;
Through them my heart at last finds just revenge;
My soul must be prepared for this last crime.
Ye who were once my children, mine no more,
Pay ye the forfeit for your father's crimes.
⁹⁰⁰ Awe strikes my spirit and benumbs my hand;
My heart beats wildly; vanished is my rage,
And mother love, returning, now drives out
The hatred of the wife. I shed their blood?
My children's blood? Give better counsel, rage!
⁹⁰⁵ Be far from thee this crime! What guilt is theirs?
Is Jason not their father?—guilt enough!
And, greater guilt, Medea calls them sons.

They are not sons of mine, so let them die!
Nay, rather let them perish since they are!
910 But they are innocent!—my brother was!
Waverest thou? Do tears make wet thy cheek?
Do wrath and love like adverse tides impel
Now here, now there? As when the winds wage war
And the wild waves against each other smite,
915 And warring tides run high, and ocean raves,
My heart is beaten, and love drives out wrath,
As wrath drives love. My anger dies in love.
Dear sons, sole solace of a storm-tossed house,
Come hither, lock your arms about my neck;
920 You may be safe for him, if safe for me!
But I am driven into exile, flight;
Torn from my bosom weeping, soon they'll go
Lamenting for my kisses—let them die
For father and for mother! Once again
925 Rage swells, hate burns; again the fury seeks
Th' unwilling hand—I follow where wrath leads.
Would that the children that made proud the heart
Of Niobe were mine, that I had borne
Twice seven sons! In bearing only two
930 I have been cursed! And yet it is enough
For father, brother, that I have borne two.—
Where does that horde of furies haste? whom seek?
For whom prepare their fires? or for whom
Brandish the infernal band the bloody torch?
935 The huge snake hisses writhing, as they lash
Their serpent scourges; with her hostile brand
Whom does Megæra seek? What dim-seen shade
Is that which hither brings its scattered limbs?
It is my brother, and he seeks revenge;
940 I grant it, thrust the torches in my eyes;
Kill, burn; the furies have me in their power!
Brother, command the avenging goddesses
To leave me, and the shades to seek their place
In the infernal regions without fear;
945 Here leave me to myself, and use this hand
That held the sword—your soul has found revenge.
[*Kills one of her sons.*]
What means this sudden noise? They come in arms
And seek to slay me. Having thus begun
My murders, I will go upon the roof,
950 Come, follow thou, I'll take the dead with me.
Strike now, my soul, nor longer hide thy power,
But show the world thy strength.

[*She goes out with the nurse and the living boy, and carries with her the body of her dead son.*]

Scene III

Jason in the foreground, Medea with the children appears upon the roof.

    Jason. Ye faithful ones, who share
In the misfortunes of your harassed king,
955 Hasten to take the author of these deeds.
Come hither, hither, cohorts of brave men;
Bring up your weapons; overthrow the house.
    Medea. I have recaptured now my crown throne,
My brother and my father; Colchians hold
960 The golden fleece; my kingdom is won back;
My lost virginity returns to me!
O gods at last appeased! Glad nuptial day!
Go, finished is the crime. Not yet complete
Is vengeance, finish while thy hand is strong
965 To smite. Why stay, why hesitate, my soul?
Thou art able! All thine anger falls to nought!
I do repent of that which I have done!
What hast thou done, O miserable one?
What, miserable? Though I should repent,
970 'Tis done, great joy fills my unwilling heart,
And, lo, the joy increases. But one thing
Before was lacking—Jason did not see!
All that he has not seen I count as lost.
    Jason. She threatens from the roof; let fire brought,
975 That she may perish burned with her own flame.
    Medea. Pile high the funeral pyre of thy sons,
And rear their tomb. To Creon and thy wife
I have already paid the honors due.
This son is dead, and this one too shall die.
And thou shalt see him perish.
980   *Jason.* By the gods,
By our sad flight together, and the bond
I have not willingly forsaken, spare
Our son! If there is any crime, 'tis mine;
Put me to death, strike down the guilty one.
985   *Medea.* There where thou askest mercy, and canst feel
The sting, I thrust the sword. Go, Jason, seek
Thy virgin bride, desert a mother's bed.
    Jason. Let one suffice for vengeance.
    Medea. Had it been
That one could satisfy my hands with blood,
990 I had slain none. Although I should slay two,
The number is too small for my revenge.

    Jason. Then go, fill up the measure of thy crime,
I ask for nothing but that thou should'st make
A speedy end.
    Medea. Now, grief, take slow revenge;
995 It is my day; haste not, let me enjoy.

[*Kills the other child.*]

    Jason. Slay me, mine enemy!
    Medea. Dost thou implore
My pity? It is well! I am avenged.
O vengeance, no more offerings can I give,
Nothing is left to immolate to thee!
1000 Look up, ungrateful Jason, recognize
Thy wife; so I am wont to flee. The way
Lies open through the skies; two dragons bend
Their necks, submissive to the yoke. I go
In my swift car through heaven. Take thy sons!

[*She casts down to him the bodies of her children, and is borne away in a chariot drawn by dragons.*]

1005   *Jason.* Go through the skies sublime, and in thy flight
Prove that there are no gods where'er thou goest.

PHÆDRA

DRAMATIS PERSONÆ

Hippolytus.
Theseus.
Phædra.
Nurse.
Messenger.
Chorus.

Scene: *Athens*.

PHÆDRA

ACT I

Scene I

Hippolytus, and his Huntsmen.

Hippolytus. Cecropians, go gird the shadowy groves,
And ridges of the mountains; traverse swift
The places that 'neath rocky Parnes lie,
Where, swiftly flowing through Thessalian vales,
5 The river roars; ascend the hills that shine
White ever with Rhipean snow. Where stand
The tangled woods of lofty elder, go;
Go where fields stretch o'er which sweet Zephyr blows
With dewy breath that wakens vernal herbs,
10 Where flows Ilissus' narrow, sluggish stream
Through barren lands and with its niggard thread
Touches the sterile sands. Turn leftward, ye,
To where the wooded highlands open out
Toward Marathon, where nightly for their young
15 The does seek food; go ye where, breathed upon
By the soft south wind, harsh Acharnæ's cold
Is tempered; tread ye sweet Hymettus' cliffs:
Seek ye Achidnæ small; too long has lain
Immune the land where on the curved sea shore
20 Sunion presses. If a huntsman's pride
Is felt by any, Phlius calls to him—
There dwells that fear of husbandmen, the boar,
Dreaded, well known, already scarred with wounds.
Give to the dogs that silent track the game
25 Free rein, but hold the swift Molossian hounds
In leash, and let the savage Cretans pull

On the stout chains with straining necks. Bind fast,
With care, by firmest knots, the Spartan dogs;
Daring and eager for the chase are they.
30 The time draws near when through the hollow rocks
Shall sound their baying. While it is but dawn
And while the dewy earth still shows the tracks,
With nostrils wide, sagacious let them snuff
The air, and with their noses to the ground
35 Search for the quarry's scent. Let some make haste
To carry on their backs the nets, and some
To bear the noose; and let the feathered snare,
Red dyed, with empty terror fill the prey.
Thou shalt the light dart poise; in both hands, thou,
40 Direct the heavy spear; thou, lying hid,
Shalt with thy clamor drive the wild beasts forth,
And thou, now victor, with curved slaughtering knife
Lay bare the victim's heart. Be present now
To us thy comrades, goddess hero-souled,
45 To whom the secret parts of earth lie bared,
Whose darts unerring ever find their prey
Whether the quarry drink Araxes' stream
Or on the frozen Hister play. Thy hand
Has slain Gætulian lions, and the deer
50 Of Crete; and now with lighter hand the flight
Of the swift doe is stayed. The tiger yields
To thee, to thee the rough-haired bison yields
And the wild, broad-horned ox. Whatever finds
In solitary places pasture land,
55 Whate'er the needy Garamantian knows,
Whate'er the Arabs in their fertile groves,
Or the Sarmatian wanderers in waste plains,
Whate'er the Pyrenees' wild summit hides,
All that Hyrcania's wooded pastures know,
60 Diana, fear thy bow. When to the woods
A worshipper accepted takes thy grace,
The toils hold conquered game, no foot breaks through
The net, the groaning wagon bears the spoils,
The muzzles of the dogs are wet with blood,
65 And joyously the rustics seek again
Their huts. Thou art propitious, goddess, now!
The signal by the loud-mouthed dogs is given,
Lo, to the woods I'm called; the shortest way
I follow.

Scene II

Phœdra, Nurse.

70   *Phœdra.* O mighty Crete, thou ruler of wide seas,
Whose ships unnumbered sail by every coast,
Through every sea which Nereus' prows divide,
Far as Phœnician soil, why driv'st thou me
To pass my youth in sorrow and in tears,
75 A hostage given to the hated race,
And wedded to a foe. Lo, far away,
My husband Theseus is a fugitive
And keeps such faith as he is wont to keep.
Through the dense shadows of the infernal lake
80 That knows no backward path bold Theseus swam,
Pirithous' friend, that he might carry thence,
As bride, the infernal monarch's ravished wife;
He goes, the friend of folly, unrestrained
By fear or shame; in lowest Acheron
85 The father of Hippolytus seeks out
Unlawful marriage and adultery.
Yet other, greater griefs than this weigh down
My sad heart, neither quiet night nor sleep
Frees me from care: my grief is fed and grows,
90 And glows within me as the vapor glows
In Etna's depths. The web of Pallas lies
Neglected, from my idle hands the flax
Has fall'n; no longer am I glad to pay
My votive offerings at the holy shrines,
95 Nor to be present with the Attic choir
Among the altars, and to wave the torch
In sacred, silent rites, nor to approach
With pious ceremony and chaste hands
Her who was guardian goddess of the earth
100 Declared. My only pleasure is to hunt
Wild beasts, and with my supple hands to hurl
The heavy dart. O whither dost thou tend,
My soul? Why dost thou madly love the woods?
I feel my wretched mother's fatal sin:
105 Our family has been wont within the woods
To sin for love. O mother, I am moved
With pity for thee: to a shocking crime
Stirred, thou didst boldly love the savage lord
Of the wild herd, that fierce adulterer,
110 Impatient of the yoke, of untamed bands
The leader—yet for something he felt love!
What god, what Dædalus will aid my fires?

       Not if again he could return himself,
       Potent in Attic arts, who safely hid
115   Our minotaur within the labyrinth,
       Could any aid to my distress be given.
       Venus, against the offspring of the sun
       Most deeply angered, by our homage now
       Avenging both herself and Mars, weighs down
120   The race of Phœbus with most shameful crime.
       No daughter of unfaithful Minos' house
       Is free from love—love ever joined with crime.
              Nurse. O wife of Theseus, Jove's illustrious child,
       From thy chaste bosom swiftly thrust such sin,
125   O quench these fires, nor yield to cruel hope.
       Whoever from the first contends against
       And conquers love, is safe, but those who nurse
       The evil with sweet blandishments too late
       Refuse to bear the yoke themselves assumed.
130   And yet I am not ignorant, in truth,
       How the proud spirit of the princess spurns—
       Haughty and arrogant—a guiding hand.
       I'll bear whatever outcome fate may bring;
       Approaching freedom makes the aged brave.
135   To wish for honor nor to go astray
       From the right path is best, yet near to this
       Is shame that one has known the thought of sin.
       Where goest thou, unhappy one? wouldst spread
       Thy household's infamy? Wouldst thou surpass
140   Thy mother? Greater is thy crime than hers;
       Thou must impute the minotaur to fate,
       Thy crime is offspring of thine own self-will.
       If thou, because thy husband sees no more
       The light of upper day, shouldst deem thy sin
145   To be committed safely, without fear,
       Thou errst. Though Theseus is in depths profound
       Of Lethe hidden, though forevermore
       He dwell in Stygian darkness, yet why deem
       That he who gives the law to many lands
150   And rules the waters with his empery wide
       Would let so base a crime go undivulged?
       Wise is a father's care.—Yet shouldst thou think
       That we by subtlety or guile might hide
       Such evil from him, wherefore shouldst thou think
155   Thy mother's parent who pours forth his light
       On all things, or the father of the gods
       Who shakes the world when in his flashing hand
       He waves the thunderbolt from Etna's forge
       Will see it not? Dost thou indeed believe
160   That it is possible to do this deed

In sight of these thy ancestors, who see
All thou wouldst hide? Yet should some favoring god
Conceal the shameful union, grant to lust
Protection hitherto denied to crime,
165 What of the everpresent punishment,
The conscious terror of a guilty mind,
The heart that knows its fault and fears itself?
Some crimes are safe, no sinner feels secure.
Stifle the flames of guilty love, I pray,
170 Do not a sin which never yet was done
In barbarous lands, not on the level plains
Of wandering Getæ, nor the unfriendly heights
Of Taurus, nor in lonely Scythia.
Make thy mind chaste, drive out the horrid thought,
175 And mindful of thy mother, fear to try
Strange unions. Wouldst thou give one marriage bed
To son and father, in thy impious womb
Conceive a progeny so basely mixed?
Forth then, and with thy bestial fires o'erthrow
180 The laws of nature; why should monsters fail?
Why empty leave thy brother's labyrinth?
As often as a Cretan woman loves
Shall she not dare unwonted prodigies?
Shall nature not withdraw from her own laws?
185   *Phædra.* I know that what thou callst to mind is true,
Love's fire compels me choose the worser part.
My soul hastes downward not unknowingly,
And seeking saner counsels, vainly turns
Backward. So when his heavy boat is driven
190 By adverse currents does the sailor use
In vain his labor, and his conquered ship
Yields to the racing current. What avail
Is reason? Madness has o'ercome and reigns;
The potent god within my breast holds sway.
195 The unbridled, winged one in all the world
Holds sway, he burns with unrelenting, flames
Ev'n wounded Jove, the warlike Mars has felt
Those torches, and the artisan who makes
Jove's triple thunderbolts has felt them too,
200 He, who Mount Etna's ever blazing forge
Keeps busy, with this tiny spark grows hot;
Phœbus himself, who from his bow directs
Sure darts, is by the boy's more certain shafts
Transfixed; they fly alike to earth and heaven.
205   *Nurse.* Base lust, crime-maddened, feigns that love's a god,
Those who have wished great liberty have given
Falsely the name of deity to lust.
Yea, doubtless, Venus sends her son to roam

Through every land! He with his tender hand
210 Prepares his shameless darts! So great a realm
The least of all the gods can claim! Mad souls
Created empty fables and have feigned
Venus' divinity, the love god's bow.
Whoever too much joys in happy days
215 And languishes in luxury desires
Some unaccustomed pleasure, then comes lust,
Ill-omened comrade of the fortunate:
Accustomed feasts no longer satisfy,
Nor home well-ordered, nor cheap wine to drink.
220 Why does this plague, selecting dainty roofs,
So rarely seek the poorer dwelling-place?
Why is it holy love abideth still
In humble homes, that temperate passions sway
The saner multitude of common folk
225 To practise self-restraint and soberness?
Why do the rich and powerful desire
More than is lawful? Who already has
Too much desires that he cannot have.
Thou knowest what is fitting her who sits
230 Upon the throne; honor and fear the crown
Of him who will return.

    Phædra. Love's empery
In me, I think, is greatest and no more
I fear returns. He never more has seen
The convex upper world who enters once
235 The home of silence and perpetual night.

    Nurse. Yet though Death bars his realm and though the gates
Are ever guarded by the Stygian dog,
Theseus e'er finds forbidden paths.

    Phædra. Perchance Theseus will find indulgence for our love.
240   *Nurse.* He has been, even to a faithful wife,
Most harsh. Antiope the Amazon
Made proof of his hard hand. Yet couldst thou bend
Thine angered husband's will, canst thou control
Hippolytus' hard heart? The very name
245 Of woman he abhors and flies them all;
Harshly he vows his years to singleness,
Shuns marriage: such the Amazonian race!

    Phædra. It pleases me through woods and lofty hills
To follow him, when on the snowy top
250 He stays his steps, or mocks the cruel rocks
With his swift foot.

    Nurse. And will he stay his steps
And, softened, give himself to thy caress?
Will he for rites of unchaste Venus give
His chastity? Perchance his hate of thee

255 Is but the reason why he so hates all.
He cannot be by any prayers o'ercome.
> *Phædra.* Wild is he but we know wild beasts are tamed by love.
> *Nurse.* He'll flee thee.
> *Phædra.* Though through seas he flee, I'll follow him.
> *Nurse.* Recall thy father's fate.
> *Phædra.* My mother's I'll recall.
260 > *Nurse.* He hates thy kind.
> *Phædra.* I shall be free from rivals in his love.
> *Nurse.* Thy husband will return—
> *Phædra.* Pirithous' friend?
> *Nurse.* Thy father'll come.
> *Phædra.* For Ariadne's send.
> *Nurse.* I pray thee by the silvery locks of age,
265 And by this heart o'erwearied with its cares
And by the breast which nursed thee, curb thy rage.
Call up thy strength; who wishes to be well
Is partly healed.
> *Phædra.* Shame has not wholly fled
From my chaste spirit; nurse, I yield to thee.
270 Let love that wishes not to be controlled
Be overcome. Thee will I not allow,
O honor, to be stained. One way remains
One only refuge from my misery;
My husband I will follow, hinder crime
By death.
275 > *Nurse.* O daughter, moderate the rush
Of thoughts unbridled, curb thy passion's force.
Now that thou thinkest thou art worthy death,
I think thee worthy life.
> *Phædra.* Death is decreed;
I only wait to seek the kind of death.
280 Shall I destroy my life with twisted noose,
Or fall upon the sword? Or shall I leap
Headlong from Pallas' lofty citadel?
> *Nurse.* In my old age, shall I permit thee thus
To perish by a violent death? Restrain thy impulse mad.
285 > *Phædra.* No reason can prevent
The death of one who has resolved to die,
Who ought to die, we therefore arm our hand
To vindicate our chastity.
> *Nurse.* Sole stay
Of wearied age, if thus hot passions press
290 Upon thy heart, think not of thy fair fame:
Fame seldom sides with truth; kindest it is
To those who merit least and to the good
Most harsh. That soul intractable and stern
We will attempt; my labor let it be

295 To meet the youth and bend his fierce, wild will.

Scene III

Chorus.

    O goddess, daughter of the stormy seas,
Whom Cupids twain call mother, how thy boy,
Ungoverned, wanton, smiling, from sure bow
Lets fly his fiery shafts! the wound when given
300 Shows no wide scar, but hidden deep within
Devours the heart. That freakish boy can know
No peace; he scatters swiftly through the world
His arrows: all who see the rising sun,
Or toward the bounds of Hesperus may dwell,
305 Or underneath the cold Parrhasian Bear,
Or fervid Cancer—ever-wandering tribes,—
They know those fires. In youth he wakes fierce flames,
Recalls to wearied age its long cooled heat,
Inflames with unaccustomed fires the hearts
310 Of virgins, and compels the gods to leave
Their heaven and in disguise to dwell on earth.
Phœbus Apollo shepherded the sheep
Of Thessaly and put aside his lyre
And called the bulls with unaccustomed pipe.
315 How often has he taken milder forms,
Who moves the sky and clouds: once, like a bird,
White wings he moved, and with a sweeter voice
Than dying swan he sang; then with fierce front,
A wanton bull, he took upon his back
320 The sportive maid, like slow oars moved his hoofs,
Breasted the deep, and through his brother's waves,
An unaccustomed realm, he took his way,
Made timid by the plunder rich he bore.
The shining goddess of the dark world burned
325 With love, forsook the night, her bright car gave
Into her brother's unfamiliar hand—
He learned to drive the chariot of the night
And turn a shorter circuit, while the wheels
Trembled beneath the heavier weight they bore;
330 Nor did the night retain its wonted length:
The day with tardy rising came to earth.
Alcmena's son, his quiver laid aside,
Put by the mighty lion's threatening spoil,
Suffered his fingers to be decked with gems,
335 Submitted to the comb his unkempt locks,
And bound his limbs about with shining gold,
While yellow sandals on his feet were tied,

And with the hand accustomed to the club
From the swift flying spindle drew the thread.
340 The Persians saw, saw too the men who dwell
In fertile Lydia's realm, the lion's skin
Put by, and on the shoulders that had borne
The skies the dainty Tyrian mantle laid.
Believe the wounded: sacred is love's fire
345 And all too potent. In whatever land
The deep surrounds, where'er the bright stars run
Their courses through the heavens, the cruel boy
There reigns: the Nereid's king has felt his dart
Within the depths of ocean, and the flame
350 No waters could extinguish; his hot fires
The winged ones knew well; the bull with love
Instinct will boldly for the whole herd war;
The timid stags will fight, if for their does
They fear; the swarthy Indian trembles then
355 At sight of the striped tiger; the fierce bear
Makes sharp his wounding tusks and all his mouth
Is foam; the Carthaginian lion then
Tosses his mane and gives a dreadful roar,
The sign of love conceived. When love compels,
360 The forests echo with the murmur harsh.
The monsters in the restless sea feel love
And the Lucanian bull; unto himself
Love arrogates all natures, nought is free,
And hatred perishes at Love's command;
365 Old angers are by passion's fires quelled.
What can I further say—love overcomes
The cruel stepdame.

ACT II

Scene I

Phædra, Nurse, Chorus.

    Chorus. Say, nurse, what news thou bear'st; how does the queen?
How burn the cruel fires?
    Nurse. No hope can soothe
370 Such troubles, and the fires can know no end;
Smothered, they still in secret grow more hot,
Conceal it how she will, her face betrays
Her passion; from her eyes the fire breaks forth,
Her pale cheeks hate the light, her troubled soul
375 Is pleased with nothing, and uncertain grief
Drives her from place to place. She totters now
With weak steps, and she seems about to die:

Scarce can her neck sustain her drooping head;
Now to repose she turns, but, sleep forgot,
380 In sad laments she wears away the night;
She bids me lay her down, then raise her up,
To loose her hair, to bind it up again;
Her dress she changes, ever with herself
Impatient. Not for food or health she cares;
385 Her strength is failing, with uncertain steps
She moves; no more her shining face is tinged
With health's rich red; her eyes, which used to show
Some sparks of Phœbus' torch, no longer shine
With light which proves her race and native land;
390 Her tears flow ever and with constant dew
Keep moist her cheeks, as when from Taurus' top
The melted snows flow down in warm, full streams.
    But see, the palace opens; she herself,
Reclining on her golden couch, rejects,
395 In her insanity, her wonted robe.
    Phædra. The garments wrought of gold and purple, slaves,
Remove; bring not the red of tyrian conch,
The web the distant Eastern peoples weave
From fiber of the trees; my flowing robe—
400 Upgathered—let a girdle bind; take off
The necklace from my neck; the pearls, rich gift
Of Indian seas, shall not adorn my ears;
Free from Assyrian odors, let my hair
Hang loose; at random thus about my neck
405 And shoulders shall my unbound locks flow free,
And as I fly shall by the winds be blown;
The quiver in my left hand, in my right
The sharp Thessalian spear. Like her who left
The frozen seas and with her maiden hosts
410 From Tanais and Mæotis touched the soil
Of Athens—with loose hair and crescent shield
She came, in guise like hers I seek the woods.
    Chorus. Cease thy laments: complaints will not avail
Thy sorrow; to the goddess of the woods,
415 The guardian god of virgins, make thy prayer.
    Nurse. Queen of the groves, who on the mountain tops
Lovest to dwell alone, we pray thee turn
To better omens thy unkindly threats.
O mighty goddess of the woods and vales,
420 Bright star of heaven, glory of the night,
Who with alternate shining dost relume
The world, O triformed Hecate, favoring shine
On this attempt; sway thou th' unbending mind
Of stern Hippolytus, that he may lend
425 A willing ear; Oh, soften his hard heart,

Teach him to love; Oh, charm his savage breast
To feel responsive fires, to Venus' laws
Submit his savage, harsh, and hostile soul.
Exert thy power; come thus with shining face,
430 Ride through the rifted clouds with crescent bright,
Be no Thessalian incantation strong
To draw thee from the starry sky of night
Through which thou ridest: let no shepherd take
Glory from thee. O goddess now invoked,
435 Be present, look with favor on our prayers.
Himself I see, who worships only thee;
Alone he comes. Why hesitate? Chance gives
Both time and place. Arts now must be employed.
Why do I fear? It is not light to dare
440 Crime's mandate. He who fears a queen's commands
Must banish thought of honor from his breast;
Poor servant of the royal will, indeed,
Is loyalty to duty.

Scene II

Hippolytus, Nurse.

Hippolytus. O faithful nurse, why hither dost thou toil,
445 With aged, wearied steps; why bearest thou
This troubled face, this set and anxious brow?
Safe is my father, surely? Phædra safe?
Safe the two well-loved pledges of their love?
Nurse. Put by thy fears; most prosperous is the realm,
450 By happy fortune blessed, thy family thrives.
But live thou gladlier in this fair estate,
For anxious am I in my care for thee,
Because thou dost so harshly rule thyself.
He may be pardoned who, by fate compelled,
455 Is wretched, but if any uncompelled
Gives himself up to trouble willingly,
Tortures himself—who knows not how to use
The goods of fortune well may forfeit them.
Rather be mindful of thy years, give rein
460 To thy free spirit, lift on high thy torch
On festal nights, let Bacchus lighten care;
Enjoy thy youth, it flies with nimble feet.
Thy bosom now is free, love smiles on youth,
Oh, let thy heart be glad; why dost thou keep
465 A widowed couch? Make cheerful thy sad youth,
Make haste, let loose the reins, life's richest days
Allow not to flow from thee unenjoyed.
God for each age provides its office fit,

       And leads from step to step; a happy brow
470 Befits the young, austerity the old.
       Why keep thyself in check and strangle thus
       Thy rightful nature? To the husbandman
       That grain gives increase that with pliant stem
       Runs riot in the joyous fields, the tree
475 Cut or restrained by no unfriendly hand
       Rises above the grove with lofty top;
       So upright natures will the better gain
       True glory, if unhampered liberty
       Nourish the noble soul. Why dost thou pass
480 An austere youth, fair Venus all forgot,
       Inhabiting the woods, fierce, ignorant
       Of life? Dost deem this part alone to be
       Assigned to men: that they should hardships bear,
       Should learn in the swift race to drive the horse,
485 And wage, with streaming blood, most savage wars?
       What various modes of death drag mortals down
       And sweep away the throngs of men! the sea,
       The sword, and treachery! But shouldst thou deem
       That thou art safe from these—of our own will
490 We seek black Styx before our time when youth
       Would pass its life in barren singleness.
       These peoples that thou seest will endure
       But one age, in themselves will come to nought.
       The first great parent of the world took care,
495 When ravenous thus he saw the hand of fate,
       That ever a new offspring should replace
       The lost. Should Venus, who renews again
       The race destroyed, withdraw from man's affairs.
       The world were dark indeed, the sea would lie
500 Bereft of fish, the air would have no birds,
       The woods no beasts, and all the ether be
       A path for sun and winds alone. Make haste
       To follow nature, the true lord of life;
       Frequent the city, live among thy kind.
505   *Hippolytus.* No other life there is more free from fault,
       More full of liberty, which better keeps
       The ancient customs, than the life of one
       Who loves the woods and leaves the city walls;
       No passion of the sordid soul inflames
510 Him who to mountain tops commits himself
       Unstained; no voice of popular applause,
       No common peoples false to honor's claims,
       No deadly envy, no inconstant fame.
       He serves no realm, nor, striving for a throne,
515 Pursues vain honor, perishable wealth;
       Free both from fear and hope, black hungry spite

Attacks him not with his vile tooth, the crimes
Nourished among the folk who dwell in towns
He does not know, nor does he shrink afraid
520 At every sound, nor coin false words, nor seek
A home with columns numberless made rich,
Nor proudly hide his rafters 'neath much gold;
Blood in abundance does not overflow
His pious altars, nor a hundred bulls,
525 Sprinkled with sacred meal, their white necks bow
Beneath the sacrificial knife for him.
His are the lonely fields, and innocent
He roams beneath the open sky, he knows
Only to build the cunning trap for beasts,
530 When worn with labor, in Ilissus' stream
He finds refreshment; now he skirts the banks
Of swift Alphæus, now through thickets dense
Of the high groves he presses where flows down
Through silent ways, with pure and shining shoals,
535 Cold Lerna's stream, and where the querulous birds
Murmur, whence softly smitten by the winds
The mountain ash trees and the ancient beech
Tremble. He loves to lie upon the banks
Of winding rivers, or upon the sod
540 To find sweet sleep, whether abundant streams
Pour down swift floods or through fresh flowers flows
The slender brook and murmurs a sweet song.
Fruit gathered from the woods supplies his food,
And berries gathered from the thickets quench
545 His thirst. I wish not royal luxuries;
The proud man drinks from golden cup, the cause
Of anxious care; how sweet it is to drink
From hollowed hand the water of the spring!
A surer rest refreshes him who rests
550 On his hard bed secure: he does not seek,
Shameless, in secret corners, in the dark,
Intrigues, nor does he, fearful, hide himself
In hidden dwellings: but the light and air
He seeks; with heaven for his witness lives;
555 Lives like the men of old who with the gods
Mingled. No blind desire for gold was theirs,
No judge with boundary stones set off their lands,
Not yet were vessels, rashly confident,
Sailing the deep; only his own home seas
560 Each knew. They did not build about their towns
Vast walls and frequent towers, the warrior then
Knew not to use stern weapons, nor to break
Closed gates with warlike engines armed with stones;
Earth knew no master, nor was made a slave

⁵⁶⁵ To the yoked oxen, but the fields unfilled
Brought forth their fruit, nor feared mankind's demands,
The woods gave natural wealth, the shadowy caves
Natural homes. Unholy thirst for gain,
And headlong wrath, and lust which fires the heart
⁵⁷⁰ Broke first this order; fierce desire to rule
Arose, the greater preyed upon the less,
And might made right. Man then with naked hands
Fought, and to weapons turned the stones and trees,
He was not armed with the light cornel spear
⁵⁷⁵ Pointed with iron, nor the sharp-edged sword,
Nor crested helmet; anger made such arms.
New arts by warlike Mars were learned, new ways
To kill, and blood polluted every land,
The sea was red with blood. Then everywhere
⁵⁸⁰ Was crime forever found, no evil deed
Was left untried; brother by brother's hand,
Parent by son's, was slain, the husband fell
By the wife's sword, and impious mothers killed
Their children. I pass over stepdame's wrath.
⁵⁸⁵ She is nowise less savage than the beasts.
But woman was the leader in all wrongs;
This bold artificer of crime beset
All hearts: so many cities are consumed,
So many peoples wage destructive war,
⁵⁹⁰ So many kingdoms ruined lie o'erthrown,
By reason of her vile adulteries.
Of others I am silent—Ægeus' wife
Medea shows how savage women are.
    Nurse. Why make all guilty of the crimes of one?
⁵⁹⁵   *Hippolytus.* I hate, I fear, I loathe, I flee from all.
Say it is reason, nature, passions wild,
It pleases me to hate; sooner shall join
Water and flame, and vessels sooner find
In the uncertain Syrtes friendly depths,
⁶⁰⁰ Sooner from farthest confines of the west
Shall Tethys bring the day, and to the lambs
Shall wolves prove kindly, than I, overcome,
Turn friendly looks on woman.
    Nurse. Love has oft
About the stubborn cast his charms, and changed
⁶⁰⁵ Their hate to love. Look at thy mother's realm,
The Amazons felt Venus' yoke, thou prov'st
This truth—one son of Amazonian blood.
    Hippolytus. For mother lost, one consolation's mine—
I may hate womankind.
    Nurse. As cliffs resist
⁶¹⁰ The waves, invincible on every side,

And hurl far back the waters that assail,
He spurns my words. But see, where Phædra comes
With headlong steps, impatient of delay.
Where leads her passion? What will fortune give?
615 Lifeless she falls; the color, as in death,
Deserts her face. O nursling, lift thy head,
Speak, see, Hippolytus embraces thee.

Scene III

Hippolytus, Phædra, Nurse.

Phædra. Who gives me back my sorrow, brings again
My passion's heavy weight upon my soul?
620 How gladly would I put an end to life!
   Hippolytus. Why wish to flee the gift of life restored?
   Phædra. Be bold, my soul, accomplish now thy will.
Though scorned, speak fearless words; who asks in fear
Teaches denial. Of my sin great part
625 Is done: it is too late for modesty;
I have loved basely. If I follow up
This my attempt, perchance the marriage torch
May hide my crime; success makes certain sins
Respectable. Lo, now begin, my soul!
630 I pray a little nearer bend thine ear,
Lest any of thy comrades should be nigh.
   Hippolytus. The place is free from any witnesses.
   Phædra. My lips refuse a passage to my words:
'Tis a great pow'r that urges me to speak,
635 A greater holds me silent. O ye gods,
I call on you to witness: what I wish
   Hippolytus. And one who wishes something cannot speak?
   Phædra. Light cares find words, but heavy ones are dumb.
   Hippolytus. Mother, commit thy cares to me.
640 *Phædra.* The name of mother is an honorable name,
And all too powerful; a humbler one
Befits our love. Call me, Hippolytus,
Sister or slave, slave rather; I will bear
All servitude. If thou shouldst bid me go
645 Through deepest snows, Mount Pindus' frozen top
Would give me no annoy, or if through fire
And hostile battle lines, I would not shrink
From giving to the ready sword my breast.
Take back the scepter to my charge consigned,
650 Receive me as thy slave; it is not meet
A realm of cities by a woman's hand
Should be defended. Thou who flourishest
In the first bloom of youth, thy father's realm

Govern, O take thy suppliant to thy breast,
655 Pity the widow and protect the slave.
    Hippolytus. This omen may the sovereign gods avert!
My father presently will come again.
    Phædra. The ruler of the realm whence none return
And of the silent Styx has made no way
660 Back to the upper air. Will he send back
The violator of his marriage couch?
Unless, perchance, now merciful to love,
He, too, inactive sits.
    Hippolytus. The upright gods
Will truly give him back to earth. But while
665 God holds our wish ungranted, I will shield,
With duteous love, my brothers; care for thee
So that thou'lt no more feel thyself bereft
Of husband. I myself will fill for thee
My father's place.
    Phædra. O lover's trusting hope!
670 Deceitful love! Have I not said enough!
With prayers I will assail him. Pity me,
Hear my unspoken prayers; I long to speak,
Yet dare not.
    Hippolytus. What is this that troubles thee?
    Phædra. What thou wouldst hardly think could overtake a stepdame.
675   *Hippolytus.* Doubtful words thou utterest: speak openly.
    Phædra. My heart is all aflame
With love and madness, fiercest fires burn hot
Within my vitals, hidden in my veins,
As o'er the lofty roof the swift flame plays.
680   *Hippolytus.* With wifely love for Theseus dost thou rage?
    Phædra. Hippolytus, 'tis so; I love the form,
The face that Theseus in his boyhood bore,
When first his cheeks were darkened by a beard,
And he beheld the winding labyrinth
685 Where dwelt the Theban monster; by a thread
He found his path. How glorious was he then!
A fillet bound his locks, a modest blush
Reddened his tender cheeks, on his soft arms
Were iron muscles. Thy Diana's face,
690 Or my Apollo's had he, or thine own!
Lo! such he was when he made glad his foe,
Thus proudly did he hold his head; in thee
Shines forth his manly beauty unadorned
But greater; all thy father is in thee,
695 And yet some part of thy stern mother's look,
A Scythian sternness on thy Grecian face.
If thou with him had crossed the Cretan straits,
For thee my sister would have loosed the thread.

O sister, in whatever part of heaven
₇₀₀ Thou shinest, I invoke thee in a cause
Both thine and mine; one house has snatched away
Two sisters, thee the father, me the son.
Lo! fallen at thy feet a suppliant lies,
Child of a kingly race. Unstained I was,
₇₀₅ Pure, innocent—'tis thou hast wrought this change.
See, to entreaty I have sunk: this day
Must either end my sorrow or my life.
Have pity on my love.
    Hippolytus. O king of gods,
Dost thou so mildly hear, so mildly see
₇₁₀ Such baseness? When will fly the thunderbolt
Sent from thy hand, if thou art now unmoved?
Oh! Let the firmament be rent apart,
The daylight be by sable clouds concealed,
The backward driven stars be turned aside
₇₁₅ To run inverted courses. Thou bright sun,
Chief of the stars, canst thou behold the crimes
Of this thy offspring? Let thy light depart!
Fly to the shades! Ruler of gods and men,
Why is thy right hand idle, hurling not
₇₂₀ Thy triple thunderbolt against the world?
Thunder upon me, pierce me with thy bolt,
And swiftly burn me with thy smiting fires.
Guilty I am, I have deserved to die,
For I have pleased my stepdame. Lo, was I
₇₂₅ Worthy of incest deemed? Did I alone
Seem to thee facile subject for thy crimes?
Is this what my austerity deserved?
O thou in crime surpassing all thy kind,
More wicked than thy mother thou art found!
₇₃₀ She stained herself with lust most infamous,
And though her crime was long a secret held,
The two-formed offspring brought at last to light
The mother's guilt—the child's ambiguous form
Betrayed her crime—of that womb thou art born.
₇₃₅ O thrice, O four times happy call I those
Destroyed and given to a violent death,
By stepdame's hate and treachery o'ercome.
Father, I envy thee! This scourge is worse,
Worse than thy Colchian stepdame.
₇₄₀   *Phædra.* I also recognize our family's fate,—
Fleeing we find it; yet I o'er myself
No more have power; I'll madly follow thee,
Through flames and seas, through rocks and raging streams;
Where'er thou turnst thy steps my love drives me.
₇₄₅ Again, O proud one, at thy feet I fall.

Hippolytus. Withdraw from my chaste body thy foul touch.
Ha, what is this? She falls upon my breast!
The sword shall slay her, she shall meet just death.
See, I bend backward by the twisted hair
With my left hand her shameless head; ne'er fell
Upon thy altars, goddess of the bow,
Blood shed in better cause.
   Phædra. Thou giv'st me now
My wish, Hippolytus. Thou mak'st me sane.
Better is this than aught that I could wish.
I'm saved, with honor by thy hand I die!
   Hippolytus. Live, yet go hence lest somehow, by thy prayers,
Thou shouldst avail—and let this sword, denied
By thee, my chaste side leave. Could Tanais' stream,
Or the Mæotis, or the Euxine sea,
Cleanse me—e'en Neptune could not wash away,
With all the waters of the mighty deep,
So great impurity. O wilderness!
O forests!

Scene IV

Phædra, Nurse.

   Nurse. The fault is known; why rest inactive? Up,
Throw back on him the blame; sin must be hid
By sin. The safest way for one in fear
Is to attack. Since no one saw the crime,
Who shall be witness whether we first dared
Or suffered ill? Athenian women, haste!
Help, faithful band of slaves; Hippolytus,
The ravisher, pursues, attacks the queen;
He threatens death, and with the sword attacks
That virtuous one. Lo, headlong has he fled,
Affrighted, in his hasty flight has left
His sword; we hold the token of his crime.
First bring again to life the fainting form:
Leave as they are her torn and loosened locks,
Proofs of the crime attempted; bear her forth
Into the city. Mistress, take thou heart;
Why shouldst thou wound thyself and shun all eyes?
Unchastity lies not in chance but thought.

Scene V

Chorus.

    As swiftly as the hurricane he fled,
    More swiftly than the hurricane that drives
    The clouds before it, swifter than swift flame
785 That burns when meteors, driven by the winds,
    Send forth long fires. On thee, Hippolytus,
    Shall fame confer all beauty that aroused,
    In ages past, man's wonder; lovelier shines
    Thy form than, when her crescent orbs have poured
790 Their fires, Diana moves with glowing face
    All night, full-orbed, in her swift car through heaven,
    And lesser stars no longer show their face.
    So Hesperus, the messenger of night,
    At twilight shines, fresh bathed in ocean's waves;
795 So Lucifer drives darkness into flight.
    Thou Thyrsus-bearing Liber, Indian born,
    Whose unshorn locks shine with immortal youth,
    Who fightest tigers with thy vineclad staff,
    Who bindest with broad bands thy horned head,
800 Thou art not fairer than Hippolytus;
    Nor shouldst thou think too highly of thy form,
    For fame has blazoned through all lands his fame
    Whom Phædra's sister did to Bromius
    Prefer.
805 O beauty, doubtful gift to mortals given.
    A fleeting good that but a moment stays,
    With what swift feet thou flyest. Not so soon,
    When noon glows hot and night a brief course runs,
    Does burning summer's breath deprive the fields
810 Of all the comeliness of early spring.
    As the pale flowers of the lily fall,
    So falls the hair, the glory of the head;
    The glow which brightens on the tender cheek
    Is in a moment gone, and one day spoils
815 The body's grace. A transitory thing
    Is beauty: who may in so frail a good
    With wisdom trust? Oh! use it while thou mayst:
    Time silently destroys thee, and each hour
    Is worse than that which just has passed away.
820 Why shouldst thou seek the desert's loneliness
    Beauty is no more safe in pathless ways
    Thee will the saucy bands of wanton nymphs,
    Accustomed to imprison lovely youths
    In streams, surround at midday in the wood;

825 And dryads, who upon the mountain tops
    Follow some Pan, will in thy sleep assail;
    Or from the starry heavens, beholding thee,
    The planet that since old Arcadian folk
    Sprung loses power to drive her shining car.
830 Lately she blushed, no sordid cloud obscured
    Her shining face; but by her angry light
    Disturbed, and fearing dark Thessalian charms,
    We offered prayers—thou wast her trouble's cause,
    And thou the cause of her unwonted stay;
835 Because the goddess of the night saw thee,
    She checked her rapid course.
    Did bitter winds blow less upon thy face,
    Didst thou less oft expose it to the sun,
    Whiter than Parian marble would it shine.
840 How pleasant is thine austere, manly face,
    The sternness of thy brow! that glorious neck
    Thou mayst with bright Apollo's well compare,
    His hair about his shoulders flowing free,
    Knowing no bond, adorns and covers him,
845 Thy hirsute front, thy shorter, uncombed locks,
    Become thee. Thou mayst with the gods contend
    In battles stern and conquer by thy strength,
    For equal is thy strength with Hercules',
    Broader thy breast than that of warlike Mars.
850 If it had pleased thee on a horse to ride,
    Thou couldst have reined the Spartan Cyllarus
    More easily than Castor. With thy hand
    Make tense the bowstring, and with all thy strength
    Direct the shaft: the Cretan, apt to learn
855 The art of shooting, not so far could send
    The slender arrow; if in Parthian wise
    Thou shootest skyward, not a dart descends
    Without a bird: within the warm breast hid
    It brings its prey from out the very clouds.
860 Seldom has man been beautiful and safe:
    Look at the ages. May a kindlier god
    Leave thee in safety, and thy beauty gain
    The aspect of unbeautiful old age!
    What will a woman's passion leave undared?
865 She plots 'gainst youth and innocence base crime.
    Behold the sinner! she would find belief
    By her torn locks, the glory of her hair
    Is all dishevelled, and her cheeks are wet;
    Her woman's cunning doth devise all frauds.
870 But who is this that comes with kingly form,
    And lofty bearing? To Pirithous
    How like his face, were not his cheeks so pale,

His unkempt hair so rough about his brow.
Ah! Theseus comes, returned again to earth!

ACT III

Scene I

Theseus, Nurse.

875 *Theseus.* I have at last escaped the land where reigns,
Eternal darkness, where night holds the dead
In its vast prison. Hardly can my eyes
Endure the brightness of the hoped-for day.
Four times the plow, gift of Triptolemus,
880 Has cut Eleusis' soil, four times the Scales
Have measured day the equal of the night,
Since first the doubtful toils of unknown fate
Have led me twixt the ills of life and death—
To me, though dead, a part of life remained,
885 The sense of ills. Alcides was their end.
He when he carried off from Tartarus
Th' unwilling dog, brought me as well to earth.
My wearied body lacks its ancient strength,
My footsteps tremble—ah! how hard the task
890 It was to seek the far-off upper air
From lowest Phlegethon, to flee from death
And follow Hercules.
                    What sound is this
Of lamentation strikes upon my ears?
Ah, some one, tell me! Grief, and tears, and woe,
895 And sad lament, e'en at my very door
Assail me; truly, worthy auspices
For one who as a guest from Hades comes.
    Nurse. Phædra maintains her firm resolve to die,
She spurns our prayers, and is resolved on death.
    Theseus. What cause is there for death?
900 Why should she die,
Her husband come again to life?
    Nurse. E'en this
Hastens her death.
    Theseus. I know not what may mean
The riddle of thy words. Speak openly.
What heavy sorrow weighs upon her mind?
905 *Nurse.* To none she tells it, she conceals her woe,
Determined that her ills shall die with her.
But haste, I pray thee, haste, for there is need.
    Theseus. Unbar the portals of my royal house.

Scene II

Phædra, Nurse, Theseus.

Theseus. O wife, dost welcome thus my late return?
₉₁₀ Dost thus behold thy husband's longed-for face?
Let go the sword and take me to thy breast,
Tell me what makes thee seek to flee from life.
    Phædra. Alas, great Theseus, by thy scepter's might,
And by the inborn nature of thy sons,
₉₁₅ And by thy coming from the shades again,
Yes, by thy ashes, suffer me to die.
    Theseus. What reason urges thee to die?
    Phædra. The fruit of death would perish if its cause were known.
    Theseus. None other than myself shall hear the cause.
₉₂₀   *Phædra.* A virtuous wife dreads but her husband's thoughts.
    Theseus. Speak, hide thy secret in my faithful breast.
    Phædra. That which thou wouldst not have another tell, tell not thyself.
    Theseus. Death shall not have the power to touch thee.
    Phædra. Death can never fail to come to him who wills it.
₉₂₅   *Theseus.* Tell me what the fault thou must by death atone.
    Phædra. The fault of life.
    Theseus. And art thou not affected by my tears?
    Phædra. The sweetest death is one by loved ones mourned.
    Theseus. Thou wilt keep silence? Then with blows and chains
₉₃₀ Thy aged nurse shall be compelled to speak
What thou wouldst not. Now cast her into chains,
Let blows drag forth the secrets of her mind.
    Phædra. Cease, I myself will speak.
    Theseus. Why turn away thy mournful face, why cover with thy robe
₉₃₅ The tears that wet so suddenly thy cheek?
    Phædra. O father of the gods, on thee I call
To witness, and on thee, bright light of heaven,
From whom our family springs; I strove to stand
Against his prayers, my spirit did not yield
₉₄₀ Either to threats or steel. Yet to his force
My body yielded; this the stain my blood
Must wash away.
    Theseus. Who was it, tell me who thus stained our honor?
    Phædra. Him thou least suspectest.
    Theseus. I earnestly entreat thee, tell me who.
₉₄₅   *Phædra.* The sword will tell thee, that the adulterer left,
When by approaching tumult terrified,
He feared the gathering of the citizens.
    Theseus. Alas, what crime is this which I behold?
What awful thing is this I look upon?
₉₅₀ The royal hilt of ivory, carved and bright,
The glory of Actæon's race! But he—Where has he fled?

Phædra. His fear and hasty flight these slaves beheld.
Theseus. O holy piety!
O ruler of the sky, and thou who holdest
955 The kingdom of the waters! Whence has come
This foul infection of my sinning son?
Did Greek soil nourish him, or was he reared
On Scythian Taurus, and by Colchis' stream?
The child repeats the father, and base blood
960 Bespeaks its primal source. This passion comes
From that armed race that hated ties of love
And, too long chaste, made common to the crowd
Their bodies. O vile people, to no laws
Of milder climes obedient! Even beasts
965 Shun sins of love and with unconscious awe
Obey the laws of nature. Where that face,
That feigned majesty and manner stern,
That seeking after old austerity,
That sad affected gravity of age?
970 O treacherous life, thou carriest hidden thoughts,
And hidest with fair form a sinful soul;
A modest bearing covers shamelessness,
Gentleness boldness, seeming goodness crime;
The false looks true, and harshness tender seems.
975 O dweller in the woods, wild, virgin, chaste,
Unconquered, hast thou kept thyself for me?
Wilt thou first try thy manhood with such crime,
In my own bed? Now to the gods above
Be praises that Antiope has fallen,
980 Struck by my hand; that when I sought the Styx
Thy mother was not left behind for thee.
O fugitive, seek unknown climes afar,
By ocean's plains shut off in earth's last bounds,
Be hid within the region 'neath our feet.
985 Shouldst thou have crossed the realms of bitter cold,
And deep within its farthest nook be lost,
Or, placed beyond hoar frost and winter snows,
Have left behind cold Boreas' bitter threats,
Thou yet shalt pay the penalty for crime;
990 Undaunted, fast upon thy flying steps,
Through every lurking place I'll follow thee.
Long, diverse, difficult, and pathless ways,
Aye, ways impossible shall we pass through;
Nothing shall hinder. Whence I have returned
995 Thou knowest. Whither arrows cannot go
I'll send my curse. Neptune has promised me
Three wishes by his favor gratified,
And has confirmed his promise with an oath
Sworn by the river Styx. My stern desire

1000 Perform, O ruler of the restless seas!
Let not Hippolytus behold again
The day's fair light, but let the youth go down
Among the wrathful spirits of the dead—
Wrathful because of me. O father, bring
1005 Thy son thy dreaded aid—I had not asked
Of thy divinity this gift supreme
But that such heavy evil pressed me sore.
Even within the depths of Tartarus,
Dread realm of Dis, and threatened by the wrath
1010 Of the infernal king, I still withheld
This wish. Fulfil thy promise. Why delay?
Why, father, are thy waters silent still?
Black clouds with driving wind should hide the sky,
Snatch from the heavens the stars, upheave the deep,
1015 Arouse the monsters of the sea, call forth
The swelling floods from Ocean's farthest bounds!

Scene III

Chorus.

O nature, mighty mother of the gods,
And thou of fiery Olympus king,
Who speedest through the flying firmament
1020 The scattered constellations, and the stars'
Uncertain courses, and the heavens that turn
So swiftly, why continue with such care
To keep the pathway of the airy heights
That in its season winter's cold and snow
1025 Lay bare the forests, that the leafy shade
Returns, that summer's constellation shines
And ripens with its fervid heat the grain,
That milder autumn comes? But since thou rul'st,
Since by thy power alone the balance weight
1030 Of the vast universe revolves, why, then,
No longer careful of the race of men,
Careless to punish evil or reward
The good, dost thou desert Hippolytus?
Fortune by ways unordered rules man's life;
1035 The worse she cherishes, and blindly flings
Her gifts, and base desire conquers law,
And fraud is king within the palace walls,
The populace rejoice to give the base
High office and to hate the very man
1040 Whom they should honor. Rigid virtue finds
The recompense of evil, poverty
Follows the pure in heart, and strong in crime

Th' adulterer reigns. O reputation vain!
O empty honor! But with headlong steps
1045 Why comes the messenger with tear-wet cheeks!

ACT IV

Scene I

Theseus, Messenger.

Messenger. O hard and bitter lot, grim servitude!
Why am I called by fate to bring such news?
　　Theseus. Be brave to speak, e'en of the bitterest woes.
I have a heart not unprepared for grief.
1050　　*Messenger.* Alas, alas, Hippolytus is dead!
　　Theseus. The father knew long since his son was dead.
Now dies the ravisher, but tell me how?
　　Messenger. When he, a fugitive, with troubled steps,
Had left the city, taking his swift course
1055 With flying feet, he quickly yoked his steeds,
With bit and bridle curbed them; with himself
Revolving many things, he cursed his land
And oft invoked his father. With loose rein
He shook his lash, impetuous. Suddenly
1060 The depths of ocean thundered, and its waves
Smote on the stars; no wind blew on the sea;
And nowhere were the quiet heavens stirred,
The tempest moved the placid deep alone.
No south wind e'er blew up Sicilia's straits
1065 Like this, nor did the wild Ionian sea
E'er rise before the northwest wind like this,
When cliffs shake with the beating of the waves,
And the foam flashes white on Leucas' top.
The great deep rose in billows mountain high,
1070 But not for ships was this disaster planned,
The earth was threatened; not with gentle roll
The waves swept onward, some strange thing the surge
Bore on its burdened bosom. What new world
Slowly upheaves its head? What island new
1075 Rises among the Cyclades? While thus
Questioning we gazed, the whole wide ocean roared,
The cliffs on every side sent back the sound;
His head all dripping with the driving spray,
Belching the flood from out his cavernous jaws,
1080 Foaming and vomiting the waters forth,
Through the great straits was dragged a monster vast;
The mound of waters, smitten, sank amazed,
Opened, and on the shores spewed out a beast

Most terrible. The deep with landward rush
1085 Followed the monster—at the thought I quake!
Ah, that huge body, what a form it had!
A great bull with blue neck, it lifted up
On a green brow a lofty crest, its ears
Were shaggy, and of changing hue its eyes;
1090 Such form the wild herd's lord on earth might have,
Or bull of ocean born. Its eyes shot flame,
Wondrously with the ocean blue they shone;
A thick mane grew upon its brawny neck,
With every breath it snorted; breast and throat
1095 Were green with clinging moss, its monster sides
Were dotted with red lichens; backward thence
It showed a monstrous form, a scaly fish,
Vast, horrible, dragging huge length along;
Such are the fish that in the outer seas
1100 Swallow swift ships or wreck them. The land shook,
The frightened herds fled madly through the fields,
The shepherd was not mindful of the lambs,
The wild beasts in the wooded pastures fled,
The huntsmen stood alarmed and faint with fear.
1105 Hippolytus, alone untouched by fear,
With tight rein curbed his horses, checked their flight,
And with his well-known voice encouraged them.
A pathway wide bends through the parted hills
Into the fields, along the ocean strand;
1110 That mound of flesh there armed him for the fight,
Lashed up his rage, and having taken heart
And stretched himself, he then essayed his strength;
He sped along, scarce touching in his flight
The surface of the ground, and stayed his course
1115 Before the frightened horses. With fierce look
Thy son arose to meet its menaces,
Nor was he silent; with loud voice he cried:
'My courage is not mastered by this threat,
To conquer bulls has been my family's task.'
1120 The horses, disobedient to the rein
And turning from the way, dragged off the car;
Where'er blind terror drove them there they went;
They fled among the rocks, but he, thy son,
Guided the chariot as the pilot guides
1125 His vessel in a storm, nor lets it turn
Aslant the wave, and by his skill escapes.
Now with tight rein he pulled upon the bit;
Now with the twisted lash he smote the steeds.
The fish, a constant comrade, followed him,
1130 Devouring now the ground with equal pace,
Now lying in the way the car was turned,

And causing greatest fear on every side.
Nor farther was it possible to flee,
For the great horned monster of the deep
1135 Lying in wait with open mouth assailed.
Then the excited horses, mad with fear,
Freed themselves from the guidance of the rein
And rearing struggled from the yoke to tear
Themselves. They hurled their burden to the ground,
1140 Headlong he fell, entangled in the lines;
The more he fought against the tightening noose,
The more its knots were strengthened. What they'd done
The frightened horses felt, and, driverless,
Where fear impelled they rushed with the light car.
1145 So through the air the horses of the sun,
Not recognizing their accustomed load
And angry that a false god brought the day,
Upon their devious course hurled Phaethon forth!
The field was red with blood, his wounded head
1150 Rebounded from the cliffs, the brambles tore
His hair, hard rocks destroyed his lovely face,
His ill starred beauty marred by many wounds
Perished. Upon the wheels his dying limbs
Were whirled about; pierced through the midst at last
1155 By a burnt stake, upon its point was fixed
His trunk, the car was stayed a little while
Held fast by its prone driver, and the steeds
At the disaster stayed their hasty course,
Then broke through all delays and tore away
1160 Their master. Brambles cut the lifeless form,
Each stinging brier and sharp thorn took part
Of that torn trunk. The band of sorrowing slaves
Followed through all the field where, dragged along,
Hippolytus in bloody characters
1165 Marked the long path, the howling dogs tracked out
Their master's members, but most loving care
Could not find all. Is this his noble form?
Illustrious sharer of his father's throne,
And certain heir, who like a star in heaven
1170 Shone bright, he now was gathered from all sides
For the last honors, for his funeral pyre
Was brought together from the plain.
    Theseus. O nature, all too potent, with what chains
Thou holdst the parent's heart! we cherish thee
1175 Although against our will. I wished to slay
The guilty one and now I weep his loss.
    Messenger. What one has wished not always makes one glad.
    Theseus. This is, I think, the farthest reach of ill:
That chance should make me curse the thing I loved.

1180 *Messenger.* Why wet thy cheeks with tears for one thou hat'st?
Theseus. Not that I lost but that I slew I weep.

Scene II

Chorus.

How many chances rule the lot of man!
Fortune against the humble least is roused,
The god more lightly smites the little worth;
1185 Obscurity finds peace and quietness
The cottage offers undisturbed old age.
The pinnacles that tower toward the skies
Most feel the east wind and the south wind smite,
Endure the savage north wind's menaces,
1190 The blowing of the rainy north-west wind;
The moist vale seldom feels the thunderbolt,
But lofty Caucasus, the Phrygian grove
Of mother Cybele, are often shaken
By thundering Jove's attack, for Jupiter,
1195 Fearing their nearness to his heavenly heights,
Aims there his bolts. Beneath the humble roofs
Of lowly homes great tumults never come.
Fickle and restless is the hour's flight,
And faith with none does flying fortune keep.
1200 Theseus, who left the gloomy shades of night,
And sees the starry skies, the sunny day,
Must sadly mourn his sorrowful return,
And find his native land more full of grief
Than dread Avernus.
1205 Chaste Pallas, venerated by the Greeks,
Because thy Theseus sees the upper world
And has escaped the waters of the Styx,
Thou owest to thy robber uncle naught;
The tyrant finds hell's number still the same.
1210 What voice from out the mourning palace sounds?
With weapon drawn why comes sad Phædra forth?

ACT V

Scene I

Theseus, Phædra.

Theseus. What fury animates thee, and with grief?
Wherefore that sword, and why those sad laments?
Why beat thy bosom for such hated dead?
1215 *Phædra.* Me, me, O cruel ruler of the seas,

Assail, and send the blue sea's awful shapes
To war on me—whate'er far Tethys bears
Within its inmost bosom, whatsoe'er
Ocean, embracing with its restless waves
1220 The world, conceals within its farthest flood!
Theseus, ever most unfeeling one,
Thou ne'er returnest safely to thy home.
Father and son must pay for thy return
By death; thou, ever guilty, dost destroy
1225 Thy home with love or hate. Hippolytus,
Such as I made thee do I see thee now?
Did Sinis or Procrustes scatter thus
Thy members, or some savage Cretan bull,
Half man, half beast, refilling with its roar
1230 The labyrinth of Dædalus, destroy
With its great horns? Oh! whither now is fled,
My star, the glory of thy brilliant eyes?
Dost thou lie lifeless? Come, one moment come,
And hear my words, 'tis nothing base I speak!
1235 With my own hands I'll pay thee what I owe,
Into this sinful breast will thrust the sword,
Will by one deed take Phædra's life away,
And cleanse her from her sin, and follow thee
Madly through floods, through Tartarean lake,
1240 Through Styx and fiery rivers. Let me die—
Let me placate the spirit of the dead:
Receive the lock of hair here cut for thee,
It was not lawful that our souls should wed,
But still, perchance, we may in fate be one.
1245 Let me, if chaste, die for my husband's sake,
And if unchaste, die for the loved one's sake!
Shall I approach my husband's marriage bed
That am with such crime stained? This one sin lacked:
That I, as one unstained, should still enjoy
1250 That bed as if it were my right. O death,
The only solace for the pains of love;
O death, last grace of injured chastity,
To thee I fly, take me to thy calm breast!
Hear me, Athena, let his father hear—
1255 He than the cruel stepdame sterner found—
Falsely have I accused him of a crime
Which I myself in my mad heart conceived;
I spoke a lie. Thou, father, hast in vain
Sought punishment; of all incestuous crime
1260 The youth is pure, unstained and innocent.
Recover now thy former spotless fame,
The sinful breast lies bare for justice' sword;
My blood is offered to a holy man.

Theseus. What thou should'st do,
O father, for thy son thus snatched away,
Learn from his stepdame. Seek the Acheron!
O jaws of pale Avernus and ye caves
Of Tænarus, ye waves of Lethe's stream
So welcome to the wretched, stagnant fens,
Hide ye the wretched one, with endless woes
O'erwhelm! Ye cruel monsters of the deep,
Great sea, and whatsoever Proteus hides
Within the farthest corner of his waves,
Be present now; into the whirling deeps
Drag me, so long rejoicing in such crimes.
O father, ever all too easily
Approving of my wrath, I am not meet
To suffer easy death—I who have strewn
My son's torn members in unheard of ways
Through all the fields. Crime did I truly find
When, as the harsh avenger, I pursued
One falsely charged with crime. The seas and stars
And land of shadows by my crimes are filled;
No place remains, me the three kingdoms know.
Have I returned for this? Was upward way
Opened but that I might behold the dead,
That, widowed, childless, I might with the torch
Light the sad funeral pyres of wife and son?
Giver of light, Alcides, take thy gift
Back to the sable groves of shadowy Dis,
Restore me to the Manes whence I came.
Me miserable! Vainly I invoke
The death that I deserted. Bloody one,
Artificer of death, contrive thou now
And bring to light unheard of means of death,
Inflict upon thyself just punishment.
Shall a great pine be bent until the top
Touches the earth, then, being freed again,
Upspringing, bear me with it to the stars?
Or shall I fling myself from Sciron's cliffs?
Yet heavier punishment than that I've seen,
Which Phlegethon compels the guilty souls
Prisoned within its circling waves of fire
To suffer: well I know the dwelling place,
The bitter penalties reserved for me.
Ye guilty souls give place and let the rock
That to the ancient son of Æolus
Gives ceaseless labor weigh these shoulders down,
Weary these hands; let rivers, flowing near
My thirsty lips, ever elude their touch.
Let the fierce vulture, leaving Tityus,

Hover about my liver and increase
My punishment. Mayst thou have rest at last,
Thou father of my friend Pirithous:
1315 On the swift flying wheel that never stays
Its turning let my limbs be whirled about.
Earth, open! Dire chaos, take me back!
Take me! The pathway to the shades of hell
Is mine by better right; I follow him!
1320 O thou who rul'st the spirits of the dead,
Fear not, for we who come to thee are chaste.
Receive me to thy everlasting home,
There will I stay. My prayers the gods hear not,
But had I asked their help in evil, deeds,
How ready had they been!
1325   *Chorus.* Eternity
Is thine, O Theseus, for lament; pay now
The honors due thy son, and quickly hide
In earth his scattered members so dispersed.
        Theseus. O hither, hither bring the dear remains,
1330 Give me the parts from many places brought.
Is this Hippolytus? The crime is mine,
'Twas I destroyed thee; and not I alone—
A father, daring crime, I called to aid
My father, I enjoy a father's gift!
1335 How bitter is such loss to broken age!
Embrace whatever of thy son is left,
And clasp him to thy bosom, wretched one.
The mangled body's separated parts,
        Chorus. O father, in their rightful order place
1340 Restore the severed members to their place.
Lo, here the place the strong right hand should rest,
And here the left that learned to hold the reins;
I recognize the marks on his left side.
How great a part is absent from our tears!
1345   *Theseus.* For this sad duty, trembling hands, be strong;
O cheeks be dry, and let abundant tears
Be stayed, the while I count my son's torn limbs,
And form his body. What is this I see,
Lacking in beauty, base, with many wounds?
1350 What part of thee it may be I know not,
Yet part of thee it is. Here, here repose,
Not in thine own but in a vacant place.
Is this the face that like the bright stars shone?
His eyes that overcame his enemy?
1355 Thus has his beauty fallen? Bitter fate!
O cruel kindness of the deity!
And is my son thus given back to me,
As I have wished? O son, in fragments borne

Forth to thy burial, from thy father take
1360 These funeral rites; thee shall the fire burn,
Lay wide the house with dismal murder filled,
Let Mopsopia sound with loud lament.
Ye, to the royal funeral pyre bring flame,
And ye, seek out his body's scattered parts
1365 Through all the fields. When she is buried,
[*Turning to Phædra's body*] Let earth lie heavy on her, let the soil
Weigh down her impious head!

ŒDIPUS

DRAMATIS PERSONÆ

Œdipus.
Creon.
Tiresias.
Phorbas.
Jocasta.
Manto.
A Corinthian.
Messenger.
Chorus.

Scene: *Thebes.*

OEDIPUS

ACT I

Scene I

Œdipus, Jocasta.

    Œdipus. Already night has fled, dim dawns the day
The morning star looks darkly through the gloom,
The woeful light in baleful flame appears
And sees our homes made desolate by plague;
5 And day will show what havoc night has wrought.
Who would be glad at being made a king?
Deceitful honor, how thy flattering face
Conceals untold misfortune. As the ridge
Of mountain summits by the wind is swept,
10 As rocky headlands, even when the sea
Is calm, by breakers at their jutting base
Are lashed, so fortune's storms attack the heights
Of kingly power. 'Twas but right to flee
The scepter of my father Polybus.

15 An exile, free from care and unafraid,
    (I call to witness heaven and the gods)
    Idly I happened on a kingdom's throne.
        I fear an impious crime: lest slain by me
    My father die; for so admonished me
20 The Delphic laurel, and of greater crime
    Forewarned me. Could there be a greater crime
    Than murder of a father? Woe is me,
    It shames me but to give the crime a voice;
    For Phœbus threats a marriage infamous,
25 A parent's bed dishonored by a son,
    Incestuous union, and a bridal torch
    That fits such wedding feast. This fear it is
    Made me an exile from my father's house.
    Not as a fugitive I left my home,
30 But, fearing to myself to trust myself,
    Nature, thy holy laws I made secure.
    Although thou loath'st the sin, yet none the less
    Fear that which seems to be impossible,—
    I greatly feared and trusted not myself.
35   E'en now the fates prepare some grievous ill—
    This plague, so hostile to the Cadmean land,
    And spreading such disaster, spares but me;
    For what worse evil then am I reserved?
    Amid the city's ruins, 'mid new deaths,
40 That ever with new tears must be bewept,
    'Mid slaughter of my people, I stand safe—
    Apollo's hand is plain. How can I hope,
    Destined for crimes like these to hold secure,
    A healthful realm? 'Tis I infect the air.
45 No gentle wind with cool breath cherishes
    The hearts that labor under burning suns;
    Light Zephyr blows not; Titan, pressing close
    The lion of Nemea's flanks, augments
    The dog-star's heat; the river beds are dry;
50 The green deserts the herbage; Dirce's fount
    Fails, and Ismenus' stream is but a thread
    Whose waters scarce make moist the barren shoals:
    Apollo's sister moves obscured through heaven,
    And earth is sad and wan with clouded day;
55 No night serene is lighted by the stars,
    But o'er the earth brood black and heavy mists;
    Infernal darkness veils the heavenly heights,
    The dwelling of the gods; her ripened fruit
    Ceres withholds—just as the golden ear
60 Lifts itself trembling on the thirsty stalk
    The grain dies fruitless; nought remains secure
    From ruin; every age and sex alike

Is smitten, son with father, youth with age,
   In ghastly ruin, and one funeral pyre
65 Serves wife and husband, so that neither mourns
   Nor weeps beside the bier of a dead spouse.
   Nay more, the rigor of such heavy woes
   Makes dry the eyes, and tears, the wonted gift
   Of sorrow, may not fall. Here going forth,
70 A grieving father carries out his child;
   Or there a grief-stunned mother brings her son,
   To burn his body on the last dread fire;
   Swiftly they go, returning to perform
   The same sad office for another child.
75 New sorrow rises from the sorrow's self,
   And they who came to bear the dead away
   Fall dead; on strangers' pyres their forms are burned,
   And fire made common spoil; woe knows no shame;
   No separate tombs enclose the holy dead;
80 It is enough the bodies should have blazed,
   How small a part to ashes really burns!
   No space remains for graves, the woods refuse
   To furnish funeral pyres for the dead.
   When once the plague has smitten, art nor vows
85 Can save. Physicians fall while minist'ring,
   And sickness seizes him who offers help.
   Prostrate before the altars here I stretch
   My suppliant hands, implore a speedy death;
   I would outrun my country's overthrow,
90 Die ere all perish, live not as the last
   Of all my kingdom. O too cruel gods!
   O heavy lot! Death, that so swiftly smites
   My people, is to me alone denied,
   Lay down the scepter from thy fatal hands;
95 Flee from the tears, the funerals, and the air
   So full of pestilence, which thou, a guest
   Ill-omened, brought'st with thee; fly swiftly hence,
   Although to home and parents thou must flee.
      Jocasta. Why add lament to sorrow? knowest thou not
100 'Tis kingly to endure unflinchingly
   Whatever adverse fortune choose to give?
   Although prosperity decline, the strength
   Of mighty empire totter to its fall,
   The king should stand unshaken; it is base
   To turn the back to fortune.
105   *Œdipus.* Far from me
   Be the reproach of sins of cowardice;
   My spirit does not know ignoble fear.
   If hostile dart, if bristling might of war
   Attack me, I would boldly hold my own—

110 Against the Giants even. When the Sphinx
Proposed her riddle, I was not afraid;
Nor did I fear before the bloody jaws
Of that dread prophetess, though all the ground
Was white with scattered bones; and when she stooped
115 From the high cliff, and, ready for her prey,
Spread her broad wings, and, lashing with her tail,
Threatened to pounce as a fierce lion does,
I asked her for her riddle; o'er my head
Wildly she sang, impatient ground her teeth,
120 And tore the rocks with claws that fain would tear
My heart. The twisted riddle of the Sphinx,
The double speech, the baleful prophecy
That fierce bird sang, I solved. Thou foolish one,
Why yearn too late for death? 'Twas possible
125 Then to have died; this scepter was the meed
Of honor, and Jocasta the reward
Allotted thee for slaying of the Sphinx.
But from the ashes of the monster comes
This curse against me, and that perished plague
130 Now ruins Thebes. No safety now remains,
If Phœbus does not show us safety's path.

Scene II

Chorus of Theban women.

O noble sons of Cadmus' race, ye die
With all your city! Wretched Thebes! alas,
Thy homes are left unto thee desolate.
135 Bacchus, thy soldiery is snatched away
By death—those gallant comrades who dared ride
To farthest India and the distant east,
And plant thy banners on earth's utmost bounds;
They saw the woods of Araby the blest
140 Fragrant with breath of cinnamon; they saw
The flying Parthian cavalry who shoot
Their treacherous arrows backward as they flee;
They saw that Red Sea's shore, where first the sun
Springs from the waters, bringing up the day,
145 There where the naked Ethiopian feels
His nearer flame.
Sons of a race unconquered, thus we fall;
We pass snatched hence by cruel destiny;
Each hour new sacrifice is led to death;
150 The long train of the sad procession hastes
Down to the shades, and all the ways are blocked,
And, for the throngs that seek the place of tombs,

The seven gates of Thebes are not enough;
Corpse upon corpse the bodies of the dead
155 Are heaped together.
The stolid sheep feel first the touch of death,
The sick lambs scarcely crop the juicy herbs.
The priest stands ready for the sacrifice,
But as his hand is raised to strike the blow,
160 The bull that waited it with gilded horns
Sinks slowly; as the heavy ax descends,
Relaxed beneath the blow his huge neck falls,
But yet by no red blood the steel is stained,—
A humor black and foul flows from the wound.
165 The horse, o'erwearied in the course, drops dead
And throws his rider prone; what sheep still live
Lie helpless in the fields; the bull grows weak
Among the herd; the shepherd fails his flock,
Fainting and dying 'mid the wasting young;
170 The hinds no longer fear the plundering wolf;
No more the angry lion roars; no more
The shaggy bear is fierce; the lurking snake
Loses its sting, shrivels and perishes,
Its venom dried.
175 The woods no longer from their leafy boughs
Shed dusky shadows on the mountain side;
No more the land grows green with springing grain;
No more the vines' full branches downward bend
With weight of Bacchus' gifts; earth feels our woes.
180 The Tartarean band of sisters, armed
With fatal torch, have burst apart the gates
Of Erebus profound, the Phlegethon
Has changed its course, and with Sidonian streams
The Styx is mingled. Black Death's eager jaws
185 Gape for us, wide he spreads his mighty wings.
The hard old ferry-man who guides the boat
That plies between the gloomy river's banks,
Sore taxed with frequent poling to and fro,
Can hardly lift his over-wearied arms,
190 Too weak to bear the thronging dead across.
'Tis said the dog of hell has burst his chains,
Forged of Tænarian iron, and now haunts
Our country; earth makes moan, and misty forms,
Larger than human, wander through the groves;
195 The Cadmean woods twice trembled and shook down
Their weight of snow, and twice the troubled fount
Of Dirce welled with blood, Amphion's dogs
Howled on the silent night.
Oh, strange and dreadful kind of death, far worse
200 Than death itself! A heavy lassitude

Binds fast our listless limbs, the feverish red
Flames in the face, and spots defile the brows;
The body's citadel, the head, is burnt
With scorching heat, the cheeks are swelled with blood,
205 The eyes are fixed, and on the drooping limbs
A foul corruption feeds, a ringing noise
Sounds in the ears, black blood flows from the nose
And bursts the veins agape; quick, racking groans
Are wrung from quivering hearts; some seek to cool
210 Their glowing fever on the icy rocks,
And some in empty homes, the watcher gone,
Make haste to seek the fountain, but their thirst
Grows as they drink. Before the altars lie
A prostrate throng and pray for speedy death,
215 For death alone the gods consent to give.
They crowd the shrines, not with their votive gifts
T' appease the wrathful gods, but with themselves
To glut the greedy anger of the gods.

ACT II

Scene I

Œdipus, Creon, Chorus.

Œdipus. Who is it hither comes with hasty steps?
220 Is it not Creon, great in deed and race?
Or does my sick soul view the false as true?
    Chorus. 'Tis Creon—he whom all desire to see.
    Œdipus. I tremble, for I dread the trend of fate;
My fearful heart is torn by two desires:
225 Where joy with sorrow mingled lies in doubt
The soul, uncertain, longing still to know,
Still fears to know. Dear brother of my wife,
If any hope thou bringst to wearied hearts,
I pray thee now be swift to tell it me.
230 *Creon.* The oracle a doubtful answer gave.
    Œdipus. Who gives us doubtful safety, gives us none.
    Creon. The Delphic oracle is wont to hide
Her secret meaning in a double sense.
    Œdipus. Though it be doubtful, tell it, since to read
235 Dark sayings is to Œdipus allowed.
    Creon. The god commands that murder of the king
Should be atoned by exile, Laius' death
Avenged; not otherwise shall cloudless day
Arise, nor any breathe untainted air.
240   *Œdipus.* Who slew the noble king? what man is he
Whom Phœbus names? Speak, that he may atone.

Creon. I pray it may not be unsafe to tell
The horrid tale of what I saw and heard.
A numbness lies upon my limbs, chill fear
245 Congeals my blood: when I, with suppliant feet,
Within the temple of Apollo came,
And with observance due had lifted up
Pure hands, and made my prayer, Parnassus' peak
Thundered, Apollo's drooping laurel shook,
250 And swayed its leaves, the holy stream that flows
From the Castalian fountain ceased; the seer,
Moved by the god, shook back her unkempt locks,
Nor had she reached the cave when from its depths
A thundering voice greater than human came:
255 'The kindly stars will not again return
To Cadmus' city till the stranger guest
Whom even as a child Apollo knew—
The stranger guilty of king Laius' death—
Shall flee from Dirce. Thou may'st not retain
260 The pleasant fruit of slaughter, long enjoyed;
Thou with thyself shalt war, and shalt bequeath
War to thy sons, so basely hast thou turned
Again to her who bore thee.'
   Œdipus. At command
I am prepared to do the god's behests,
265 For it is meet this man be offered up
To Laius' ashes, that the sanctity
Of kings be not by treachery profaned;
For kings have need to guard the life of kings.
Him who alive was feared none think of dead.
270   *Creon.* 'Twas terror drove out thought of him who died.
  Œdipus. Can any fear prevent a reverent care?
  Creon. The Sphinx, her gloomy song of threatened crime.
  Œdipus. This wrong, at heaven's command, shall be avenged.
Ye gods who look with favor on our realm,
275 Whoe'er ye be, both thou whose laws control
The whirling firmament, thou brightest star
Of heaven, who governest the twice six signs
Diversely, whose swift wheel rolls off slow time;
And thou Diana, wanderer through the dark,
280 Who still returnest to thy brother's side;
Thou too almighty ruler of the winds,
Who driv'st thy azure car through ocean's plains;
And thou whose dwelling shuns the holy light,
Be present. Grant that he who slew the king
285 May find no peaceful home, no household gods,
Nor hospitable land; may he lament
A shameful marriage, offspring odious;
Let him commit the crime from which I fled—

What worse could it be possible to wish?
290 Nor shall a place of grace remain for him.
I swear by this my kingdom, where I dwell
A guest, and by the kingdom that I left,
And by my household gods; by thee I swear,
Great father Neptune, who dost softly bathe
295 My dear land's double coast with gentle waves;
By thee I swear, who camest to inspire
The Delphic priestess' words of prophecy:
So may my father on his lofty throne
Live out his age secure in length of days,
300 And Merope no other marriage know
Than that of Polybus, as I will show
The guilty man no favor. Tell me where
The impious crime was done, did Laius fall
In open war or slain by treachery?
305   *Creon.* He sought the leafy grove, Castalia's fount,
Treading the way o'ergrown with thorny vines;
From thence three roads stretch forth into the plain;
One leads through Phocis, land to Bacchus dear,
Whence high Parnassus lifts its double peak
310 And, seeking heaven, rises from the fields
By gentle slopes; another to the land
Of Sisyphus, whose shores two oceans wash;
Into the valley lands of Olenos
The other leads, and, by a sinuous course
315 Meeting at last the wandering waters, slips
Across the cool ford of th' Elean stream;
Here unexpectedly, when all seemed safe,
Robbers assailing, wrought the hidden crime.
But summoned by Apollo's oracle,
320 Tiresias comes in haste, with trembling steps,
And Manto, his companion, hither leads
The sightless seer.

Scene II

Œdipus, Tiresias, Manto, Creon in the background.

    Œdipus. Near to Apollo, sacred to the god,
Speak, tell the answer; whom does justice seek?
325   *Tiresias.* In truth it hardly fits thee, great-souled one,
To wonder that the tongue is slow to speak,
And asks delay; truth, to the blind, lies hid.
Yet whither Phœbus or my country calls
I follow, and Apollo's oracle
330 Shall be made known. If youth's hot blood were mine,
I might receive the god within my breast;

But to the altars bring the white-backed bulls
That never on their necks have borne the yoke;
And thou, who to a father reft of light
Art guide, my daughter, tell me what the marks
Of the prophetic sacrifice.
    Manto. There stands, fronting the altars, an abundant gift.
    Tiresias. In hallowed words invoke the gods on high,
Heap up the altars with the fragrant gift of eastern incense.
    Manto. On the sacred fire the frankincense has been already cast.
    Tiresias. What of the flame? Has it yet seized the gift?
    Manto. It shone a moment with a sudden light,
Then fell again as suddenly.
    Tiresias. But say
If clear and bright the fire now burns, if shoots
To heaven a straight, pure flame, until its crest,
Upstreaming, melts away in liquid air?
Or does it fluttering creep about the sides
And flicker dark with undulating smoke?
    Manto. Th' inconstant flame has not one form alone:
As Iris, the rain-bearer, intertwines
Her various colors, and her bow, stretched forth
Across the heavens, by its painted arc
Announces showers—you may not tell the tints,
Blue mingles with the gold, then disappears
And glows again blood red, then sinks at last
Into the dark. The stubborn flame is split
In two, and one discordant half divides
Again. I shudder, father, at the sight!
To Bacchus the libation has been poured,
And see, it turns to blood; a heavy smoke
O'erhangs the king, is densest round his head,
And hides the murky light with heavy cloud.
Father, what means it? Say.
    Tiresias. What can I say?
Amid the tumult of a mind confused
I grope; what shall I say? The ills are dire,
But hidden. By a less uncertain sign
The gods are wont to manifest their wrath;
What is it that they wish yet do not wish
Should be revealed? Why hide they thus their wrath?
Something there surely is that shames the gods.
Bring near the victims, scatter on their necks
The salted meal: do they with placid mien
Suffer the priest's approach and lifted hand?
    Manto. Turned toward the east, the bull throws back his head,
Shrinks from the day, and, overcome with fear,
He dreads the sun's face and her radiant beams.
    Tiresias. By one blow fall they, to the earth struck down?

Manto. The heifer gave herself to death, o'erthrown
380 By the first blow; the bull, by two strokes felled
Rolls madly here and there, until at last,
Wearied, his struggling life is forced away.
    Tiresias. Springs the blood swiftly from a narrow cut,
Or does it slowly moisten the deep wounds?
385   *Manto.* The blood in rivers from the heifer's side
Flows forth, but from the bull's deep wound the stream
Is scant, though from his mouth and eyes there wells
Much blood.
    Tiresias. An unpropitious sacrifice
Foretells most terrible events. But say
390 What signs undoubted do the entrails show?
    Manto. My father, what is this? The inward parts
Not with the wonted gentle quivering
Are moved, but shake the hand in which they're held,
And from the veins new blood flows forth; the heart
395 Is sick and withered, and lies covered up;
The veins are leaden blue, the bowels lack
The greater part, the liver is decayed
And covered up with froth of inky gall,
And, omen ever fraught with ill for kings,
400 See from the lobe two equal heads arise;
A slender membrane covers either head
Denying lurking place for hidden things;
The hostile side in sturdy strength lifts up
Its seven veins; all these an oblique ridge
405 Cuts off, preventing them from turning back.
Changed is the natural order, nothing lies
Where it is wont, inverted is the whole:
Not on the right is found the bloody lung,
Breather of air, nor on the left the heart;
410 Nor does the membrane with its soft embrace
Surround the viscera's rich folds, no law
Is here observed, and nature's ways are changed.
Let us examine whence this order strange.
What shocking prodigy is this I see?
415 In a new place, an unaccustomed way,
The foetus of the unwed heifer fills
The parent, moves its members with a moan,
Stirs with a quivering motion its weak limbs;
Black blood pollutes the tissues, the torn trunk
420 Attempts to move, the lifeless heifer seeks
To rise and with its horns attack the priest;
The entrails fly the hand; that sound you hear
Is not the lowing of the noble herd,
Is not the voice of the affrighted flocks—
425 The altars shake, the altar-fires resound.

Œdipus. Say freely what these fearful signs presage,
Unfrighted shall my ears drink in thy words.
    Tiresias. Those ills for which thou seekest help, thou'lt grudge
Thyself to help.
    Œdipus, Tell that high heaven ordains;
430 What hand destroyed the king, defiled the realm?
    Tiresias. Alas, not wandering bird that on light wing
Cleaves the blue depth of heaven, nor fiber torn
From out the living breast can tell the name.
Another way must needs be found, the king
435 Must from the region of eternal night
Be called, must be sent forth from Erebus,
That he may name the author of his death;
The earth must open and relentless Dis
Must be invoked, and hither must be brought
440 The dwellers of the nether Styx. Declare
To whom thou wilt this office delegate;
For as the king 'tis not permitted thee
To see the land of shades.
    Œdipus. This task demands,
Creon, thy care, for thou art next myself.
445   *Tiresias.* While open wide we lay the Stygian depths,
Ye Thebans, raise a song in Bacchus' praise.

Scene III

Chorus of Thebans.

Wreathe with the nodding vine your flowing locks,
Take the Nysean thyrsus in your hands.
    O Bacchus, light and glory of the skies,
450 Be present while the noblest in thy Thebes
Raise supplicating hands and prayers to thee;
With favoring glance turn hitherward thy head
So virginal, dispel with starry look
The clouds, the menaces of Erebus
455 And eager fate. To twine the flowing hair
With vernal flowers well beseemeth thee;
To bind about thy head the Tyrian crown,
Or wreath with berried ivy thy smooth brows;
To let thy loosened hair fall unrestrained,
460 Or in a careful knot to bind it back.
Thus didst thou grow, fearing a stepdame's wrath,
Under false seeming; wore thy flaxen locks
In virgin fashion, girded up thy robe
And flowing syrma; thus the regions wild
465 Of eastern lands, of men who drink the streams
Of Ganges, or who break the Araxes' ice,

Saw thee reclining in thy golden car,
Thy lions half concealed beneath thy robe;
On his mean ass Silenus followed thee,
His swollen temples with green vine leaves bound,   470
And wanton priests thy hidden mysteries held.
Thy company of Bassarids, thy band
Of chosen followers led the Edonian dance
Now on Pangæus, now on Thracian soil
Of Pindus' heights; among the Cadmean dames   475
The Mænad, Theban Bacchus' comrade, came,
Her body with a sacred fawn skin girt,
The slender thyrsus in her waving hand.
The bacchanals who mangled Pentheus' limbs,
When madness left them and their limbs relaxed,   480
Gazed on their deed as on an unknown crime.
   Surrounded by her train of ocean nymphs,
Cadmean Ino, shining Bacchus' aunt,
Rules o'er the ocean; and the wandering youth,
Divine Palæmon, Bacchus' kin, gives laws   485
That still the raging of the mighty deep.
Thee, when a child, Etrurian shepherds stole,
But Nereus stilled the raging of the sea—
Plane trees and laurel groves to Phœbus dear
Sprang green with early leaves, a garrulous bird   490
Sang in the branches, riotous ivy held
The oars, and vines o'erhung the lofty mast;
In the ship's prow the Idæan lion roared,
A tiger from the Ganges held the poop.
The frightened pirate leaped into the sea,   495
And as he sank a new form covered him—
A sinuous dolphin followed the swift ship.
Pactolus that with rushing waters sweeps
Its golden banks away, has carried thee
On its rich current; the Massagetes,   500
Who mix with blood their drink of milk, unbent
Their conquered bows and freed their Getan shafts;
Lycurgus' ax-armed people recognize
The sway of Bacchus; the wild Dacian land,
The wandering tribes that feel the north wind's blast,   505
The nations where the cold Mæotis flows,
And those on whom look down from heaven's heights
The wagons twain and star of Arcady
Have felt his power. The scattered Geloni
He overcame, and took away their arms   510
From the fierce maiden warriors by his might.
The virgin troops that by Thermodon dwell.
To Mænads turned, cast from them their light shafts
And sank to earth with drooping face. The mount

515 Of blest Cithæron flowed with Theban blood;
And Prœtus' daughters wandered in the woods;
In Juno's presence Argos honored him;
Naxos, surrounded by the Ægean sea,
Brought him a maid deserted for his bride,
520 And with a better husband thus replaced
Her loss. The Bacchic river freely flowed
From the dry rock, its bubbling rills divide
The turf, the deep earth drank the honey's stream,
And fountains of white milk and Lesbian wine
525 Mingled with odorous thyme.
Bacchus led up his bride to heaven's height;
With loose hair, Phœbus sang the bridal song,
Twin Cupids waved aloft the bridal torch;
At Bacchus' coming Jove laid by his dart
530 Of fire, and loathed the dreaded thunderbolt.
As long as old earth's starry heavens turn,
As long as ocean with its waves surrounds
Th' encircled earth, and while the full-orbed moon
Continues to relight her dying fires,
535 As long as Lucifer foretells the dawn,
As long as high Arcturus touches not
The azure ocean, we will pay our vows
To fair Lyæus' bright divinity.

ACT III

Scene I

Œdipus, Creon.

Œdipus. Thy face betrays the signs of tears, but speak,
540 Whose life must be an offering to the god?
Creon. Thou bid'st me tell what fear would have me hide.
Œdipus. If thou remain'st unmoved by suffering Thebes,
Thy kindred's fallen scepter bids thee speak.
Creon. Thou'lt yearn to know not what thou fain would'st know.
545 *Œdipus.* A want of knowledge is an idle balm
For ills. Would'st thou conceal the evidence
That brings us public health?
Creon. When medicine is bitter, painful is it to be healed.
Œdipus. Tell what thou heard'st or thou shalt learn to know,
550 Conquered by heavy punishment, what power
The weapons of an angry king may have.
Creon. Kings hate the words their own commands call forth.
Œdipus. Unless thy voice lay bare the oracle
Thou shalt be sent to dusky Erebus, a sacrifice for all.
555 *Creon.* O grant the boon of silence.

Can a lesser liberty be sought for from a king?
 Œdipus. Such liberty
Oft harms both king and kingdom more than words.
 Creon. What boon is left when silence is forbid?
560 *Œdipus.* He weakens royal power who, told to speak, keeps silence.
 Creon. Hear unmoved, I pray, the words forced from me.
 Œdipus. What man, being urged to speak,
Was ever punished for obedience?
 Creon. Near the Dircean region of moist vales,
565 Afar from Thebes, there stands an ilex grove,
The cypress, ever green, lifts up its head
Above the wood, and aged, spreading oaks
Stretch out gnarled, rotten branches; wasting years
Have rent the cypresses, and from their roots
570 Great oaks have fall'n and lean 'gainst neighboring trunks;
The bitter-berried laurel, the slim lime,
The Paphian myrtle, and the alder tree
Destined to move as oars through the wide deep,
The pine around whose slender bole the winds
575 Play and whose summit stretches to the sun,
Are here, and in their midst a mighty tree
Spreads o'er the lesser grove its heavy shade,
And darkens all beneath its spreading boughs.
In shadow, knowing neither light nor sun,
580 And stiff with everlasting frost, there lies
A melancholy pool; an oozy swamp
Surrounds the sluggish spring; here came the priest,
Nor knew delay—the place itself brought night.
The earth was hollowed out and brands were laid,
585 Brands snatched from funeral pyres; the seer put on
The somber robe and smote upon his brow,
Even to his feet his unkempt vestments flowed.
With mourning guise the sad old man advanced,
The gloomy yew upon his hoary locks.
590 Black two-year sheep were brought and jet-black bulls;
The flame destroyed the sacrifice, the sheep
That still were living feared the deadly fire.
Then he invoked the manes, thee invoked,
King of the shades, and him who blocks the gates
595 Of the Lethean waters; and his song
Rolled magically forth, wild threats he sang,
Compelled and calmed the airy shades, and poured
Offerings of blood, and burned the victims whole—
He saturated all the grot with blood.
600 Libations too with the left hand he poured
Of snow-white milk and wine, and sang again,
And looking down he called with dreadful voice
The manes. Hecate's train bayed back, the cave

Thrice grimly thundered, all the earth was moved.
605 'I have been heard,' the prophet said, 'my words
Have proved effectual, the dark abyss
Is broken open and a way is made
For Pluto's people to the upper air.'
The forest shook and lifted up its leaves,
610 The oaks were split, a shudder shook the grove,
Earth groaned and opened; either not unmoved
Could hell behold her hidden depths assailed,
Or earth, that she might give the dead a path,
Rent wide her surface, thundering, or the dog,
615 Three-headed Cerberus, in anger shook
His heavy chains. Earth yawned and opened wide
Her mighty breast, I saw the darksome lake
Amid the shades, I saw the pallid gods
And very night. My frozen blood stood still.
620 The savage band leaped forth, that warlike race
Of brothers sprung from Dirce's dragon's teeth,
Leaped into life full-armed; th' Erinyes shrieked,
Horror, blind Fury, and whatever else
Eternal night creates and keeps concealed,—
625 Grief tearing out its hair, and dread disease
Propping its weary head, and dull old age,
And shrinking fear, and evil pestilence,
All eager to destroy the Theban land.
My spirit fainted; Manto, who knew well
630 The ancient ceremonies, stood aghast;
Her fearless father, by his blindness bold,
Called up from cruel Dis the bloodless throng—
Straightway they hover like a fleecy cloud,
And breathe free air beneath the open sky.
635 More than the falling leaves of Eryx' height,
Or flowers that bloom at Hybla in the spring
When bees swarm round them, more than waves that break
Against the shores of the Ionian sea,
More than the birds that flee the Thracian cold
640 And, cleaving heaven, change the northern snows
For Nile's warm air, are they the prophet's voice
Evoked. The trembling spirits eagerly
Fly to the coverts of the leafy groves.
First Zethus rises from the earth, he grasps
645 The horns of a fierce bull in his right hand,
Then comes Amphion, whose left hand supports
The harp that with sweet music drew the rocks;
The haughty child of Tantalus held up
Proudly among her sons her drooping head
650 And, safely glorying, beheld their shades;
Insane Agave, yet more wretched, came,

The wild Bacchantes, who destroyed the king,
Behind her, and, still uttering horrid threats,
Poor, mangled Pentheus followed the mad train.
₆₅₅ Often invoked, Laius last advanced
His shame-crowned head; afar from all the train
He stands and hides himself; the priest renewed
His Stygian prayers, until the shade revealed
To open day the face he fain would hide.
₆₆₀ I tremble as I speak—with bloody limbs
Dreadful to look upon he stood, his hair
Unkempt and covered o'er with shameful filth.
With angry lips he spoke; 'Cadmean house,
Savage and ever glad in kindred blood,
₆₆₅ Shake the wild thyrsus, with inspired hand
'Twere better thou should'st rend thy sons; the love
A mother bears her child is Thebes' worst crime.
Alas, my country, not by angry gods,
By sin art thou despoiled. No baleful wind
₆₇₀ Breathed from the south it is that injures thee,
Nor does the earth, too little wet with showers,
Slay with dry breath; a blood-stained king destroys,
Seizing upon a scepter, prize of crime,
And on his mother's marriage bed. Base son!
₆₇₅ But yet more wretched than her son is she
Who twice was bearer of unhallowed seed.
He turned again to her who gave him birth,
And has through her created odious sons,
Has done what beasts scarce do, unto himself
₆₈₀ Begotten brothers,—evil intricate,
And prodigy more doubtful than his Sphinx.
O, thou who in thy right hand dost sustain
A bloody scepter, it is thee I seek,
And all thy realm; a father unavenged,
₆₈₅ I'll bring for bridesmaids to thy marriage-feast
The dread Erinyes, I will bring the scourge,
Thy home impure will ruin, crush thy house
With impious war. Drive therefore from thy land
In haste the exiled king, and let him bend
₆₉₀ Whithersoe'er he will his fatal steps;
The earth will then grow green with flowery spring,
Her herbs revive, the vital air will breathe
Pure winds, and once again the forests know
Their former beauty. Ruin, pestilence,
₆₉₅ Disaster, death, corruption, and distress,
His worthy henchmen, will with him depart;
He shall desire with flying feet to leave
Our kingdom, but with wearisome delays
I'll stay his steps so he shall creep along

700 Uncertain of the road, shall grope his way
With the sad steps of age. Up, drive him forth
From earth—from heaven I will shut him out.
    Œdipus. An icy trembling fills my flesh and bones,
Accused am I of doing what I feared;
705 Merope joined with Polybus disproves
The crime of marriage; Polybus unharmed
Absolves my hand from guilt of parricide;
Father and mother prove me free from sin
Of murder and adultery, what room
710 Remains for crime? Thebes mourned for Laius' death
Long ere my foot had touched Boeotia's land.
Is the seer mocked, or is the god himself
Faithless to troubled Thebes? Ah, now I know
The shrewd accomplices in guile; the seer
715 Invents this lie, using the gods as cloak,
And promises my scepter shall be thine. [*To Creon.*]
    Creon. Could I then wish my sister thus dethroned?
If sacred ties of kinship held me not
Within my station, yet would Fortune's self,
720 Too often tempted, make me fear such deed.
Now may'st thou lay aside the weight of power,
Nor, laying it aside, be crushed. Oh, take
In safety now a place of lower rank.
    Œdipus. Thou counselest me freely lay aside
This heavy scepter?
725   *Creon.* Those who still might choose
I would advise, but thou must bear thy lot.
    Œdipus. For those who wish to rule, the surest way
Is praise of moderate fortunes, ease, and sleep;
The restless often counterfeit such calm.
730   Creon. Is faith so long maintained so little worth?
    Œdipus. Pretended faith has oftentimes made safe
The pathway to perfidious faithlessness.
    Creon. Set free from all the burdens of the crown,
I still enjoy the benefits of power;
735 The citizens come thronging to my door,
And no day rises with alternate change
On which our lares are not overflowed
With gifts from royal kindred: splendid feasts,
Rich clothing, safety by my favor won,
740 And countless offerings. Could I deem I lacked
Aught in such happy fortunes?
    Œdipus. Those thus blessed lack ever moderation.
    Creon. Shall I then fall as if guilty, though my cause unheard?
    Œdipus. Has my life's fate been fully told to thee,
745 Or has Tiresias heard me plead my cause?
Yet seem I guilty. Ye have led the way, I follow.

Creon. What if I am innocent?
Œdipus. Kings ever fear uncertainty no less than certain evils.
Creon. He whom empty fears alarm, deserves the true.
750 *Œdipus.* Who once has sinned, when pardoned comes to be an enemy.
Let all that's doubtful fall.
Creon. Thus enmity is gendered.
Œdipus. He who fears such hate too much
Has never learned to rule; fear guards the realm.
755 *Creon.* The king who holds his throne with cruel sway
Must fear the fearful; on its author's head will fear return.
Œdipus. [*To his followers.*] Shut up the criminal
Within a rocky cave, and guard him well.
I go to seek again my palace walls.

Scene II

Chorus.

760 Thou art not author of our many woes,
'Tis not for thee Fate seeks Thebes' royal house;
'Tis the gods' ancient wrath pursues us still,
Castalia's grove to the Sidonian guest
Gave shelter, Tyrian colonists were bathed
765 By Dirce's fount, when great Agenor's son,
Weary of seeking over all the world
The sister Jove had ravished, stood afraid
Beneath our trees, adoring Jove himself:
At Phœbus' bidding he forsook his flight,
770 Followed the footsteps of the straying cow
That never yet had felt the ploughshare's weight
Nor bent beneath the great cart's curving yoke;
He from the fatal heifer gave a name
To the new people. Since that time the land
775 Has ever borne new monsters; the dread snake,
Born in deep valley, o'er the aged oaks
Hisses, and rears above the pines its head,
While on the ground its greater length is spread;
Or earth by birth unnatural brings forth
780 That armored host: from winding horn there went
The signal, from the trumpet's twisted brass
The strident note, but not before the band
Had tried their ready lips with warlike noise
Of unknown speech. The field by kindred hosts
785 Was held, fit offspring of the scattered seed;
They measured out their life in one short day—
After the day-star paled were born, and fell
Ere Hesperus had risen. Horror seized
The stranger at such marvels, and he feared

790 The new-born nations' war, until they died
And earth, their mother, saw the sons she bore
Returned within her lap. Let civil war
Rise thence, and let the Thebes of Hercules
From them learn bitter fratricidal wars.
795 Why tell the lot that Cadmus' grandson bore,
When with the antlers of the long-lived stag
His brow was hidden, and the hounds pursued
Their master? Swift Actæon headlong fled
Through woods and mountains, and, 'mid fields and rocks
800 Roaming with nimble feet, he feared to see
A feather moved by Zephyr, feared the toils
Himself had placed; and, mirrored in the waves
Of the untroubled fountain where had bathed
The virgin goddess bitterly ashamed,
805 He saw reflected bestial form and horns.

ACT IV

Scene I

Œdipus, Jocasta.

Œdipus. My mind is full of cares which fear recalls.
The gods of heaven and hell deem Laius slain
By crime of mine, but still my guiltless soul,
Known better to myself than to the gods,
810 Denies the charge; yet memory recalls
Faintly how with my lifted staff I felled
And gave to Dis that proud old man whose car
Hindered my path; but far from Thebes he fell
Where in Phocaea's plain three pathways meet.
815 I pray thee solve the riddle, dear-loved wife:
Dying, how many years had Laius lived?
Fell he in bloom of youth, or weak with age?
    Jocasta. 'Twixt youth and age, but somewhat nearer age.
    Œdipus. Were many in the train that followed him?
820   *Jocasta.* Uncertain of the way, the greater part
Were lost, a faithful few alone remained beside his car.
    Œdipus. Did any others fall, partakers of the royal fate?
    Jocasta. Alas!
One brave and faithful follower shared his lot.
825   *Œdipus.* Still I seem guilty. Number, place, agree.
But when—
    Jocasta. Since then ten harvests have been reaped.

Scene II

Œdipus, An Old Citizen of Corinth.

Corinthian. [*To Œdipus.*] King Polybus has found eternal rest,
And Corinth calls thee to thy father's throne.
    Œdipus. How fortune buffets me on every side!
Tell me, I pray thee, by what fate he fell.
    Corinthian. A quiet sleep set free the old man's soul.
    Œdipus. Not murdered and yet dead my father lies.
Bear witness: fearless now of any crime,
As fits a son, I may lift up pure hands
To heaven.—But of the destiny foretold
That which I most have need to fear remains.
    Corinthian. Thy father's throne will banish every fear.
    Œdipus. My father's throne I willingly would take,
But fear my mother.
    Corinthian. Canst thou be afraid
Of her who anxiously for thy return is waiting?
    Œdipus. Filial love has made me flee.
    Corinthian. And wouldst thou leave her widowed?
    Œdipus. Thou hast named the thing I dread.
    Corinthian. Reveal the hidden fear
That weighs upon thy mind, for I am wont
To guard the secrets of my lords.
    Œdipus. Alas!
Warned by the Delphic oracle, I fear a mother's marriage bed.
    Corinthian. Thy empty fears
Put by, no longer tremble, Merope
Was not thy mother.
    Œdipus. In a spurious son what gain was hoped for?
    Corinthian. Children make more firm
A kingdom's proud security.
    Œdipus. What means
Hadst thou to learn the secrets of the bed?
    Corinthian. A child, I gave thee to thy mother's arms.
    Œdipus. Thou gavest me to her; who gave me thee?
    Corinthian. A shepherd from Cithæron's snowy top.
    Œdipus. What fortune took thee to those wooded heights?
    Corinthian. I followed on the hills my horned flock.
    Œdipus. Show some undoubted marks upon my flesh.
    Corinthian. Thou borest deep-cut scars of iron bonds,
And from thy bruised and swollen feet arose thy name.
    Œdipus. Again I ask, what man was he
Who gave my body to thee for a gift?
    Corinthian. He fed the royal flocks and under him
Was placed a company of humbler men.

Œdipus. His name?
Corinthian. Our earliest recollections fail
With age, and, wearied, slip away with years.
Œdipus. Shouldst thou be able by his face and form
To know again the man?
Corinthian. Perchance I might;
A trifle oft calls back a thing forgot.
Œdipus. Assemble all the herdsmen and their flocks
Before the altars; slaves, go, hither call
Swiftly the men who shepherd all the flock.
Corinthian. Permit the thing so long a time unknown
Still to lie hid, for often fraught with ill
Is truth for him who drags her to the light.
Œdipus. What greater ill than this is possible?
Corinthian. That must be great which is with great toil sought.
Here meet the public safety and thy own,
The two are equal, take a middle path;
Seek nothing, let the fates unfold themselves.
Œdipus. He who disturbs auspicious fate does ill,
But when affairs are at their last extreme one acts with safety.
Corinthian. Seekest thou a race nobler than that of kings?
Look lest thou loathe when thou hast found thy parents.
Œdipus. I will know
My birth, although it prove of little worth.
But Phorbas, keeper of the royal flocks,
Comes; dost thou know the old man's name or face?
Corinthian. His form awakes a memory, but his face
Is yet not clearly known, though not unknown.

Scene III

Œdipus, Corinthian, Phorbas.

Corinthian. Didst thou upon Cithæron's summits herd
The fruitful flock when Laius ruled in Thebes?
Phorbas. Cithæron gave each summer to our flocks
Her fertile meadows and rich pasturage.
Corinthian. Dost thou not know me?
Phorbas. Dimly I recall—
Œdipus. Speak, didst thou ever give to him a child?
Thy cheeks change color, dost thou hesitate?
What answer seekest thou? Truth shuns delay.
Phorbas. Thou stirrest memories that time had dimmed.
Œdipus. Speak out, lest pain compel thee to the truth.
Phorbas. I gave this man the child—a useless gift,
The boy could not enjoy the light of heaven.
Corinthian. Far be the omen! Still he lives and still long may he live!
Œdipus. Why sayest thou the child no longer lives?

      Phorbas. His tender limbs were bound
By iron bonds that pierced through both his feet,
The wound had caused a swelling, and the flesh
Was even then by foul corruption touched.
      Œdipus. [*Aside.*] What wouldst thou further? Do the fates draw near?
[*To Phorbas.*] Who was the child?
      Phorbas. A promise seals my lips.
      Œdipus. What, ho! bring fire; let flames draw forth the truth.
      Phorbas. Through such inhuman ways shall truth be sought?
I pray thee, be content with ignorance.
      Œdipus. If fierce I seem to thee, and uncontrolled,
Thou hast a ready vengeance. Speak the truth,
Who was the child? What mother gave him birth? His father, who?
      Phorbas. His mother is thy wife.
      Œdipus. Earth, open! Prince of darkness, king of shades,
Take back to shades Tartarean the fate
That overthrows the laws of lineage!
Cast stones at this base head, ye men of Thebes;
Slay me with darts; let sons and fathers come
With lifted sword; ye brothers, husbands, wives,
Take arms against me; and ye, plague-sick men,
Snatch from the pyres the brands to hurl at me.
A shame to men and hated of the gods
I wander, overthrowing holy laws,
Already worthy death when breathing first
The unfamiliar air. Give back at last
Thy baneful life; dare now to do some deed
Worthy thy crimes; haste with swift steps to seek
The royal palace, wish thy mother joy
Of home and children.

Scene IV

Chorus.

If I could govern at my will my lot,
Soft Zephyr only on my sails should blow,
Nor should my trembling sailyards feel the gale;
A light and soft-breathed air should gently waft
My fearless boat; my path of life should lie
Along the safe mid course. The foolish youth
Who feared the Cretan king, to untried ways
Trusted himself, sought like true bird to guide
Through air his flight, but with unnatural wings:
He gave the waters where he fell a name.
Old Dædalus more shrewdly winged his way
Through middle air, and, stooping 'neath the clouds,
Waited his nursling (as the bird collects

Its scattered young that fly the hawk in fear)
Until the boy, in ocean struggling, moved
Hands he had shackled for his daring flight.
950 Whoever dares just limits to exceed
Hangs poised in place unsure. But what is this?
The door creaks, see, the palace servant comes;
He sadly shakes his head. [*To the servant.*] What word dost bring?

ACT V

Scene I

Chorus, Messenger.

Messenger. When overtaken by his fate foretold,
955 He recognized his loathsome origin,
And stood convicted of his crime, the king
Condemned himself and sought with hasty steps
The hated house. So rages through the land
The Lybian lion that with threatening front
960 Shakes back its tawny mane. His eyes were wild,
His face with anger stern; he sighed and groaned
And over all his limbs a cold sweat ran;
His foaming lips gave forth mad threatenings,
His anguish overflowed, and in its depths
965 O'erwhelmed him; raging, with himself he planned
Some evil monstrous as his monstrous fate.
'Why hinder punishment,' he cried, 'the sword
Should pierce this cursed breast; with scorching flame
Or stones let one subdue it; what fierce bird,
970 What tiger will upon my vitals feed?
Thou that hast been a harbor wide of crime,
Sacred Cithæron, from thy forests send
Wild beasts or rabid dogs to do me ill.
Give back Agave. Soul, why fear'st thou death?
975 'Tis death alone can snatch me from my fate
Guiltless.' He spoke and on his sword-hilt leaned
His impious hand, and drew the sword;—'To die,—
Canst thou with such brief punishment atone
Crimes such as thine; with one blow pay for all?
980 Die! For thy father, surely 'tis enough.—
But for thy mother, for the loathsome sons
Thou causedst to see light, thy mourning land
Which suffers for thy crime with widespread death;
What wilt thou give for these? Thou canst not pay;
985 Thou art a bankrupt. Nature's very self,
Who, Œdipus, for thee alone reversed
Her changeless laws of birth, for thee must find

New punishment. Oh, could I live again,
And die again, and ever be reborn,
990 And offered ever to new punishment!
Poor wretch, thy subtlest wit is needful here,
The punishment that only once can fall
Must be enduring; slow death must be sought.
Find out a place where mingled with the dead
995 Yet far from those who live, thou mayest roam.
Die, but not with thy father's death! My soul,
Delayest thou?' A sudden rain of tears
O'erflowed his face, his cheeks were wet with grief.
'Is it enough to weep? Enough that thus
1000 My eyes should flow with tears? The eyes themselves
Shall follow, from their sockets shall be torn;
Ye gods of marriage, is not this enough?'
His threat'ning face with savage fire glowed red,
His eyeballs hardly seemed to hold their place
1005 Within their sockets; furious, desperate,
Enraged of mien and wild, he cried aloud,
And turned his vengeful hand against himself;
His eyes expectant stood, and willingly
Followed his fingers, rushed to meet the wound.
1010 With eagerness his crook'd hands sought his eyes,
Digged out the eyeballs by their deepest roots,
Then, lingering still within the vacant space,
Tore with their nails the empty sockets' folds
And hollow corners, raging overmuch
1015 And vainly. Then he raised his head to seek
The day, and scanning heaven with sightless eyes
Found night; whatever from his mangled brow
Still hung he rent away, and conquering cried
To all the gods: 'Behold, I pray thee, spare
1020 My country, I have paid the debt was due,
Have borne the penalty was merited;
A night that fits my marriage has been found.'
Foul drops bedewed his face, his mangled head
Poured from the broken veins a stream of blood.
1025 *Chorus*. The sport of fate are we, yield then to fate.
Unquiet cares ne'er changed that distaff's thread,
Whatever we, the race of men, endure,
Whatever we may do, comes from above;
Lachesis, with a hand that turns not back
1030 Her distaff, spinneth out the thread of life;
All walk a path prepared, and man's first day
Foretells his last; not Jupiter himself
May make the spindle of the fates turn back;
The order of her turning, fixed for all,
1035 No prayers can change. Fear oftentimes has proved

To many fatal, many meet their fate
When most they fear and shun it. Hark, the gates
Open, the sightless king comes sadly forth
Without a leader.

Scene II

Œdipus, Chorus.

1040   *Œdipus.* 'Tis well; 'tis finished; I have paid in full
All that was due my father. Welcome night!
What god appeased has scattered on my head
Black darkness? Who forgives the criminal?
I have escaped the day's all-seeing eye.
1045 The murderer of thy father to thy hand owes nothing.
Light has fled thee; such a face is meet for Œdipus.
    Chorus. Behold! Behold!
Jocasta rushes forth, with rapid steps,
Frantic and wild; thus wild and frantic once
1050 A Theban mother rent her son and learned,
Too late, her crime. She fears and hesitates,
Yet longs to speak to the afflicted king.
Her shame gives place to sorrow, but her words
Come hesitating from her lips.

Scene III

Œdipus, Jocasta, Chorus.

1055   *Jocasta.* What shall I call thee? Son? Why hesitate?
Thou art my son, why blush to hear the name?
Speak to me, son, although unwillingly;—
Why turn away thy head, thy sightless eyes?
    Œdipus. Who is it who forbids me to enjoy
1060 My darkness, gives me back again my sight?
A mother's voice! Alas, my work is lost!
It is no longer lawful we should meet;
Vast seas shall separate the criminals,
And unknown lands shall part them; and if one
1065 Stay here, the other under alien stars
And distant suns must dwell.
    Jocasta. The fault was Fate's, none sins in living out his destiny.
    Œdipus. O mother, spare thy words, and spare my ears;
By what remains of this my mangled form,
1070 By all the fatal tokens of our race,
By all the good and evil of our name, I do beseech thee.
    Jocasta. What, my soul, dost sleep?
Why to the sharer of his crime refuse

Due punishment? Incestuous one, through thee
1075 The beauty of the laws of human kind,
Confused, hath perished; die, and let the sword
Cut short thy sinful life. If, shaking heaven,
The father of the gods himself should hurl
With savage hand his flashing thunderbolt,
1080 A mother infamous, I could not still
Endure sufficient penalty for crime.
I long to die, let but a way be found;
If thou hast slain thy father, lend thy hand
No less to me thy mother. This last deed
1085 Remains; draw now thy sword, by that sword fell
My husband. Why not freely speak his name?
He is my husband's father,—shall I thrust
Within my breast the sword, or plunge it deep
Into my ready throat? Ah, knowest thou not
1090 To choose the place where thou shalt strike the blow?
Seek out, my hand, the fruitful womb that bore husband and sons.
  Chorus. She falls, struck down by death;
Her hand still lingers in the wound, the blood drives out the sword.
  Œdipus. Foreteller of the truth,
1095 And god of truth, I make my prayer to thee:
Only a father's murder was foretold,
But twice a parricide, beyond my fear
Guilty, I've slain my mother; she lies dead
Through this my guilt. O Phœbus, lying god,
1100 I have exceeded all the ills foretold.
With fearful steps tread now thy gloomy way;
Through nights obscure, with hesitating feet,
Advance and with thy trembling hand feel out
Thy pathway; hasten on with trembling steps;
1105 Fly hence!—Yet stay, lest o'er thy mother's corpse
Thou fall. Ye weary ones, with fell disease
Burdened, behold I go; draw breath again,
Lift up your heads: a milder sky will shine
When I am gone; whoever still retains
1110 His life, though weak and prostrate, still shall draw
Lightly the breath of life. Hence, end thy work!
The earth's death-dealing poison I will take;
Harsh fates, the black and haggard plague, the chill
Of dreadful sickness, and wild grief shall come
1115 With me,—with me! Such guides for me are meet.

AGAMEMNON

DRAMATIS PERSONÆ

Ghost of Thyestes.
Agamemnon.
Ægisthus.
Eurybates.
Strophius.
Orestes.
Pylades.
Clytemnestra.
Electra.
Cassandra.
Nurse of Clytemnestra.
Chorus of Trojan Women
Chorus of Argive Women.

Scene: *Before the palace of Agamemnon.*

AGAMEMNON

ACT I

Scene I

The Ghost of Thyestes.

    Leaving the dark abode of gods of hell,
    I come from depths profound of Tartarus,
    Uncertain which abode I hate the more;
    Thyestes flees both heaven and hell. My soul
5   Is filled with dread, I tremble; lo, I see
    My father's home—nay, more, my brother's home!
    This is the portal of the ancient house
    Of Pelops; here Pelasgia's kingly crown
    Is consecrated; here upon their throne
10 They sit who wield the scepter, this the place
    Where meets the great assembly, this the place
    Of feasting. I am glad I have returned!
    Were it not better by the mournful streams
    To dwell? Were not the watch-dog of the Styx
15 That shakes his threefold necks and inky manes
    Better? Where, bound upon the flying wheel,
    That form is borne; where oft that useless toil
    By the still backward rolling wheel is mocked;
    Where on the heart that ever grows anew

20 The eager birds feed ever; where, consumed
With burning thirst, he stands amid the waves
Whose lips deceived still seek the flying stream,
Grim penalty for other feasts—how small
Compared with ours is that old man's crime!
25 Let us consider all those guilty ones
Who by the Gnosian judge have been condemned:
Thyestes overtops them all in crime.
By my own brother I was overcome,
With my three sons was sated, they in me
30 Have found a sepulcher; my flesh and blood
I ate. And not this only; Fortune stained
The father, but another, greater crime
Was added to that sin—Fate bade me seek
With my own daughter union infamous;
35 Nor did I, fearful, shrink from her behest,
I did the deed. So, that I might make use
Of flesh of all my children, she, my child,
Compelled by fate, bore fruit of me, her sire,
Most worthy. So is nature backward turned;
40 So have I by my crime confusion made,
Have father's father with the father blent,
The father with the husband, with the son
The grandson, day with night! But now, though late,
And coming after death to one long tried
45 With evil fortunes, the dark prophecy's
Uncertain promise is at length fulfilled.
The king of kings, the one of leaders lord,
Dread Agamemnon, following whose flag
A thousand vessels broidered with their sails
50 The Trojan seas, now, after ten long years,
Troy being conquered, is at home again,
About to give him to his wife's embrace.
Now shall the house in blood of vengeance swim:
I see sword, spear, and battle-ax; I see
55 The royal head divided by the blow
Of two-edged ax, already crimes are near,
Already guile, blood, slaughter; yea, and feasts
Are spread. Ægisthus, now the hour draws nigh
For which thou wast begot. Why droops the head
60 In shame? Why, doubtful, shrinks the trembling hand?
Why with thyself take counsel, turn away,
And ask if this is right for thee to do?
Behold thy mother; know that it is so.
Why suddenly does summer's fleeting night
65 Linger as does the winter's longer dark?
Why holds it in the sky the failing stars?
Do I delay the coming of the sun?

Let daylight to the world return again. [*Goes out.*]

Scene II

Chorus of Argive Women.

O Fortune, how deceitful are thy gifts!
70 The lofty thou dost place in doubtful seats
And hazardous, the sceptered never know
A rest serene, nor can they for a day
Be certain of their power, care on care
Fatigues them, ever new storms vex their souls.
75 The waters of the Libyan Syrtes rage
Less wildly in the change of ebb and flood;
Less wildly from its lowest depths heaved up,
Surges the water of the Euxine sea,
Northward, where never dipped in waters blue
80 Boötes drives his starry wain, than turns
The headlong fate of kings on Fortune's wheel.
All things that make them fear, they long to have
Yet tremble to possess; refreshing night
Brings not to them repose, and conquering sleep
85 Frees not their breasts from care. What citadel
Has not by mutual treachery been o'erthrown,
Or vexed by impious war? Law, modesty,
The sacred faithfulness of marriage vows,
Forsake the court; with hand that thirsts for blood,
90 Bellona, baleful goddess, follows it,
And follows, too, that fury who inflames
The proud, attendant on those o'er-proud homes
That from their lofty height shall sometime fall.
If arms were idle and deceit should cease,
95 They yet would sink beneath their very weight,
And fortune underneath its own load fail.
The sails on which the favoring south wind blows
Too fiercely fear the breeze; the lofty tower
Whose summit pierces to the very clouds
100 Is beaten by the tempests, and the grove
That spreads abroad its heavy shadow sees
Its old oaks shattered; lofty halls are struck
By thunderbolts; great bodies are exposed
The more to sickness, when the lean herds roam
105 The arid pastures; 'tis the broadest back
That feels the wound.
Whatever Fortune to the heights has raised
Is lifted up but for a deeper fall,
But moderate possessions longer bide.
110 Happy the man contented with his lot

Among the common throng, who skirts the shore
Before safe winds, and, daring not to trust
His vessel to the open ocean, sails
Near land.

ACT II

Scene I

Clytemnestra, Nurse.

Clytemnestra. Why waver, slow of heart?
115 Why seek safe plans?
The better way is closed. Unstained I kept
My marriage vows, my widowed scepter held
In chaste fidelity; now, virtue, law,
Fidelity and honor, piety,
120 And modesty which gone comes not again,
All these have perished. Give the rein to lust,
Let loose thy passions, crime must make crime safe.
Whatever faithless wife, with secret love
Made mad, whatever stepdame's hand, has dared;
125 Whate'er that ardent and unnatural maid
Who fled from Colchis in Thessalian boat
Has dared: sword, poison.—With thy lover leave
Mycena and thy home in secret flight!
Why, timid one, of secrecy, and flight,
130 And exile, speak? Those things thy sister sought,
A greater crime is more befitting thee.
  Nurse. O Argive queen, of Leda's race renowned,
Why broodest thou in silence? Of control
Impatient, why with swelling heart resolve
135 So fiercely? Thou art silent, but thy grief
Speaks in thy face; therefore, whate'er it be,
Give thyself time and space; delay oft heals
What reason cannot heal.
  Clytemnestra. So great the pains
That torture me, I cannot brook delay.
140 The flames are burning up my heart and reins;
Fear, mingled with my grief, applies the scourge;
Hate drives me on, and base desire's yoke
Presses upon me, nor will be denied.
And midst the fires that thus besiege my soul,
145 Shame, wearied, sunken, conquered, once again
Rises. By varying tempests am I driven!
As when the winds and tides drive different ways
The depths of ocean, and the doubtful seas
Know not to whether evil they must bow,

150 So I have dropped the rudder from my hands,
And wheresoever rage, or hope, or grief
May bear me, thither do I go; my boat
Is given to the waves. When one knows not
The way, 'tis best to follow chance.
    Nurse. Who seeks
155 In chance a leader, he is blindly rash.
    Clytemnestra. He has no need to fear a doubtful chance,
Whose fortunes are at lowest ebb.
    Nurse. Thy crime will be unknown and safe, if so thou wilt.
    Clytemnestra. The sins of royal houses shine abroad.
160   *Nurse.* Repentest thou the old crime, planning yet a new?
    Clytemnestra. The man is fool indeed who keeps
A limit in his sinning.
    Nurse. He, who hides his crime with crime, increases what he fears.
    Clytemnestra. The sword and fire are oft best medicine.
165   *Nurse.* But no one tries at first the uttermost.
    Clytemnestra. In evil one must seize the quickest way.
    Nurse. Ah, let the sacred name of wife deter.
    Clytemnestra. For ten years looked I on my husband's face?
    Nurse. The children that thou barest him call to mind.
170   *Clytemnestra.* My daughter's marriage torches I recall,
My son-in-law Achilles. Here, indeed, maternal faithfulness abides.
    Nurse. She freed
From long delay the fleet becalmed, she stirred
The sluggish languor of the moveless sea.
175   *Clytemnestra.* O grief, O shame! A child of Tyndarus,
Of heavenly race, I bore a child to be
A lustral offering for the Doric fleet!
I think upon my daughter's marriage-bed,
Which, worthy Pelop's house, was then prepared
180 When he, her father, at the altar stood,
The sacrificing priest! What nuptial fires!
The prophet Calchas at his own response
Recoiled, the altars shrank away. O house,
Still overcoming crime with crime, with blood
185 We purchase favoring winds, buy war with death.
But were a thousand ships by her death freed,
The ships were not set free by favoring god,
'Twas Aulis drove the impious vessels forth.
With auspices like these he wages not
190 A warfare fortunate. A slave's slave made
By love, unmoved by prayers, that old man held
The booty from Apollo Smintheus torn,
Already burning for the sacred maid.
Dauntless Achilles could not with his threats
195 Bend him, nor he who saw (none else) earth's fate—
The prophet to us faithful, to the slave

Most mild, nor troubled people, nor the pyres
Relighted. Conquered, though by no foe's hand,
Midst the last ruins of the falling Greeks
200 He slept, had time for lust, renewed his loves.
Nor ever was his lonely couch unpressed
By barbarous mistress; he it was who took
The virgin of Lernessus, rightful spoil
Of great Achilles, hot ashamed to seize
205 The maiden from the hero's bosom torn.
Lo, this is Priam's enemy! And now
He feels again the wounds of love, inflamed
With passion for the Phrygian prophetess;
The winner of the Trojan trophies turns
210 Again toward Ilium, husband of a slave,
And son-in-law of Priam! Up, my soul!
No easy war is that thou now wouldst wage!
Crime must be used. O weak and slow of heart,
What day dost thou await? Till Phrygian maid
215 Shall hold the scepter in great Pelop's house?
Do orphaned virgins keep thee still at home?
Or does Orestes keep thee, he so like
His father? All the ill about to come
Upon them, all the storms that overhang,
220 Shall move thee. Wretched one, why longer pause?
The raging stepdame of thy sons is here.
If thou canst do no otherwise, the sword
Shall pierce thy side, shall slay both thee and him.
Now mingle blood with blood; in dying, kill
225 Thy husband; 'tis not misery to die,
When thou art with thy enemy destroyed.
    Nurse. Queen, curb thy spirit, cease from wrath, recall
How great the day: he comes, the conqueror
Of savage Asia, Europe's punisher,
230 Who drags in triumph captured Pergamus
And Phrygians all too long victorious.
Wouldst thou with secret crime attack him now,
Whom Hercules, although his eager hand
Was grimly armed, touched not with cruel sword,
235 Nor Ajax, though he deemed that death was sure,
Nor Hector, to the Greeks the sole delay
In war, nor Paris' weapon surely aimed,
Nor Memnon black, nor Xanthus bearing down
Bodies and armor mingled in its waves,
240 Nor Simois' stream that flowed encarnadined
With slaughter, nor the ocean god's white son,
Cygnus, nor Thracian phalanx led to war
By Rhesus, nor the bucklered Amazon
With ax and quiver? Dost thou think to slay

245 This one, returned? To stain with murder base
The altars? Will victorious Greece endure
This crime and not avenge? See now the steeds,
And weapons, and the sea thick strewn with ships,
The soil with blood of noble Greeks made wet,
250 And all the fate of Troy, turned back on us!
Restrain thy fiery passion, calm thy soul.

Scene II

Ægisthus, Clytemnestra, Nurse.

Ægisthus. The time that ever with my heart and soul
I feared, is here indeed—for me the end.
Why turn away? Why, at the first attack,
255 Lay down thy arms? Thou mayest certain be
That vengeful gods prepare a fearful fate
And dread disaster for thee. Thy vile head
Make bare, Ægisthus, for all martyrdoms:
Receive with ready breast the sword and flame;
260 One finds in death so met no punishment.
My comrade oft in danger, Leda's child,
Be thou my ally now; that leader base,
That father harsh, shall give thee blood for blood.
But wherefore dost thou tremble? Wherefore flies
265 A pallor to thy cheeks? With drooping lids
Why stand amazed?
    Clytemnestra. The love I owe as wife
Conquers and turns me back. To fealty
From which it was not ever right to turn
I'm brought again, again I seek chaste truth;
270 For never is the hour too late to seek
The path of virtue, who repents his sin is almost innocent.
    Ægisthus. Thou art insane;
Dost thou believe or hope there yet remains
For thee, with Agamemnon, marriage truth?
275 Though naught within thy soul should make thee fear,
Yet, arrogant and by too strong a breath
Of favoring fortune borne, his pride would swell
Beyond control; while Troy yet stood, his men
Ill brooked his pride, why trust a nature fierce
280 Now Troy is his? He was Mycena's king;
He comes as tyrant, for prosperity
Increases pride. Surrounded by a throng
Of concubines, he comes; but midst the throng
The servant of the truth-foretelling god
285 Is eminent and holds Mycena's king.
If thou wouldst with another woman share

Thy husband's bed, yet she, perchance, would not.
The greatest ill a wife can know is this:
A concubine possessing openly
₂₉₀ Her husband's home. Nor mistresses, nor kings
Can share their power.
      Clytemnestra. Why wouldst thou drive me back,
Ægisthus, to the steep, why fan the rage
That lives already in the flame? Perchance
The victor has allowed himself to use
₂₉₅ Some licence t'ward the captive maid—'tis meet
Neither for mistress of the house nor wife
To think on that. The throne has other laws
Than has the humbler couch. Of shameful crime
Conscious, my soul may not too harshly judge
₃₀₀ My husband's sins. He readily forgives,
Who needs forgiveness.
      Ægisthus. Is it so indeed?
Is mutual indulgence then allowed?
Are then the laws of kings unknown to thee,
Or new? To us harsh judges, to themselves
₃₀₅ Most mild, they deem their greatest pledge of power
To be the right to do what is forbid to others.
      Clytemnestra. Helen's sin has been forgiven,
With Menelaus she returns again
Through whom on Europe and on Asia came like dangers.
₃₁₀   *Ægisthus.* But no woman ever filled
With secret passion Menelaus' heart,
Nor made him faithless to his wife. This man
Seeks crime in thee, desires to find excuse;
And if, indeed, thou hadst done nothing base,
₃₁₅ What profits innocence and blameless life?
When thy lord hates thee he inquires not—
Thou must be guilty. Exiled, fugitive,
Wouldst seek Eurotas, Sparta, and thy home?
Whom kings divorce are not allowed to flee,
₃₂₀ With empty hopes thou wouldst allay thy fears.
      Clytemnestra. None but the true have knowledge of my sin.
      Ægisthus. None true e'er cross the threshold of a king.
      Clytemnestra. With wealth I'll buy fidelity.
      Ægisthus. The faith that can with gold be bought, more gold can shake.
₃₂₅   *Clytemnestra.* My former shame arises in my breast,
Why harass with thy words? With kindly voice
Why urge thy evil counsels? Dost thou think
The noble queen who braves the king of kings
Will marry thee, an exile?
₃₃₀   *Ægisthus.* Why should I less noble seem to thee than Atreus' son,
I who was born Thyestes' son?
      Clytemnestra. Say too his grandson, if the son is not enough.

Ægisthus. I was begotten by Apollo's will;
I need not blush, since such my ancestry.
335   *Clytemnestra.* Dost call Apollo source of that base stock?
Thou drov'st him from the sky, night fell again,
And he recalled his steeds. Why make the gods
The sharers of dishonor? Taught by fraud
To steal the pleasures of another's bed,
340 Whom through illicit love alone we proved
A man, begone, and take from out my sight
My home's dishonor; leave the palace pure for king and husband.
    Ægisthus. I am used to ills,
And exile is not new; if thou, O queen,
345 Commandest, not alone from home I go
And Argos—I delay not at thy word
To pierce with steel this heart weighed down with grief.
    Clytemnestra. A bloody child of Tyndarus, indeed,
Would I become should I allow this deed;
350 She owes thee fealty who sinned with thee.
Come with me, that together we may find
A means to free us from the threatening storm.

Scene III

Chorus of Argives.

Sing songs in praise of Phœbus, noble youths!
For thee the festal throng enwreathe their hair,
355 For thee the unwed Argives wave the boughs
Of laurel and their tresses virginal
Unbind. O ye who drink the icy wave
Of Erasinus' or Eurotas' stream,
Or of Ismenus flowing silently
360 Between green banks; thou too, O Theban guest,
Join in our chorus; so Tiresias' child,
Foreknowing Manto, bade with sacred feasts
To venerate the gods, Latona's twins.
Victorious Phœbus, peace once more restored,
365 Unbend thy bow, and from thy shoulder loose
Thy quiver heavy with swift shafts, and smite
With fingers swift the tuneful lute, I would
That it may sound no stern or lofty strain,
But as thou usest to the gentle lyre
370 To modulate a simple melody,
When to the strain the skilful muse gave ear.
Sound too the graver chords as thou hast sung
When gods beheld the Titans overcome
By thunder; or when mountains superposed
375 On mountains built a pathway to the skies

For monsters fierce—Ossa on Pelion stood,
Pineclad Olympus weighed upon them both.
O sharer of the greater sovereignty—
Both wife and sister, Juno, queen, be near!
380 Thy chosen band who in Mycena dwell,
We honor thee. Thou only dost protect
Thy troubled Argos that now prays to thee.
Thou holdest peace and war within thy hand,
Take, Victress, Agamemnon's laurels now.
385 To thee the boxwood flute with many stops
Sounds now the sacred notes of praise; to thee
The maidens touch the tuneful strings in song
Of sweet accord; the Grecian matrons wave
To thee the votive torch; before thy shrine
390 Is slain the snow-white consort of the bull,
Untaught to plow, whose neck has never felt
The yoke. And thou, O child of mighty Jove,
Illustrious Pallas, thou who oft hast sought
The Trojan turrets with thy hostile spear,
395 Thee, in the woman's chorus, old and young
Adore; thy priestess, at thy coming, opes
The temple doors, the great procession comes.
Wearied and bent with years, the aged bring
To thee their thanks for wishes gratified,
400 And pour with trembling hand the wine to thee.
Thee too, as we are wont, we supplicate,
Diana of the crossways; thou didst first,
Lucina, bid thy native Delos stand,
That here and there among the Cyclades
405 Was driven by the winds, nor rooted fast—
Her land is fixed, she yields not to the winds
That once she followed, offers vessels now
Firm haven. Number now, victorious one,
The deaths that Niobe bewailed, she stands
410 A mournful rock on Sipylus' high top,
And from the ancient marble ever flow
New tears; both men and maids pay reverence due,
Twin goddess, to thy bright divinity.
O guide and father, with thy thunderbolt
415 Excelling, at whose nod the heavens bow,
O Jove, great author of our race, accept,
Thou more than all, the gifts we offer thee;
Look kindly on thy not degenerate sons.
But see, a soldier comes with hasty steps,
420 And bears the evidence of joy, for lo,
His spear is wreathed with laurel; he is here,
The ever-faithful servant of the king.

ACT III

Scene I

Eurybates, Clytemnestra.

Eurybates. O shrines and altars of the heavenly ones,
O lares of my fatherland, sore worn
And scarcely crediting myself, I stand
A suppliant, after many weary years,
And worship thee! Pay now thy vows to God,
The glory of Argolis comes at length,
The victor Agamemnon, to his own.
  Clytemnestra. Glad words I hear. Through ten long years desired,
Where tarries he? Upon the land or sea?
  Eurybates. Unharmed, with glory rich, with honor great,
He sets his foot upon the longed-for shore.
  Clytemnestra. Let us with sacred offerings celebrate
This late-come, prosperous day, and reverence
Gods slow if favoring. Tell me, lives he yet—
My husband's brother? Say where now abides my sister?
  Eurybates. Better fate is theirs than ours,
I hope and pray, yet cannot surely tell,
Since most uncertain are the changing seas.
The scattered fleet was smitten by the waves,
Nor ship saw ship, and Atreus' son himself
Bore greater ills at sea than in the war.
The victor comes as vanquished, bringing back
Few ships of all his fleet and these half wrecked.
  Clytemnestra. What chance befell our ships?
Upon the deep. How were our leaders parted?
  Eurybates. Bitter news thou askest. Thou wouldst have me mix with joy
Most grievous tidings, and my spirit fears
To tell the sorrows, trembles at the woe.
  Clytemnestra. Yet tell me all. Who shuns to know his loss
Increases fear; the ills that torture most are those half known.
  Eurybates. When Pergamus had fall'n
Before the Doric brands, and all the spoil
Had been divided, each one sought the sea
In haste; the soldier, wearied with the sword,
Unbound it from his side, through all the poop
The bucklers lay neglected; to the oar
The warriors put their hands, and each delay
Seemed long to those who hasted to be gone.
Again the standard on the royal ship
Shone out, again the trumpet's silver note
Recalled the joyful rowers, and again

The golden prow marked out the way, made plain
465 The pathway which a thousand ships should take.
At first a gentle air impels the ship,
Touching the sails, the tranquil waves scarce stir
Beneath light Zephyr's sighing breath. The sea
Is splendid with the fleet that covers it.
470 With joy we look on Troy's deserted shores,
With joy we leave behind Sigeum's waste.
The youths make haste to ply the ready oar
And aid the winds; they move their sinewy arms
With strokes alternate, and the furrowed waves
475 Flash up and strike against the vessel's sides,
The white foam covers up the ocean's blue.
But when a stronger breeze fills up the sails,
They lay aside the oars and to the winds
They trust the ships. The soldiers stretch themselves
480 Upon the rowing benches, or from far
They watch how fast the vessel leaves behind
The flying land, or tell the deeds of war:
Brave Hector's threats, the chariot, and the corpse
Brought back by Priam for the funeral pyre,
485 And Jupiter Herceus' altars, red
With blood of kings. Then dolphins on the foam
Sported and leaped across the swelling waves
With curving backs, and played about the sea,
And moved in circles, and beside the keel
490 Swam, joying now to follow, now to lead
The fleet, now capered round the first ship's beak
The choric band, now round the thousandth frisked.
Already all the coast had disappeared,
The shore was hidden and Mount Ida's top
495 Was dim with distance, and the smoke of Troy
Appeared an inky cloud which keenest sight
Alone could see. Already from the yoke
Was Titan setting free his weary steeds,
Already day was done, and mid the stars
500 The daylight was departing; a light cloud,
Increasing ever from an inky spot,
Made dim the bright rays of the setting sun;
The many colored sunset made us fear
A storm. At first, night showed a starry sky,
505 The sails, deserted by the wind, dropped loose.
Then from the summits of the hills there fell
A murmur deep that threatened graver things,
And the long shore and rocky headlands groaned,
The waves rolled up before the coming wind;
510 Then suddenly the moon is hid, the stars
Vanish, and to the skies the deep is tossed,

The heavens disappear. 'Tis doubly night,
A thick mist hides the darkness, all light flees,
And sea and sky are mingled. From all sides
515 The winds together blow upon the sea
And hurl the waters from their lowest depths—
The east and west winds strive, the north and south,
Each sends his darts, and all in hostile wise
Stir up the straits, a whirlwind sweeps the sea.
520 The Thracian northwind whirls the snow about,
The Libyan southwind drives along the sands,
Nor holds the south wind; Notus blows along
Dense rain clouds, adds its waters to the waves,
And Eurus shakes the orient, stirs the realm
525 Of Nabathæa and the eastern straits.
How from the sea wild Corus lifts his head!
You would believe the world to be hurled down
From every quarter and the gods themselves
To be from out their inner heavens torn,
530 And in the night of Chaos all things lost.
The stormy sea attacks the stormy sky,
The winds hurl back the waves, the ocean's bed
Is all too small, the rain clouds and the waves
Mingle their floods. In such calamity
535 This comfort even fails: to see, at least,
And know, the evil by whose means we die;
For darkness weighs upon us, and the night
Of Hades, and ill-omened Styx is there.
Yet fires shine forth and from the rent clouds gleams
540 The baneful lightning; to our burdened hearts
This fearful light is sweet, its glare desired.
The fleet destroys itself, prow batters prow,
And side 'gainst side is driven. Opening wide,
The yawning ocean swallows up a ship,
545 Then spews it forth again upon the deep;
Here sinks a vessel with its freight, and here
One to the waters yields its shattered hulk;
A great wave covers one, one floats despoiled
Of all its rigging, neither sails nor oars
550 Nor upright masts that bear the lofty yards
Remain, it tosses on th' Icarian sea
A broken wreck. Experience brings no aid,
Nor reason; skill avails not in such ills.
Cold terror seizes all, the sailors leave
555 Their post of duty, stupefied with fear;
The hand lets fall the oar; the dread of death
Compels the wretched ones to pay their vows
To heaven, and Greeks and Trojans make one prayer.
What may not fate accomplish! Pyrrhus now

560 Envies his father; great Ulysses feels
Envy of Ajax; Atreus' younger son
Of Hector; Agamemnon fain would share
The lot of Priam. Whoso fell at Troy
Is now called happy, who at honor's post
565 Deserved to die, who lives to fame and lies
Beneath the conquered soil. 'Shall sea and waves
O'erwhelm us where no noble deed is dared,
And shall a coward's fate consume the brave?
Must death be useless? Whatsoever god
570 Thou art who art not yet, with all our ills,
Appeased, calm now at length thy face divine;
Troy even would have tears for our distress.
If still thy wrath endures and thou wouldst send
The Doric race to ruin, why must these
575 On whose account we perish, with us die?
Oh, calm the hostile sea! This fleet contains
Both Greeks and Trojans.' So they cried, nor more
Were able, for the waters drowned their words.
Behold another woe: Athena comes
580 Armed with the thunderbolt of angry Jove,
And threats with all the power her spear may claim,
Her ægis and the Gorgon's wrath, or fire
Of Jove, her father; tempests blow anew.
Ajax alone is still invincible,
585 And wrestles with the storm; while yet he strives
With straining rope to guide his vessel's sails,
The lightning strikes him; then another bolt
Is leveled: Pallas, imitating Jove,
With hand drawn back lets drive with all her force
590 This well-aimed bolt, it passes through the ship
And Ajax, and bears down both it and him;
He, nothing moved, firm as the rugged cliff,
Rises half burned from out the briny deep,
Divides the boisterous sea, and breasts the waves,
595 And seizing with his hand the vessel's side,
He seems to draw the flame, and Ajax stands
Shining above the dark expanse of sea
Which mirrors back his glory. When at length
A rock is reached, he madly cries aloud:
600 'Glad am I to have conquered sea and flame,
Glad am I to have vanquished sky and sea,
The thunderbolt and Pallas; I fled not
In fear before the war god, nor drew back
Before the darts of Phœbus. I o'ercame
605 These with the Phrygians, shall I now know fear?
Thou sent'st another's weapon with weak hand.
But what if he himself should send a dart?'

Further he in his madness would have dared,
When Father Neptune, lifting up his head
610 Above the waters, with his trident smote
The cliff and overturned it, broke away
The crag, and he who in its fall was crushed
Lies overwhelmed by earth and sea and fire.
Another greater trouble waits for us,
615 Poor shipwrecked ones. There is a shallow sea,
With rough shoals treach'rous, where false Caphareus
Covers her hidden rocks with whirlpools swift;
The waters boil against the cliffs, the waves
Seethe ever with alternate change. Above,
620 A fortress frowns, it overlooks both seas;
Thy Pelops' shores on one side and, curved back,
The isthmus which divides th' Ionian seas
From Phryxus' waves; upon the other lies
Lemnos, by crime made great, Chalcedon too,
625 And Aulis which so long delayed the fleet.
This fortress Palamedes' father holds,
Upon its highest pinnacle he sets,
With impious hand, a blazing torch, whose light
Draws to the treacherous cliffs the Grecian fleet.
630 The ships are caught upon the pointed rocks,
Part go to pieces in the shoals, a part
Cling to the rocks, their prows are torn away;
One vessel strikes another as it turns,
And by the wrecked ship is the other wrecked.
635 They fear the land, prepare for open sea.
Toward dawn the storm's rage fell away; for Troy
Due satisfaction had been rendered back;
Phœbus returned and daylight showed the wreck
Of that sad night.
    Clytemnestra. Shall I be sad or glad
640 For husband given back? In his return
I take delight, but I am forced to weep
The heavy losses of our realm. Give back,
O father, shaking with thy thunderbolts
The realms sublime, give back the favoring gods
645 To Greece. [*To the Chorus.*] Now bind the brows with festal wreaths,
And let the sacred flute pour forth sweet tones,
Before great altars let white victims fall.
But see the Trojans come, a mournful band,
With hair unkempt, while high above them all
650 Apollo's untamed prophetess waves high
The laurel of the god.

Scene II

Chorus of Trojan Captives, led by Cassandra.

Alas, how sweet a woe to man is given
In love of life, when open lies the way
To flee from all misfortunes, when free death,
That haven tranquil with eternal calm,
Invites the wretched—there no terrors fright,
No storms of fortune rage, nor thunderbolts
Of mighty Jove; its deep peace fears no league
Of restless citizens, nor angry threats
Of foes victorious, nor the stormy seas
When Corus blows, nor hostile battle line,
Nor dust cloud raised before the coming ranks
Of savage horsemen, nor a city's fall
Or nation's, when the hostile flames lay waste
The walls, nor savage war.
Disdainful of the fickle god, he breaks
All bondage, who can unafraid behold
Black Acheron and gloomy Styx, and dares
To put an end to life—that man to kings
Is equal, yea is equal to the gods.
How wretched he who knows not how to die!
We saw our country's fall on that dread night,
When ye, O Doric flames, laid hold on Troy.
Not overcome by war nor arms she fell;
As once before, Herculean arrows smote.
Not Thetis' son and Peleus', not the friend
Too well beloved by Peleus' warlike son,
Conquered, when feigned Achilles glorious shone
In borrowed armor; not Achilles' self
When in his fiery heart he suffered grief,
And on the ramparts Trojan women feared
His swift attack. In evil case she lost
Misfortune's utmost honor: to go down,
By brave deeds vanquished. Twice five years she stood,
To perish by the treach'ry of a night.
We saw the seeming gift, the mighty mole
The Grecians left, and, credulous, we brought
Within the city walls, with our right hands,
The fatal offering. At the gateway oft
The great horse trembled, bearing in its womb
Leaders and war concealed. It might have been
That we had turned their guile against themselves,
So that the Greeks had died by their own fraud.
Oft rang the shaken shields, and on our ears

695 A gentle murmur smote as Pyrrhus groaned,
Slow to submit him to Ulysses' will.
Secure from fear the Trojan youths rejoice
To touch the sacred ropes. Astyanax
Leads here a company, his peers in age;
700 The maiden to Thessalian funeral pyre
Betrothed advances with another band—
These maids, those youths; glad mothers bring the gods
Their votive offerings; to the altars go
Glad fathers; through the city, on each face
705 One look is seen, and—what has never been
Since Hector's funeral pyre—sad Hecuba
Rejoices. O unhappy grief, what first,
What last, dost thou make ready to bewail?
The city walls which hands of gods built up,
710 But thy hand overthrew? The temples burned
Above their gods? There is no time to weep
Those ills! The Trojan women weep thy fate,
Great Father! In the old man's throat I saw,
I saw the sword of Pyrrhus, the slow blood
715 Scarce tinged the steel.

ACT IV

Scene I

Cassandra, Chorus of Trojan Women.

    Cassandra. O Trojan women, check thy tears that flow,
Demanded ever by the passing hours;
Or weep your own misfortunes, mine reject
Companion, cease laments for my distress;
720 I may myself suffice for all our ills.
    Chorus. Whom secret griefs disturb, they sorrow most;
We joy to mingle tears with tears, to weep
Together for our own, nor canst thou weep
Such ruin worthily, though thou art brave,
725 Heroic, and hast suffered many woes.
Not the sad song which from the vernal boughs
The mournful nightingale in varying strains
To Itys sings, not that in which laments
The Thracian swallow, who in querulous tones
730 Tells from the roofs her husband's impious loves,
Could worthily bewail thy fallen house;
Should shining Cygnus, 'mongst the snow-white swans
Abiding on the Ister and the Don,
His death-song sound; or halcyons join lament
735 For the lost Ceyx with the murmuring waves,

When to the tranquil deep they trust again
And anxiously above their wavering nests
Cherish their young; or, should the mournful throng
Of Cybele which, by the shrill flute stirred,
740 Smite on their breasts and Phrygian Atys mourn—
Should these lament and lacerate their arms
'Twere not enough. Our tears no limit have,
Cassandra, since our suffering knows no bounds.
Why from thy forehead tear the sacred bands?
745 I think the wretched most should fear the gods.

    Cassandra. Misfortunes now have conquered every fear,
Nor lift I any prayer to those in heaven;
Should they desire, they have no way to harm.
Fortune has robbed herself of all her power.
750 No father, land, or sister now is mine,
The graves and altars drank my people's blood.
Where is that joyous band of brothers now?
The palace of the sad old king is left
Empty; among so many marriage-beds
755 All save the Spartan woman's now are seen
Widowed; the mother of so many kings,
The fruitful Thracian queen, who furnished forth
So many fires of death, sad Hecuba,
Using new laws, assumes an aspect wild;
760 Madly she howls around her ruined home,
Outliving Hector, Priam, Troy, herself.

    Chorus. Apollo's priestess suddenly is still,
Her cheeks are pale, a trembling strikes her limbs,
Her fillet bristles, her soft locks rise up
765 In horror, with a stifled murmur sounds
Her throbbing heart, uncertain is her glance,
Her eyes turn to and fro or gaze unmoved;
Higher than is her wont she holds her head
Toward heaven, and moves along with haughty step;
770 Now the wild Mænad, raging with the god,
Unlocks her struggling lips or strives in vain
To close them on the message of the god.

    Cassandra. Why dost thou to Parnassus' sacred height
Impel me, goaded by the stinging lash
775 Of inspiration new, beside myself?
Depart, O Phœbus, I am thine no more.
Quench the prophetic fire in my breast.
For whom now shall I rove in holy rage?
For whom now celebrate the bacchanal?
780 Now Troy is fallen, why should I remain
A seer whose prophecies are not believed?
Where am I? Sweet light flies and night obscures
My sight, the sky lies hidden in the dark.

But see, day brightens with a twofold sun,
And Argos rises double. Ida's woods
I see; the shepherd, fatal arbiter,
Between the potent goddesses as judge
Is seated. Fear, ye kings, I warn ye fear
The bastard child; that nursling of the woods
Shall be the one to overthrow your home.
Why bears that mad one in her woman's hand
The hostile spear? With Amazonian sword
Whom seeks the Spartan woman's murderous hand?
What other face is that which draws my eyes?
The lion of Marmorica lies low,
The conqueror of wild beasts, his lofty neck
Brought down by tooth of an inglorious foe;
The daring lioness' bloodthirsty bite
He has endured. O shades of those I loved,
Why call ye me, the only one unharmed
Of all my race? O father, thee I seek,
I who have seen the burial of Troy.
O brother, terror of the Greeks, Troy's aid,
I see no more thy former grace, see not
Those hands made hot by burning of the fleet,
But lacerated limbs and grievous wounds,
Torn by the heavy chain: I follow thee,
O Troilus! Too soon thou didst engage
In battle with Achilles! Thou didst bear,
Deiphobus, a face of fear, 'twas given
By thy new bride. My soul is glad to pass
The Stygian fens, to see the savage dog
Of Tartarus, the realm of eager Dis!
To-day the boat of gloomy Phlegethon
Carries across the river royal souls,
The victor and the vanquished. O ye shades,
To you I pray; thou flood by which the gods
Make oath, to thee I pray no less; draw back
The covering of the dusky world awhile,
That toward Mycenae Phrygia's spirit horde
May turn their eyes. Behold, unhappy ones,
The fates are put to flight.
The squalid sisters threat, they wildly lash
Their bloody whips, the left hand swings the brand,
Around their shrunken limbs the sable robe
Of mourning clings, and terrors of the night
Are heard, and giant bones through time corrupt
Lie in the slimy fen. The worn old man,
Who mourns the murders that shall be, forgets
His thirst, nor strives to drink the wanton stream;
And father Dardanus in solemn dance exults.

Chorus. Already is her passion spent,
She falls on bended knee, as falls the bull
Before the altars, bearing in its neck
835 A heavy wound. Her drooping form lift up.
But lo, where Agamemnon comes at length,
With victor laurels crowned, to venerate
His gods; his wife went forth with joyous steps
To meet him, and as one with him returns.

Scene II

Agamemnon, Clytemnestra, Cassandra, Chorus of Argive Women.

840 *Agamemnon.* At length, unharmed, I find my native land.
Hail, soil beloved! To thee has spoil been given
By countless foreign nations, unto thee
Submits at last great Asia's Troy, so long
Successful. [*Sees Cassandra*] Why stretched out upon the earth
845 With drooping head lies here Apollo's maid?
Slaves, lift her up; with water cool restore
Her strength. With shrinking glance she lifts her lids.
Lift up thy heart! That longed-for port of rest
Is here. It is a day of solemn joy.
850 *Cassandra.* There was a day of solemn joy for Troy.
Agamemnon. Before the altars reverence due we pay.
Cassandra. Before the altars has my father died.
Agamemnon. We pray alike to Jove.
Cassandra. Hercean Jove?
Agamemnon. Thinkst thou, thou seest Ilium once again?
Cassandra. And Priam.
Agamemnon. 'Tis not Troy.
855 *Cassandra.* Where Helen is
Is Troy.
Agamemnon. Fear not the lady, hapless slave.
Cassandra. My freedom waits.
Agamemnon. No danger threatens thee.
Cassandra. Great danger thee.
Agamemnon. What can a victor fear?
Cassandra. What fears he not?
Agamemnon. O faithful band of slaves,
860 Restrain her till the god departs from her,
Lest in her helpless raving she should sin.
O father, who dost hurl the lightning's wrath,
Who drivest in thy train the clouds, who reignst
In earth and heaven, to whom the victor brings
865 His spoil in triumph, thee I venerate;
And thee, Argolic Juno, sister, wife
Of mighty Jove, with votive offerings

And gifts from Araby, on bended knee,
I gladly worship.

Scene III

Chorus of Argive Women.

870 O Argos, by thy noble citizens
Ennobled, Argos ever well beloved
By angry stepdame, thou dost foster still
Great nurslings. Once unequal, thou dost now
Equal the gods: thy glorious Hercules
875 Has by his twelve great labors won a place
In heaven; for him Jove, shattering nature's laws,
Doubled the hours of the dewy night,
And bade the sun to drive his flying car
Later, and bade thy steeds to turn again
880 Slowly, O pale Diana. That bright star,
Whose name alternately is changed, returned
And marveled to be called the evening star.
Aurora stirred at the accustomed hour,
But sinking back she laid her drowsy head
885 Upon her aged husband's breast. The east
Felt, and the west, that Hercules was come.
Not in a single night was such an one
Begotten. The swift moving world stood still
For thee, O child, inheritor of heaven.
890 The lion of Nemæa, by thy arm
Pressed earthward, knew thee as the Thunderer's son;
And the Parrhasian stag, that so laid waste
Arcadia's meadows, knew thee; the fierce bull,
That groaning left Dictæan pastures, knew;
895 Killed by Alcides was the fruitful snake,
He bade it ne'er again to rise from death.
With taunts he crushed beneath his falling club
The brothers twain and the three monsters dread,
From one breast borne, and to the east he brought
900 His Spanish spoil—the three-formed Geryon.
He drove the Thracian steeds; the tyrant fed
Not with the grass that grows by Strymon's stream
Or Hebrus' banks his herd; that cruel one
Offered his savage beasts the blood of guests;
905 The ruler's blood at last made red those jaws.
Untamed Hippolyte beheld the spoil
Snatched from her breast; the fierce Stymphalian birds
Fell smitten from the clouds; the tree, that bore
The golden apples never plucked before,
910 Feared greatly, and fled back into the air

With lightened boughs. The sleepless guardian heard
With fear the rattling of the golden fruit
Only when Hercules, enriched with spoil,
Of yellow gold, had left the orchards bare.
915 Dragged to the light of day by triple chain,
The dog of hell was silent and barked not
From any mouth—he feared the unknown day.
The lying house of Dardanus succumbed
Before thee, learned thy bow was to be feared.
920 When thou wast leader, in as many days
Troy fell, as it had taken years before.

ACT V

Scene I

Cassandra, Chorus.

Cassandra. Great deeds are being done within; not less
Than those of Troy's ten years. Ah, what is this?
Up, up, my soul! take thou the seer's reward:
925 We conquered Phrygians conquer! It is well!
Troy rises from its ashes! In thy fall,
Great parent, thou hast dragged Mycenae down,
Thy conqueror flees. To my foreseeing eye
Ne'er came a clearer vision: lo, I see,
930 Am present, in the vision I rejoice.
No doubtful dream deceives me now, I see!
Tables are spread within the kingly halls,
As once the Phrygian's last feast was spread;
The couch with Ilian purple shines, they drink
935 From gold the wine of old Assaracus.
Lo, decked in broidered suit the proud one lies,
He wears the kingly robe that Priam wore;
His wife entreats him now to put aside
The garments of his foes and wear instead
940 The toga woven by his faithful spouse.
I fear, my spirit at the vision shrinks;
Will he, the exile and adulterer, slay
The king and husband? Vengeance comes at last!
The festival shall see the master's death,
945 And blood shall be commingled with the wine;
The garment at the murderer's wish put on
Shall give him over, bound by treachery,
To death; its meshes bind his hands, his head
Its loose impenetrable folds surround;
950 Manlike she stabs his side, but with a hand
That trembles, nor stabs deep, the dagger stops

Midway the wound. But as in lofty wood
The bristling boar, when captured, strives in vain
For freedom and in struggling tighter draws
His chains and rages vainly, so he strives
To loose the flowing folds that everywhere
Imprison, seeks to find his enemy.
The child of Tyndarus in madness grasps
The two-edged ax; as sacrificing priest
Before the altar fixes with his eyes
The bullock's neck before he strikes the blow,
So either way she aims her weapon's stroke.
It falls, 'tis done. His partly severed head
Hangs by a slender thread, here from his trunk
Gushes the blood, there fall his groaning lips.
Not yet the murderers cease, the lifeless form
He seeks and mangles, she adds needless stabs;
Each in such crime is worthy of his own,
He is Thyestes' son, the sister she
Of Helen. Lo, the sun uncertain stands
Whether he pass along his wonted way,
Whether the Thyestean path he take.

Scene II

Orestes, Cassandra, Electra, Chorus.

Electra. O one avenger of thy father's death,
Fly, fly, and shun thy foes' death-dealing hands;
Our house is ruined and the kingdom falls!
What guest is this that drives his flying car?
O brother, in my garments hide thyself.
Yet, fool, why fly? A stranger dost thou fear?
Fear those at home. Orestes, put aside
Thy fears, it is a friend whom I behold,
A sure and faithful friend.

Scene III

Strophius, Pylades, Orestes, Electra, Cassandra, Chorus.

Strophius. I, Strophius, am from Phocis come again;
Honored at Elis with the victor's crown,
I come to welcome back with joy the friend
By whose hand smitten, after ten long years,
At last has Ilium fallen. Who is this
Whose mournful face is numbed with sorrow's tears?
What sorrowful and fearful maid is this?
I know the royal child; what cause to weep,

Electra, in this house of joy?
990   *Electra.* Alas!
My father, by my mother's crime destroyed,
Lies dead, and now to share his father's death
The son is sought. Ægisthus now controls
The palace, where he came with base desires.
995   *Strophius.* Alas! No happiness abides for long!
    Electra. I pray thee, by my father's memory,
And by the scepter known through all the world,
And by the fickle gods, take far away
Orestes; hide him, 'tis a pious theft.
1000   *Strophius.* Though Agamemnon's murder makes me fear
Like slaughter, I will hide thee willingly,
Orestes. From my forehead take the crown,
The decoration of Olympic games;
And in thy right hand take the victor's palm,
1005 Hiding thy head behind the leafy branch,
And may this palm, gift of Pisæan Jove,
Offer at once an omen and a shield.
And thou, Pylades, in thy father's car
Sitting as comrade, of thy father learn
1010 The faithfulness that friendship ever owes.
Ye steeds whom Greece has testified are swift,
Flee, flee this dreadful spot, in headlong flight.

Scene IV

Electra, Cassandra, Chorus.

    Electra. He goes, he has escaped, the flying car
Already disappears before my gaze.
1015 My enemies I now can safely wait;
Freely I offer now my hand to death.
The bloody conqueror of her husband comes,
Her garments dyed with slaughter, even now
Her hands are red with recent blood, her face
1020 Is dark with murder. To the altars' foot
I go. Cassandra, priestess, let me kneel
With thee, since equally with thee I fear.

Scene V

Ægisthus, Clytemnestra, Electra, Cassandra, Chorus.

    Clytemnestra. Foe of thy mother, bold and impious child,
What custom is it bids a virgin seek this public place?
1025   *Electra.* A virgin, I have fled the dwelling of adulterers.
    Clytemnestra. Who believes in thy virginity?

Electra. Because thy child?
Clytemnestra. Be humble with thy mother.
Electra. Dost thou teach thy daughter duty?
Clytemnestra. Thou hast manly force,
1030 A haughty heart, but thou shalt learn to show,
Subdued by torture, all thy woman's soul.
Electra. Perchance I am deceived, yet seems the sword a woman's weapon.
Clytemnestra. Mad one, dost thou think that thou with us art equal?
Electra. Sayest thou, us?
1035 What other Agamemnon hast thou found?
Speak as a widow, husband hast thou none.
Clytemnestra. An impious maid's unbridled tongue the queen
Will tame. Make answer swift, where is my son?
Thy brother, where?
Electra. Beyond Mycenæ gone.
1040 *Clytemnestra.* Now give me back my son.
Electra. Give back to me my father.
Clytemnestra. Tell me where he is concealed.
Electra. In safety; calm, and fearing no new reign.
For honorable mother 'tis enough.
Clytemnestra. Not for an angry one. To-day thou diest.
1045 *Electra.* Yet die I by thy hand. Behold I leave
The altars, if it pleases thee to plunge
Within my heart the steel, I face the blow;
Or wouldst thou, as one smites the sacrifice,
My bowed neck smite? Ready it waits the wound.
1050 All things have been made ready for the crime;
In this blood wash that foul right hand made wet
With husband's murder.
Clytemnestra. Sharer of my realm
And of my danger, come; Ægisthus, come.
Undutifully does my child insult
1055 And wound her mother, and she hides my son.
Ægisthus. Mad girl, no more assail thy mother's ears
With words insulting and with hateful speech.
Electra. Will even one most skilled in basest crimes,
One born through crime, of name ambiguous,
1060 At once his father's grandchild, sister's son, instruct?
Clytemnestra. Ægisthus, dost thou hesitate
To shear away her impious head with steel?
Let her give up her brother or her life.
Ægisthus. In a dark prison shall she pass her years,
1065 And torn by every torture shall desire,
Perchance, to render up the one she hides.
Helpless, imprisoned, poor, and sunk in filth,
Before her marriage widowed, and by all
Hated, an exile, heaven's air denied,
1070 Though late, she will at last succumb to ills.

Electra. Grant death.
Ægisthus. If thou wouldst shun it, I would grant.
Who puts an end to punishment by death is skill-less tyrant.
Electra. Is aught worse than death?
Ægisthus. Life, if thou long'st for death. Slaves, seize the maid
1075 And having carried her afar from here,
Beyond Mycenæ, to the realm's last bound,
Chain her within a cavern fenced about
With gloomy night, that so imprisonment
May finally subdue the restless maid.
1080 *Clytemnestra.* The captive mistress, the king's concubine,
Shall pay the penalty of death; away!
Drag her away, that she may follow still
The husband torn from me.
Cassandra. Nay drag me not,
I will myself precede thee, for I haste
1085 To be the first who to my Phrygian friends
Shall bear the news: the sea with wreckage strewn,
Mycenæ taken, and the king who led
A thousand leaders dead by his wife's hand,
Cut down by lust and fraud. I would not stay.
1090 Oh, snatch me hence! I thank you and rejoice
That I have lived so long beyond the fall
Of dear-loved Troy.
Clytemnestra. Peace, raging one.
Cassandra. Like rage shall fall on thee.

THYESTES

DRAMATIS PERSONÆ

Atreus.
Thyestes.
Spirit of the elder Tantalus.
Plisthenes,
Tantalus,   } Sons of Thyestes.
A boy,
Megæra.
Messenger.
Servant.
Chorus of Men of Mycenæ.

Scene: *Before the Palace of Atreus.*

THYESTES

ACT I

Scene I

Spirit of Tantalus, Megæra.

Spirit. Who drags me from my place among shades,
Where with dry lips I seek the flying waves
What hostile god again shows Tantalus
His hated palace? Has some worse thing come
5 Than thirst amid the waters or the pangs
Of ever-gnawing hunger? Must the stone,
The slippery burden borne by Sisyphus,
Weigh down my shoulders, or Ixion's wheel
Carry my limbs around in its swift course,
10 Or must I fear Tityus' punishment?
Stretched in a lofty cave he feeds dun birds
Upon his vitals which they tear away,
And night renews whatever day destroyed,
And thus he offers them full feast again.
15 Against what evil have I been reserved?
Stern judge of Hades, whosoe'er thou art
Who metest to the dead due penalties,
If something can be added more than pain,
Seek that at which the grim custodian
20 Of this dark prison must himself feel fear,
Something from which sad Acheron shall shrink.
Before whose horror I myself must fear;

For many sprung from me, who shall outsin
Their house, who, daring deeds undared by me,
25 Make me seem innocent, already come.
Whatever impious deed this realm may lack
My house will bring; while Pelops' line remains
Minos shall never be unoccupied.

Megœra. Go, hated shade, and drive thy sin-stained home
30 To madness; let the sword try every crime,
And pass from hand to hand; nor let there be
Limit to rage and shame; let fury blind
Urge on their thoughts; let parents' hearts be hard
Through madness, long iniquity be heaped
35 Upon the children, let them never know
Leisure to hate old crimes, let new ones rise,
Many in one; let sin while punished grow;
From the proud brothers let the throne depart,
Then let it call the exiled home again.
40 Let the dark fortunes of a violent house
Among unstable kings be brought to naught.
Let evil fortune on the mighty fall.
The, wretched come to power; let chance toss
The kingdom with an ever-changing
45 Where'er it will. Exiled because of crime,
When god would give them back their native land
Let them through crime reach home, and let them hate
Themselves as others hate them. Let them deem
No crime forbidden when their passions rage;
50 Let brother greatly fear his brother's hand,
Let parents fear their sons, and let the sons
Feel fear of parents, children wretched die,
More wretchedly be born; let wife rebel
Against her husband, wars pass over seas,
55 And every land be wet with blood poured forth;
Let lust, victorious, o'er great kings exult
And basest deeds be easy in thy house;
Let right and truth and justice be no more
'Twixt brothers. Let not heaven be immune—
60 Why shine the stars within the firmament
To be a source of beauty to the world?
Let night be different, day no more exist.
O'erthrow thy household gods, bring hatred, death,
Wild slaughter, with thy spirit fill the house,
65 Deck the high portals, let the gates be green
With laurel, fires for thy advent meet
Shall glow, crimes worse than Thracian shall be done.
Why idle lies the uncle's stern right hand?
Thyestes has not yet bewept his sons;
70 When will they be destroyed? Lo, even now

            Upon the fire the brazen pot shall boil,
            The members shall be broken into parts,
            The father's hearth with children's blood be wet,
            The feast shall be prepared. Thou wilt not come
75   Guest at a feast whose crime is new to thee:
            To-day we give thee freedom; satisfy
            Thy hunger at those tables, end thy fast.
            Blood mixed with wine shall in thy sight be drunk,
            Food have I found that even thou wouldst shun.
            Stay! Whither dost thou rush?
80   *Spirit.* To stagnant pools,
            Rivers and waters ever slipping by,
            To the fell trees that will not give me food.
            Let me go hence to my dark prison-house,
            Let me, if all too little seems my woe,
85   Seek other shores; within thy channels' midst
            And by thy floods of fire hemmed about,
            O Phlegethon, permit me to be left.
            O ye who suffer by the fates' decree
            Sharp penalties, O thou who, filled with fear,
90   Within the hallowed cave dost wait the fall
            Of the impending mountain, thou who dreadst
            The ravening lion's open jaws, the hand
            Of cruel furies that encompass thee,
            Thou who, half burned, dost feel their torch applied,
95   Hear ye the voice of Tantalus who knows:
            Love ye your penalties! Ah, woe is me,
            When shall I be allowed to flee to hell?
                    Megæra. First into dread confusion throw thy house,
            Bring with thee battle and the sword and love,
100   Strike thou the king's wild heart with frantic rage.
                    Spirit. 'Tis right that I should suffer punishment,
            But not that I myself be punishment.
            Like a death-dealing vapor must I go
            Out of the riven earth, or like a plague
105   Most grievous to the people, or a pest
            Widespread, I bring my children's children crime.
            Great father of the gods, our father too—
            However much our sonship cause thee shame—
            Although my too loquacious tongue should pay
110   Due punishment for sin, yet will I speak:
            Stain not, my kinsmen, holy hands with blood,
            The altars with unholy sacrifice
            Pollute not. I will stay and ward off crime.
            [*To Megæra.*] Why dost thou terrify me with thy torch,
115   And fiercely threaten with thy writhing snakes?
            Why dost thou stir the hunger in my reins?
            My heart is burning with the fire of thirst,

My parched veins feel the flame.
    Megæra. Through all thy house
Scatter this fury; thus shall they, too, rage,
120 And, mad with anger, thirst by turns to drink
Each other's blood. Thy house thy coming feels
And trembles at thy execrable touch.
It is enough; depart to hell's dark caves
And to thy well-known river. Earth is sad
125 And burdened by thy presence. Backward forced,
Seest thou not the waters leave the streams,
How all the banks are dry, how fiery winds
Drive the few scattered clouds? The foliage pales,
And every branch is bare, the fruits are fled.
130 And where the Isthmus has been wont to sound
With the near waters, roaring on each side,
And cutting off the narrow strip of land,
Far from the shore is heard the sound remote.
Now Lerna's waters have been backward drawn,
135 Sacred Alpheus' stream is seen no more,
Cithæron's summit stands untouched with snow,
And Argos fears again its former thirst.
Lo, Titan's self is doubtful—shall he drive
His horses upward, bring again the day?
140 It will but rise to die.

                Scene II

                Chorus.

If any god still cherish love for Greece,
Argos, and Pisa for her chariots famed,
If any cherishes the Isthmian realm,
And the twin havens, and the parted seas,
145 If any love Taygetus' bright snows
That shine afar, which northern winter lays
Upon its highest summits and the breath
Of summer trade winds welcome to the sails
Melts, let him whom Alpheus' ice-cold stream
150 Touches, well known for his Olympic course,
Wield the calm influence of his heavenly power,
Nor suffer crimes in constant series come.
Let not a grandson, readier for that crime
E'en than his father's father, follow him,
155 Nor let the father's error please the sons.
Let thirsty Tantalus' base progeny,
Wearied at length, give up their fierce attempts;
Enough of crime! No more is right of worth,
And common wrongs of little moment seem;

160 The traitor Myrtilus betrayed his lord
And slew him—by such faith as he had shown
Himself dragged down, he gave the sea a name;
To ships on the Ægean never tale
Was better known. Met by the cruel sword,
165 Even while he ran to gain his father's kiss,
The little son was slain; he early fell
A victim to the hearth, by thy right hand,
O Tantalus, cut off that thou mightst spread
Such feasts before the gods. Eternal thirst
170 And endless famine followed on the feast;
Nor can a worthier punishment be found
For savage feast like that. With empty maw
Stands weary Tantalus, above his head
Hangs ready food, more swift to take its flight
175 Than Phineus' birds; on every side it hangs;
The tree beneath the burden of its fruit
Bending and trembling, shuns his open mouth;
He though so eager, brooking no delay,
Yet oft deceived, neglects to touch the tree,
180 And drops his head and presses close his lips,
And shuts his hunger in behind clenched teeth.
The ripe fruit taunts him from the languid boughs,
And whets his hunger till it urges him
To stretch again his hand oft stretched in vain.
185 Then the whole harvest of the bended boughs
Is lifted out of reach. Thirst rises then,
More hard to bear than hunger, when his blood
Is hot within him and his eyes aflame;
Wretched he stands striving to touch his lips
190 To the near waters, but the stream retreats,
Forsakes him when he strives to follow it,
And leaves him in dry sands; his eager lips
Drink but the dust.

ACT II

Scene I

Atreus, Slave.

Atreus. O slothful, indolent, weak, unavenged
195 (This last I deem for tyrants greatest wrong
In great affairs), after so many crimes,
After thy brother's treachery to thee,
After the breaking of all laws of right,
Dost thou, O angry Atreus, waste the time
200 In idle lamentations? All the world

Should echo with the uproar of thy arms,
And either sea should bear thy ships of war;
The fields and cities should be bright with flame;
The flashing sword should everywhere be drawn;
205 All Greece shall with our horsemen's tread resound;
Woods shall not hide the foe nor towers built
Upon the highest summits of the hills;
Mycenae's citizens shall leave the town
And sing the warsong; he shall die hard death
210 Who gives that hated head a hiding-place.
This palace even, noble Pelops' home,
Shall fall, if it must be, and bury me
If only on my brother too it fall.
Up, do a deed which none shall e'er approve,
215 But one whose fame none shall e'er cease to speak.
Some fierce and bloody crime must now be dared,
Such as my brother seeing shall wish his.
A wrong is not avenged but by worse wrong
What deed can be so wild 'tis worse than his?
220 Does he lie humbled? Does he feel content
When fortune smiles, or tranquil when she frowns?
I know the tameless spirit of the man,
Not to be bent but broken, therefore seek
Revenge before he makes himself secure,
225 Renews his strength, lest he should fall on me
When I am unaware. Or kill, or die!
Crime is between us to be seized by one.
    Slave. Fearest thou not the people's hostile words?
    Atreus. Herein is greatest good of royal power:
230 The populace not only must endure
Their master's deeds, but praise them.
    Slave. Fear shall make
Those hostile who were first compelled to praise;
But he who seeks the fame of true applause
Would rather by the heart than voice be praised.
235   *Atreus.* The lowly oft enjoy praise truly meant,
The mighty ne'er know aught but flattery.
The people oft must will what they would not.
    Slave. The king should wish for honesty and right;
Then there is none who does not wish with him.
240   *Atreus.* When he who rules must wish for right alone
He hardly rules, except on sufferance.
    Slave. When reverence is not, nor love of law,
Nor loyalty, integrity, nor truth, the realm is insecure.
    Atreus. Integrity, truth, loyalty, are private virtues; kings
245 Do as they will.
    Slave. O deem it wrong to harm
A brother, even though he be most base.

Atreus. No deed that is unlawful to be done
Against a brother but may lawfully
250 Be done against this man. What has he left
Untainted by his crime? Where has he spared
To do an impious deed? He took my wife
Adulterously, he took my realm by stealth,
The earnest of the realm he gained by fraud,
255 By fraud he brought confusion to my home.
There is in Pelops' stalls a noble sheep,
A magic ram, lord of the fruitful herd;
O'er all his body hangs the golden fleece.
In him each king sprung from the royal line
260 Of Tantalus his golden scepter holds,
Who has the ram possesses too the realm,
The fortunes of the palace follow him.
As fits a sacred thing, he feeds apart,
In a safe meadow which a wall surrounds
265 Hiding the pasture with its fateful stones.
The faithless one, daring a matchless crime,
Stole him away and with him took my wife,
Accomplice in his sin. From this has flowed
Every disaster; exiled and in fear
270 I've wandered through my realm; no place is safe
From brother's plots; my wife has been defiled.
The quiet of my realm has been disturbed,
My house is troubled, and the ties of blood
Are insecure, of nothing am I sure
275 Unless it be my brother's enmity.
Why hesitate? At length be strong to act.
Look upon Tantalus, on Pelops look;
To deeds like theirs these hands of mine are called.
Tell me, how shall I slay that cursed one?
280   *Slave.* Slain by the sword let him spew forth his soul.
    Atreus. Thou tellest the end of punishment, I wish
The punishment itself. Mild tyrants slay;
Death is a longed-for favor in my realm.
    Slave. Hast thou no piety?
    Atreus. If e'er it dwelt
285 Within our home, let piety depart.
Let the grim company of Furies come,
Jarring Erinnys and Megæra dread
Shaking their torches twain. My breast burns not
With anger hot enough. I fain would feel worse horrors.
290   *Slave.* What new exile dost thou plot, in thy mad rage?
    Atreus. No deed that keeps the bounds
Of former evils, I will leave no crime
Untried, and none is great enough for me.
    Slave. The sword?

Atreus. 'Tis poor.
Slave. Or fire?
Atreus. 'Tis not enough.
Slave. What weapon then shall arm such hate as thine?
Atreus. Thyestes' self.
Slave. This ill is worse than hate.
Atreus. I own it. In my breast a tumult reigns;
It rages deep within, and I am urged
I know not whither, yet it urges me.
Earth from its lowest depths sends forth a groan,
It thunders though the daylight is serene,
The whole house shakes as though the house were rent,
The trembling Lares turn away their face.
This shall be done, this evil shall be done,
Which, gods, ye fear.
Slave. What is it thou wilt do?
Atreus. I know not what great passion in my heart,
Wilder than I have known, beyond the bounds
Of human nature, rises, urges on
My slothful hands. I know not what it is,
'Tis something great. Yet be it what it may,
Make haste, my soul! Fit for Thyestes' hand
This crime would be; 'tis worthy Atreus, too,
And both shall do it. Tereus' house has seen
Such shocking feasts. I own the crime is great,
And yet it has been done; some greater crime
Let grief invent. Inspire thou my soul
O Daulian Procne, thou wast sister too;
Our cause is like, assist, impel my hand.
The father, hungrily, with joy shall tear
His children, and shall eat their very flesh;
'Tis well, It is enough. This punishment
Is so far pleasing. But where can he be?
And why is Atreus so long innocent?
Already all the sacrifice I see.
As in a picture, see the morsels placed
Within the father's mouth. Wherefore, my soul,
Art thou afraid? Why fail before the deed?
Forward! It must be done. Himself shall do
What is in such a deed the greater crime.
Slave. But captured by what wiles, will he consent
To put his feet within our toils? He deems
That all are hostile.
Atreus. 'Twere not possible
To capture him but that he'd capture me.
He hopes to gain my kingdom; through this hope
He will make haste to meet the thunderbolts
Of threatening Jove, in this hope will endure

The swelling whirlpool's threats, and dare to go
Within the Libyan Syrtes' doubtful shoals,
To see again his brother, last and worst
340 Of evils deemed; this hope shall lead him on.
    Slave. Who shall persuade him he may come in peace?
Whose word will he believe?
    Atreus. Malicious hope
Is credulous, yet I will give my sons
A message they shall to their uncle bear:
345 'The wandering exile, leaving chance abodes,
May for a kingdom change his misery,
May reign in Argos, sharer of my throne.'
But if Thyestes sternly spurn my prayers,
His artless children, wearied by their woes
350 And easily persuaded, with their plea
Will overcome him; his old thirst for rule,
Beside sad poverty and heavy toil,
With weight of evil, will subdue his soul
However hard it be.
    Slave. Time will have made
His sorrow light.
355   *Atreus.* Thou errest; sense of ills
Increases daily. To endure distress
Is easy, but to bear it to the end
Is hard.
    Slave. Choose others for thy messengers
In this dread plan.
    Atreus. Youth freely dares the worst.
360   *Slave.* What now thou teachest them in enmity
Against their uncle, they may later do
Against their father; evil deeds return
Full oft upon their author.
    Atreus. If they learned
The way of treachery and crime from none,
365 Possession of the throne would teach it them.
Art thou afraid their natures will grow base?
So were they born. That which thou callest wild
And cruel, and deemst hardly to be done,
Ruthless, nor showing honor for god's laws,
370 Perchance is even now against ourselves attempted.
    Slave. Shall thy sons know what they do?
    Atreus. Discretion is not found with so few years.
They might perhaps discover all the guile;
Silence is learned through long and evil years.
375   *Slave.* The very ones through whom thou wouldst deceive
Another thou deceivest?
    Atreus. That themselves may be exempt from crime or fault of mine;
Why should I mix my children in my sins?

My hatred shall unfold itself in me.
380 Yet say not so, thou doest ill, my soul;
If thine thou sparest, thou sparest also his.
My minister shall Agamemnon be,
And know my plan, and Menelaus too
Shall know his father's plans and further them.
385 Through this crime will I prove if they be mine;
If they refuse the contest nor consent
To my revenge, but call him uncle, then
I'll know he is their father. It shall be.
But oft a frightened look lays bare the heart,
390 Great plans may be unwillingly betrayed;
They shall not know how great affairs they aid.
Hide thou our undertaking.
  Slave. Scarce were need
That I should be admonished; in my breast
Both fear and loyalty will keep it hid,
395 But loyalty the rather.

Scene II

Chorus.

The ancient race of royal Inachus
At last has laid aside fraternal threats.
What madness drove you, that by turns you shed
Each other's blood and sought to mount the throne
400 By crime? You know not, eager for high place,
What kingly station means. It is not wealth
That makes the king, nor robes of Tyrian dye,
'Tis not the crown upon the royal brow,
Nor gates made bright with gold; a king is he
405 Whose hard heart has forgotten fear and pain,
Whom impotent ambition does not move,
Nor the inconstant favor of the crowd,
Who covets nothing that the west affords,
Nor aught that Tagus' golden waves wash up
410 From its bright channels, nor the grain thrashed out
Upon the glowing Libyan threshing-floors,
Who neither fears the falling thunderbolt,
Nor Eurus stirring all the sea to wrath,
Nor windy Adriatic's swelling rage;
415 Who is not conquered by a soldier's lance,
Nor the drawn sword; who seated on safe heights,
Sees everything beneath him; who makes haste
Freely to meet his fate, nor grieves to die.
Let kings who vex the scattered Scythians come,
420 Who hold the Red Sea's shore, the pearl-filled sea,

       Or who intrenched upon the Caspian range
       To bold Sarmatians close the way, who breast
       The Danube's waves, or those who dare pursue
       And spoil the noble Seres where'er they dwell.
425   The mind a kingdom is; there is no need
       Of horse, or weapon, or the coward dart
       Which from afar the Parthian hurls and flees—
       Or seems to flee, no need to overthrow
       Cities with engines that hurl stones afar,
430   When one possesses in himself his realm.
       Whoever will may on the slippery heights
       Of empire stand, but I with sweet repose
       Am satisfied, rejoice in gentle ease,
       And, to my fellow citizens unknown,
435   My life shall flow in calm obscurity,
       And when, untouched by storm, my days have passed,
       Then will I die, a common citizen,
       In good old age. Death seemeth hard to him
       Who dies but too well known to all the world,
440   Yet knowing not himself.

ACT III

Scene I

Thyestes, Plisthenes, Tantalus, A boy.

       Thyestes. The longed-for dwelling of my native land
       And, to the wretched exile greatest boon,
       Rich Argos and a stretch of native soil,
       And, if there yet be gods, my country's gods
445   I see at last; the Cyclop's sacred towers,
       Of greater beauty than the work of man;
       The celebrated race-course of my youth
       Where oft, well known, I drove my father's car
       And carried off the palm. Argos will come
450   To meet me, and the people come in crowds,
       Perchance my brother Atreus too will come!
       Rather return to exile in the woods
       And mountain pastures, live the life of brutes
       Among them. This bright splendor of the realm
455   With its false glitter shall not blind my eyes.
       Look on the giver, not the gift alone.
       In fortunes which the world deemed hard I lived
       Joyous and brave, now am I forced to fear,
       My courage fails me, fain would I retreat,
       Unwillingly I go.
460   *Tantalus.* What see I here?

With hesitating step my father goes,
He seems uncertain, turns away his head.
    Thyestes. Why doubt, my soul? or why so long revolve
Deliberations easy to conclude?
465 In most uncertain things dost thou confide
And in thy brother's realm, and stand in fear
Of ills already conquered and found mild?
Dost fly the troubles thou hast learned to bear?
Now to be wretched with the shades were joy,
Turn while thou yet hast time.
470   *Tantalus.* Why turn away?
From thy loved country? Why deny thyself
So much of happiness? His wrath forgot,
Thy brother gives thee back the kingdom's half
And to the jarring members of his house
475 Brings peace, restores thee once more to thyself.
    Thyestes. Thou askest why I fear; I do not know.
I see not aught to fear and yet I fear.
Fain would I go and yet with slothful feet
I waver and am borne unwillingly
480 Whither I would not; thus the ship propelled
By oar and sail is driven from its course by the opposing tide.
    Tantalus. Whatever thwarts
Or hinders thee, o'ercome; see what rewards
Are waiting thy return. Thou mayst be king.
    Thyestes. Since I can die.
485   *Tantalus.* The very highest power—
    Thyestes. Is naught, if thou hast come to wish for naught.
    Tantalus. Thy sons shall be thy heirs.
    Thyestes. No realm can have two kings.
    Tantalus. Does one who might be happy choose unhappiness?
    Thyestes. Believe me, with false name
490 Does power deceive; and vain it is to fear
Laborious fortunes. High in place, I feared,
Yea, feared the very sword upon my side.
How good it is to be the foe of none,
To lie upon the ground, in safety eat.
495 Crime enters not the cottage; without fear
May food be eaten at the humble board,
Poison is drunk from gold. I speak known truth—
Ill fortune is to be preferred to good.
The humble citizen fears not my house:
500 It is not on the mountain summit placed,
Its high roofs do not shine with ivory;
No watchman guards my sleep; we do not fish
With fleets, nor drive the ocean from its bed
With massive walls, nor feed vile gluttony
505 With tribute from all peoples; not for me

Are harvested the fields beyond the Getes
And Parthians; men do not honor me
With incense, nor are altars built for me
Instead of Jove; upon my palace roofs
No forests nod, no hot pools steam for me;
Day is not spent in sleep nor night in crime
And watching. Aye, none fears me and my home,
Although without a weapon, is secure.
Great peace attends on humble circumstance
He has a kingdom who can be content without a kingdom.
    Tantalus. If a favoring god
Give thee a realm, it should not be refused,
Nor should it be desired. Thy brother begs
That thou wouldst rule.
    Thyestes. He begs? Then I must fear.
He seeks some means whereby he may betray.
    Tantalus. Full often loyalty that was withdrawn
Is given back, and true affection gains redoubled strength.
    Thyestes. And shall his brother love
Thyestes? Rather shall the ocean wet
The northern Bear, and the rapacious tides
Of the Sicilian waters stay their waves,
The harvest ripen in Ionian seas,
And black night give the earth the light of day;
Rather shall flame with water, life with death,
The winds with ocean join in faithful pact.
    Tantalus. What fraud dost thou still fear?
    Thyestes. All. Where may end
My cause for fear? His hate is as his power.
    Tantalus. What power has he to harm thee?
    Thyestes. For myself
I do not fear; my sons, for you I dread
My brother Atreus.
    Tantalus. Dost thou fear deceit?
    Thyestes. It is too late to seek security
When one is in the very midst of ill.
Let us begone. This one thing I affirm:
I follow you, not lead.
    Tantalus. God will behold
With favor thy design; boldly advance.

Scene II

Atreus, Thyestes, Plisthenes, Tantalus, A boy.

    Atreus. [*Aside.*] At last the wild beast is within my toils:
Lo, I behold him with his hated brood.
My vengeance now is sure, into my hands
Thyestes has completely fall'n; my joy
545 Scarce can I temper, scarcely curb my wrath.
Thus when the cunning Umbrian hound is held
In leash, and tracks his prey, with lowered nose
Searching the ground, when from afar he scents
By slightest clue the bear, he silently
550 Explores the place, submitting to be held,
But when the prey is nearer, then he fights
To free himself, and with impatient voice
Calls the slow huntsman, straining at the leash.
When passion hopes for blood it will not own
555 Restraint; and yet my wrath must be restrained!
See how his heavy, unkempt hair conceals
His face, how loathsome lies his beard. Ah, well!
Faith shall be kept. [*To Thyestes.*] To see my brother's face
How glad I am! All former wrath is past.
560 From this day loyalty to family ties
Shall be maintained, from this day let all hate
Be banished from our hearts.
    Thyestes. [*Aside.*] O wert thou not
Such as thou art, all could be put aside.
[*To Atreus.*] Atreus, I own, I own that I have done
565 All thou believest; this day's loyalty
Makes me seem truly base: he sins indeed
Who sins against a brother good as thou.
Tears must wash out my guilt. See at thy feet
These hands are clasped in prayer that ne'er before
570 Entreated any. Let all anger cease,
Let swelling rage forever be dispelled;
Receive these children, pledges of my faith.
    Atreus. No longer clasp my knees, nay, rather seek
My warm embrace. Ye, too, the props of age,
575 So young, my children, cling about my neck.
And thou, put off thy raiment mean and coarse;
Oh, spare my sight, put on these royal robes
Like mine, and gladly share thy brother's realm.
This greater glory shall at last be mine:
580 To my illustrious brother I give back
His heritage. One holds a throne by chance,
To give it up is noble.

Thyestes. May the gods
Give thee, my brother, fair return for all
Thy benefits. Alas, my wretchedness
585 Forbids me to accept the royal crown,
My guilty hand shrinks from the scepter's weight;
Let me in lesser rank unnoted live.
    Atreus. This realm recovers its two kings.
    Thyestes. I hold, O brother, all of thine the same as mine.
590   *Atreus.* Who would refuse the gifts that fortune gives?
    Thyestes. He who has learned how swiftly they depart.
    Atreus. Wouldst thou refuse thy brother such renown?
    Thyestes. Thy glory is fulfilled, but mine still waits:
Firm is my resolution to refuse the kingdom.
595   *Atreus.* I relinquish all my power unless thou hast thy part.
    Thyestes. I take it then.
I'll wear the name of king, but law and arms
And I shall be thy slaves, for evermore.
    Atreus. Wear then upon thy head the royal crown.
600 I'll give the destined victim to the gods.

Scene III

Chorus.

Who would believe it? Atreus, fierce and wild,
Savage and tameless, shrank and was amazed
When he beheld his brother. Stronger bonds
Than nature's laws exist not. Wars may last
605 With foreign foes, but true love still will bind
Those whom it once has bound. When wrath, aroused
By some great quarrel, has dissevered friends
And called to arms, when the light cavalry
Advance with ringing bridles, here and there
610 Shines the swift sword which, seeking fresh-shed blood,
The raging war-god wields with frequent blows;
But love and loyalty subdue the sword,
And in great peace unite unwilling hearts.
What god gave sudden peace from so great war?
615 Throughout Mycenæ rang the crash of arms
As though in civil strife, pale mothers held
Their children to their bosoms, and the wife
Feared for her steel-armed husband, when the sword,
Stained with the rust acquired in long peace,
620 Unwillingly obeyed his hand. One sped
To strengthen falling walls, to build again
The tottering towers, to make fast the gates
With iron bars; and on the battlements
The pale watch waked through all the anxious night.

625 The fear of war is worse than war itself.
But threatenings of the cruel sword have ceased,
The trumpet's deep-toned voice at last is stilled,
The braying of the strident horn is hushed,
And to the joyous city peace returns.
630 So when the northwest wind beats up the sea
And from the deep the swelling waves roll in,
Scylla from out her smitten caverns roars
And sailors in the havens fear the flood
That ravening Charybdis vomits forth,
635 And the fierce Cyclops, dwelling on the top
Of fiery Ætna, dreads his father's rage,
Lest whelmed beneath the waves, the fires that roar
Within his immemorial chimney's throat
Should be profaned, and poor Laertes thinks,
640 Since Ithaca is shaken, that his realm
May be submerged; then, if the winds subside,
More quiet than a pool the ocean lies,
Scattered on every side gay little skiffs
Stretch the fair canvas of their spreading sails
645 Upon the sea which, late, ships feared to cut;
And there where, shaken by the hurricane,
The Cyclades were fearful of the deep,
The fishes play. No fortune long endures:
Sorrows and pleasures each in turn depart,
650 But pleasure soonest; from the fairest heights
An hour may plunge one to the lowest depths;
He who upon his forehead wears a crown,
Who nods and Medians lay aside the sword,
Indians, too, near neighbors of the sun,
655 And Dacians that assail the Parthian horse,
He holds his scepter with an anxious hand,
Foresees the overthrow of all his joy,
And fears uncertain time and fickle chance.
Ye whom the ruler of the earth and sea
660 Has given power over life and death,
Be not so proud, a stronger threatens you
With whatsoever ills the weaker fears
From you; each realm is by a greater ruled.
Him whom the rising sun beholds in power
665 The setting sees laid low. Let none confide
Too much in happiness, let none despair
When he has fallen from his high estate,
For Clotho blends the evil with the good;
She turns about all fortunes on her wheel;
670 None may abide. Such favoring deities
No one has ever found that he may trust
To-morrow; on his flying wheel a god.

Spins our swift changing fortunes.

ACT IV

Scene I

Messenger, Chorus.

Messenger. Oh, who will bear me headlong through the air,
675 Like a swift wind, and hide me in thick cloud
That I no longer may behold such crime?
O house dishonored, whose base deeds disgrace
Pelops and Tantalus!
    Chorus. What news is thine?
    Messenger. What region can it be that I behold?
680 Argos and Sparta to which fate assigned
Such loving brothers? Corinth or the shores
Of the two seas? The Danube that compels
The fierce Alani frequently to flee?
Hyrcania underneath eternal snows?
685 Is it the wandering Scythians' changing home?
What land is this that knows such monstrous deeds?
    Chorus. Speak and declare the ill whate'er it be.
    Messenger. If I have courage, if cold fear relax
Its hold upon my members. Still I see
690 Th' accomplished slaughter. Bear me far from hence,
O driving whirlwind; whither day is borne
Bear me, torn hence!
    Chorus. Control thy fear, wrung heart,
What is the deed that makes thee quake with fear
Speak and declare its author, I ask not
695 Who it may be, but which. Now quickly tell.
    Messenger. Upon the heights a part of Pelops' house
Faces the south; the further side of this
Lifts itself upward like a mountain top
And overlooks the city; thence their kings
700 May hold the stubborn people 'neath their sway.
Here shines the great hall that might well contain
An army, vari-colored columns bear
Its golden architraves; behind the room
Known to the vulgar, where the people come,
705 Stretch chambers rich and wide, and far within
Lies the arcana of the royal house,
The sacred penetralia; here no tree
Of brilliant foliage grows, and none is trimmed;
But yews and cypress and black ilex trees
710 Bend in the gloomy wood, an ancient oak
Rises above the grove and, eminent

Over the other trees, looks down on all
From its great height. Here the Tantalides
Are consecrated kings, and here they seek
715 Aid in uncertain or untoward events
Here hang their votive offerings, clear-toned trumps,
And broken chariots, wreckage of the sea,
And wheels that fell a prey to treachery,
And evidence of every crime the race
720 Has done. Here Trojan Pelops' crown is hung,
Here the embroidered robe from barbarous foes
Won. In the shade trickles a sluggish rill
That in the black swamp lingers lazily,
Like the unsightly waters of black Styx
725 By which the gods make oath. 'Tis said that here
The gods of the infernal regions sigh
Through all the dark night, that the place resounds
With rattling chains, and spirits of the dead
Go wailing up and down. Here may be seen
730 All dreadful things; here wanders the great throng
Of spirits of the ancient dead sent forth
From antique tombs, and monsters fill the place
Greater than have been known, and oft the wood
With threefold baying echoes, oftentimes
735 The house is terrible with mighty forms.
Nor does the daylight put an end to fear,
Night is eternal in the grove, and here
The sanctity of the infernal world
Reigns in the midst of day. Here sure response
740 Is given those who seek the oracle;
From the adytum with a thundering noise
The fatal utterance finds a passage out,
And all the grot reechoes the god's voice.
Here raging Atreus entered, dragging in
745 His brother's sons; the altars were adorned—
Ah, who can tell the tale? The noble youths
Have their hands bound behind them and their brows
Bound with the purple fillet; incense too
Is there, and wine to Bacchus consecrate,
750 And sacrificial knife, and salted meal;
All things are done in order, lest such crime
Should be accomplished without fitting rites.
  Chorus. Whose hand took up the sword?
  Messenger. He is himself
The priest: He sang himself with boisterous lips
755 The sacrificial song, those given to death
He placed, he took the sword and wielded it;
Nothing was lacking to the sacrifice.
Earth trembled, all the grove bent down its head,

The palace nodded, doubtful where to fling
760 Its mighty weight, and from the left there shot
A star from heaven, drawing a black train.
The wine poured forth upon the fire was changed
And flowed red blood; the royal diadem
Fell twice, yea thrice; within the temple walls
765 The ivory statues wept: all things were moved
At such a deed; himself alone unmoved,
Atreus stood firm and faced the threatening gods.
And now delay at last was put aside;
He stood before the altar, sidelong, fierce
770 In gaze. As by the Ganges, in the woods,
The hungry tiger stands between two bulls,
Uncertain which one first shall feel his teeth—
Eager for both, now here now there he turns
His eyes and in such doubt is hungry still—
775 So cruel Atreus gazes on the heads
Devoted sacrifices to his rage:
He hesitates which one shall first be slain,
And which be immolated afterward;
It matters not and yet he hesitates.
780 And in the order of his cruel crime
Takes pleasure.
  Chorus. Which is first to feel the sword?
  Messenger. Lest he should seem to fail in loyalty
First place is given to his ancestor—
The one named Tantalus is first to fall.
  Chorus. What courage showed the youth? How bore he death?
  Messenger. He stood unmoved, no useless prayers were heard.
That cruel one hid in the wound the sword,
Pressing it deep within the victim's neck,
Then drew it forth; the corpse was upright still:
790 It hesitated long which way to fall,
Then fell against the uncle. Atreus then,
Dragging before the altar Plisthenes,
Hurried him to his brother: with one blow
He cut away the head; the lifeless trunk
795 Fell prone and with a whispered sound the head
Rolled downward.
  Chorus. Double murder thus complete,
What did he then? Spared he the other boy?
Or did he heap up crime on crime?
  Messenger. Alas!
As crested lion in Armenian woods
800 Attacks the herd, nor lays aside his wrath
Though sated, but with jaws that drip with blood
Follows the bulls, and satisfied with food
Threatens the calves but languidly; so threats

Atreus, so swells his wrath, and holding still
805 The sword with double murder wet, forgets
Whom he attacks; with direful hand he drives
Right through the body and the sword, received
Within the breast, passes straight through the back.
He falls and with his blood puts out the fires;
By double wound he dies.
810   *Chorus.* O savage crime!
    Messenger. Art horrified? If there the work had ceased,
It had been pious.
    Chorus. Could a greater crime
Or more atrocious be by nature borne?
    Messenger. And dost thou think this was the end of crime?
'Twas its beginning.
815   *Chorus.* What more could there be?
Perchance he threw the bodies to wild beasts
That they might tear them, kept from funeral fire?
    Messenger. Would he had kept, would that no grave might hide
The dead, no fire burn them, would the birds
820 And savage beasts might feast on such sad food!
That which were torment else is wished for here.
Would father's eyes unburied sons might see!
O crime incredible to every age!
O crime which future ages shall deny!
825 The entrails taken from the living breast
Tremble, the lungs still breathe, the timid heart
Throbs, but he tears its fiber, ponders well
What it foretells and notes its still warm veins.
When he at last has satisfied himself
830 About the victims, of his brother's feast
He makes secure. The mangled forms he cuts,
And from the trunk he separates the arms
As far as the broad shoulders, savagely
Lays bare the joints and cleaves apart the bones;
835 The heads he spares and the right hands they gave
In such good faith. He puts the severed limbs
Upon the spits and roasts them by slow fire;
The other parts into the glowing pot
He throws to boil them. From the food the fire
840 Leaps back, is twice, yea thrice, replaced and forced
At last reluctantly to do its work.
The liver on the spit emits shrill cries,
I cannot tell whether the flesh or flame
Most deeply groaned. The troubled fire smoked,
845 The smoke itself, a dark and heavy cloud,
Rose not in air nor scattered readily;
The ugly cloud obscured the household gods.
O patient Phœbus, thou hast backward fled

     And, breaking off the light of day at noon,
850 Submerged the day, but thou didst set too late.
     The father mangles his own sons, and eats
     Flesh of his flesh, with sin polluted lips;
     His locks are wet and shine with glowing oil;
     Heavy is he with wine; the morsels stick
855 Between his lips. Thyestes, this one good
     Amid thy evil fortunes still remains:
     Thou knowest it not. But this good too shall die.
     Let Titan, turning backward on his path,
     Lead back his chariot and with darkness hide
860 This foul new crime, let blackest night arise
     At midday, yet the deed must come to light.
     All will be manifest.

Scene II

Chorus.

     Oh, whither, father of the earth and sky,
     Whose rising puts the glory of the night
865 To flight, oh, whither dost thou turn thy path,
     That light has fled at midday? Phœbus, why
     Hast thou withdrawn thy beams? The evening star,
     The messenger of darkness, has not yet
     Called forth the constellations of the night,
870 Not yet the westward turning course commands
     To free thy horses that have done their work,
     The trumpet has not yet its third call given,
     The signal of declining day, new night.
     The plowman is amazed at the swift fall
875 Of supper-time, his oxen by the plow
     Are yet unwearied; from thy path in heaven
     What drives thee, O Apollo? What the cause
     That forces from their wonted way thy steeds?
     Though conquered, do the giants strive again
880 In war, hell's prison being opened wide?
     Or does Tityus in his wounded breast
     Renew his ancient wrath? The mountains rent,
     Does Titan's son, Typhœus, stretch again
     His giant body? Is a pathway built
885 By Macedonian giants to the sky,
     On Thracian Ossa is Mount Pelion piled?
     The ancient order of the universe
     Has perished! rise and setting will not be!
     Eos, the dewy mother of the dawn,
890 Wont to the god of day to give the reins,
     Sees with amaze her kingdom overthrown,

She knows not how to bathe the wearied steeds,
Nor dip the smoking horses in the sea.
The setting sun himself, amazed, beholds
895 Aurora, and commands the darkness rise
Ere night is ready, the bright stars rise not,
Nor do the heavens show the faintest light,
Nor does the morn dissolve the heavy shades.
Whate'er it be would it were only night!
900 Shaken with mighty fear my bosom quakes
Lest all the world to ruin should be hurled,
And formless chaos cover gods and men,
And nature once again enfold and hide
The land and sea and starry firmament.
905 With the upspringing of its deathless torch
Bringing the seasons, never more shall come
The king of stars and give the waiting world
Changes of summer and of winter's cold;
No more shall Luna meet the sun's bright flame
910 And take away the terror of the night,
And running through a briefer circuit pass
His brother's car; into one gulf shall fall
The heaped-up throng of gods.
The zodiac, pathway of the sacred stars,
915 Which cuts the zones obliquely, shall behold
The falling stars and fall itself from heaven.
Aries, who comes again in early spring
And with warm zephyr swells the sails, shall fall
Headlong into the sea through which he bore
920 Timorous Hella; and the Bull, that wears
The Hyades upon its shining brow,
Shall with himself drag down the starry Twins
And Cancer's claws; the Lion, glowing hot,
That Hercules once conquered, shall again
925 Fall from the skies; and to the earth she left
The Virgin too shall fall, and the just Scales,
And with them drag the churlish Scorpion.
Old Chiron, who holds fixed the feathered dart
In the Thessalian bow, shall loose his shaft
930 From the snapped bowstring, and cold Capricorn
Who brings the winter's cold shall fall, and break
For thee, whoe'er thou art, thy water-jug,
Thou Water-bearer; with thee too shall fall
The Fishes, last of stars; and Charles's Wain,
935 That never yet has sunk below the sea,
Falling shall plunge beneath the ocean wave.
The slippery Dragon, that between the Bears
Winds like a winding river, shall descend;
And, with the Dragon joined, the Lesser Bear

940 So icy cold, and slow Boötes too,
     Already tottering to his overthrow,
     Shall fall from heaven with his heavy wain.
     Out of so many do we seem alone
     Worthy to be beneath the universe
945 Buried, when heaven itself is overthrown?
     In our day has the end of all things come?
     Created were we for a bitter fate,
     Whether we've banished or destroyed the sun.
     Let lamentation cease, depart base fear;
950 Eager for life is he who would not die
     Even though with him all the world should fall.

ACT V

Scene I

Atreus.

     High above all and equal to the stars
     I move, my proud head touches heaven itself;
     At last I hold the crown, at last I hold
955 My father's throne. Now I abandon you,
     Ye gods, for I have touched the highest point
     Of glory possible. It is enough.
     Ev'n I am satisfied. Why satisfied?
     No shame withholds me, day has been withdrawn;
960 Act while the sky is dark. Would I might keep
     The gods from flight, and drag them back by force
     That all might see the feast that gives revenge.
     It is enough the father shall behold.
     Though daylight be unwilling to abide,
965 Yet will I take from thee the dark that hides
     Thy miseries; too long with merry look
     Thou liest at thy feast: enough of wine,
     Enough of food, Thyestes. There is need,
     In this thy crowning ill, thou be not drunk
970 With wine. Slaves, open wide the temple doors,
     And let the house of feasting open lie.
     I long to see his color when he sees
     His dead sons' heads, to hear his words that flow
     With the first shock of sorrow, to behold
975 How, stricken dumb, he sits with rigid form.
     This is the recompense of all my toil.
     I do not wish to see his wretchedness
     Save as it grows upon him. The wide hall
     Is bright with many a torch; supine he lies
980 On gold and purple, his left hand supports

His head that is so heavy now with wine;
He vomits. Mightiest of the gods am I,
And king of kings! my wish has been excelled
Full is he, in the silver cup he lifts
985 The wine. Spare not to drink, there still remains
Some of the victims' blood, the old wine's red
Conceals it; with this cup the feast shall end.
His children's blood mixed with the wine he drinks;
He would have drunken mine. Lo, now he sings,
990 Sings festal songs, his mind is dimmed with wine.

Scene II

Atreus, Thyestes.

Thyestes. By long grief dulled, put by thy cares, my heart,
Let fear and sorrow fly and bitter need,
Companion of thy timorous banishment,
And shame, hard burden of afflicted souls.
995 Whence thou hast fallen profits more to know
Than whither; great is he who with firm step
Moves on the plain when fallen from the height;
He who, oppressed by sorrows numberless
And driven from his realm, with unbent neck
1000 Carries his burdens, not degenerate
Or conquered, who stands firm beneath the weight
Of all his burdens, he is great indeed.
Now scatter all the clouds of bitter fate,
Put by all signs of thy unhappy days,
1005 In happy fortunes show a happy face,
Forget the old Thyestes. Ah, this vice
Still follows misery: never to trust
In happy days; though better fortunes come,
Those who have borne afflictions find it hard
1010 To joy in better days. What holds me back,
Forbids me celebrate the festal tide?
What cause of grief, arising causelessly,
Bids me to weep? What art thou that forbids
That I should crown my head with festal wreath?
1015 It does forbid, forbid! Upon my head
The roses languish, and my hair that drips
With ointment rises as with sudden fear,
My face is wet with showers of tears that fall
Unwillingly, and groans break off my song.
1020 Grief loves accustomed tears, the wretched feel
That they must weep. I would be glad to make
Most bitter lamentation, and to wail,
And rend this robe with Tyrian purple dyed.

My mind gives warning of some coming grief,
1025 Presages future ills. The storm that smites
When all the sea is calm weighs heavily
Upon the sailor. Fool! What grief, what storm,
Dost thou conceive? Believe thy brother now.
Be what it may, thou fearest now too late,
1030 Or causelessly. I do not wish to be
Unhappy, but vague terror smites my breast?
No cause is evident and yet my eyes
O'erflow with sudden tears. What can it be,
Or grief, or fear? Or has great pleasure tears?

Scene III

Atreus, Thyestes.

1035   *Atreus.* Brother, let us together celebrate
This festal day: this day it is which makes
My scepter firm, which binds the deathless pact
Of certain peace.
    Thyestes. Enough of food and wine!
This only could augment my happiness,
1040 If with my own I might enjoy my bliss.
    Atreus. Believe thy sons are here in thy embrace.
Here are they and shall be, no single part
Of thy loved offspring shall be lost to thee.
Ask and whate'er thou wishest I will give,
1045 I'll satisfy the father with his sons;
Fear not, thou shalt be more than satisfied.
Now with my own thy young sons lengthen out
The joyous feast: they shall be sent for; drink
The wine, it is an heirloom of our house.
1050 *Thyestes.* I take my brother's gift. Wine shall be poured
First to our fathers' gods, then shall be drunk.
But what is this? My hands refuse to lift
The cup, its weight increases and holds down
My right hand, from my lips the wine retreats,
1055 Around my mouth it flows and will not pass
Within my lips, and from the trembling earth
The tables leap, the fire scarce gives light,
The air is heavy and the light is dim
As between day and darkness. What is this?
1060 The arch of heaven trembles more and more,
To the dense shadows ever thicker mist
Is added, night withdraws in blacker night,
The constellations flee. Whate'er it is,
I pray thee spare my sons, let all the storm
1065 Break over my vile head. Give back my sons!

Atreus. Yea, I will give them back, and never more
Shalt thou be parted from them. [*Exit.*]

Scene IV

Thyestes.

What distress
Seizes my reins? Why shake my inward parts?
I feel a burden that will forth, my breast
1070 Groans with a groaning that is not my own.
Come, children, your unhappy father calls;
Come, might I see you all this woe would flee.
Whence come these voices?

Scene V

Atreus, Thyestis, Slave bearing a covered charger.

Atreus. Father, spread wide thy arms, they come, they come.
1075 Dost thou indeed now recognize thy sons?

[*charger is uncovered.*]

Thyestes. I recognize my brother: Canst thou bear
Such deeds, O earth? O Styx, wilt thou not break
Thy banks and whelm in everlasting night
Both king and kingdom, bearing them away
1080 By a dread path to chaos' awful void?
And, plucking down thy houses, fallest thou not,
O city of Mycenæ, to the ground?
We should already be with Tantalus!
Earth, ope thy prisons wide on every side;
1085 If under Tartarus, below the place
Where dwell our kinsmen, rests a lower deep,
Within thy bosom let a chasm yawn
Thitherward, under all of Acheron
Hide us; let guilty souls roam o'er our heads
1090 Let Phlegethon that bears its fiery sands
Down through its glowing channels, flow o'er me!
Yet earth unmoved lies but a heavy weight,
The gods have fled.
    Atreus. Take, rather, willingly
Those whom thou hast so long desired to see;
1095 Thy brother does not hinder thee. Rejoice;
Kiss them, divide thy love between the three.
    Thyestes. This is thy compact? This thy brother's faith?
Is this thy favor? Layst thou thus aside

Thy hate? I do not ask to see my sons
Unharmed; what wickedness and deathless hate
May give, a brother asks: grant to my sons
Burial; give them back, thou shalt behold
Straightway their burning. Lo, I ask thee naught,
The father will not have but lose his sons.

Atreus. Thou hast whate'er remains, whate'er is lost.

Thyestes. And do they furnish food for savage birds?
Are they destroyed by monsters, fed to beasts?

Atreus. Thyself hast banqueted upon thy sons,
An impious feast.

Thyestes. 'Tis this that shamed the gods!
This backward drove the daylight whence it came!
Me miserable! What cry shall I make,
What wailing? What words will suffice my woe?
I see the severed heads, the hands cut off,
Greedy and hungry, these I did not eat!
I feel their flesh within my bowels move;
Prisoned, the dread thing struggles, tries to flee,
But has no passage forth; give me the sword,
Brother, it has already drunk my blood:
The sword shall give a pathway to my sons.
It is denied? Then rending blows shall sound
Upon my breast. Unhappy one, refrain
Thy hand, oh, spare the dead! Who e'er beheld
Such hideous crime? Not wandering tribes that dwell
On the unkindly Caucasus' rough cliffs,
Or fierce Procrustes, dread of Attica.
Behold, the father feasts upon his sons,
The sons lie heavy in him—is there found
No limit to thy base and impious deeds?

Atreus. Crime finds a limit when the crime is done,
Not when avenged. Even this is not enough.
Into thy mouth I should have poured the blood
Warm from the wounds; thou shouldst have drunk the blood
Of living sons. My hate betrayed itself
Through too much haste. I smote them with the sword,
I slew them at the altar, sacrificed
A votive offering to the household gods,
From the dead trunks I cut away the heads,
And into tiniest pieces tore the limbs;
Some in the boiling pot I plunged, and some
I bade should be before a slow flame placed;
I cut the flesh from the still living limbs,
I saw it roar upon the slender spit,
And with my own right hand I plied the fire.
All this the father might have better done:
All of my vengeance falls in nothingness!

He ate his sons with impious lips indeed,
Alas, nor he nor they knew what he did!
    Thyestes. Hear, O ye seas, stayed by inconstant shores;
Ye too, ye gods, wherever ye have fled,
1150 Hear what a deed is done! Hear, gods of Hell,
Hear, Earth, and heavy Tartarean night
Dark with thick cloud! Oh, listen to my cry!
Thine am I, Hell, thou only seest my woe,
Thou also hast no star. I do not make
1155 Presumptuous prayer, naught for myself I ask—
What could be given me? I make my prayer
For you, my sons. Thou ruler of the heavens,
Thou mighty king of the ethereal courts,
Cover the universe with horrid clouds,
1160 Let winds contend on every side, send forth
Thy thunders everywhere; not with light hand,
As when thou smitest with thy lesser darts
Innocent homes; but as when mountains fell
And with their threefold ruin overwhelmed
1165 The Giants—use such power, send forth such fires,
Avenge the banished day, where light has fled
Fill up the darkness with thy thunderbolts.
Each one is evil,—do not hesitate—
Yet if not both, I sure am base; seek me
1170 With triple dart, through this breast send this brand:
If I would give my sons a funeral pyre
And burial, I must give myself to flames.
If nothing moves the gods, if none will send
His darts against this sinful head, let night,
1175 Eternal night, abide and hide the crime
In everlasting shadows. If thou, Sun,
No longer shinest, I have naught to ask.
    Atreus. Now in my work I glory, now indeed
I hold the victor's palm. I would have lost
1180 My crime's reward unless thou thus wert grieved.
I now believe my sons were truly mine—
Now may I trust again in a chaste bed.
    Thyestes. What evil have my children done to thee?
    Atreus. They were thy sons.
    Thyestes. The children of their sire—
1185   *Atreus.* Undoubted sons; 'tis this that makes me glad.
    Thyestes. I call upon the gods who guard the right to witness.
    Atreus. Why not call upon the gods
Who guard the marriage-bed?
    Thyestes. Who punishes a crime with crime?
    Atreus. I know what makes thee mourn:
1190 Another first accomplished the grim deed,
For this thou mournest; thou art not distressed

Because of thy dread feast, thou feelest grief
That thou hast not prepared such feast for me.
This mind was in thee: to provide like food
For thy unconscious brother, and to slay
My children with their mother's aid. One thing
Withheld thee—thou believedst they were thine.
    Thyestes. Th' avenging gods will come and punish thee;
To them my prayers commit thee.
    Atreus. To thy sons I give thee over for thy punishment.

HERCULES ON ŒTA

DRAMATIS PERSONÆ

Hercules.
Hyllus.
Philoctetes.
Dejanira.
Alcmena.
Iole.
Nurse.
Chorus of Œchalian Maidens.
Chorus of Œtolian Matrons.

Scene: *Act I, Œchalia,*
       Act II et seq., Trachina.

HERCULES ON CETA

ACT I

Scene I

Hercules, Iole, Chorus of Œchalian Maidens.

    Hercules. O father of the gods, whose thunderbolt
Both homes of Phœbus, east and west, do know,
Reign now secure, for I have brought thee peace
Wherever Nereus checks the spread of land.
There is no need to thunder, perjured kings
And cruel tyrants lie o'erthrown. I've slain
Whatever might have felt thy thunderbolt.
But father, why is heaven to me denied?
In all things, surely, I have worthy proved
Of Jove, my stepdame even witnesses
My heavenly birth. Why longer make delay?
Dost fear? Could Atlas not support the skies
If Hercules were there? Why still refuse

The star? Death sent me back to thee, all ills
15 That earth or sea or air or hell bring forth
Have yielded: through Arcadian streets no more
The lion wanders; the Stymphalian birds
Are dead; there is no stag of Mænalus;
The dying dragon sprinkled with his blood
20 The golden groves; the Hydra yields his life;
Beside the river Hebrus I destroyed
That well-known herd with blood of slaughtered guests
Made fat; and from Thermodon bore away
The spoils of war; I saw the silent shades,
25 Nor thence returned alone. The trembling day
Beheld black Cerberus. He saw the sun.
Busiris was before his altars slain;
By this one hand fell Geryon, and by this
The bull, the terror of a hundred lands;
30 Whatever hostile thing the earth brought forth
Has perished, by my right hand overcome.
If earth denies wild beasts to Juno's wrath,
Give back, I pray, a father to thy son,
Or give a constellation to the brave.
35 I do not ask that thou shouldst show the road,
If thou permit me, I will find a way;
Or if thou fear'st lest earth conceive wild beasts,
Then speed the evil while she has and sees
Thy Hercules: who else would dare assail
40 Such foes, or be, in any Argive town,
Worthy of Juno's hate? There is no land
That does not speak my fame, the frost-bound race
Of Scythians in the north, the men of Ind
Exposed to Phœbus' rays, the Libyans, too,
45 Beneath the constellation of the crab,
Have felt my hand; bright Titan, thee I call
To witness, I have gone with thee where'er
Thou sheddest light—thy light could not pursue
My triumphs, for beyond the sun's bright world
50 I passed: day was not where my metes were set,
Nor nature, earth was wanting to my steps,
She first was wearied. Night assailed my eyes,
And utmost chaos. I have come again
From whence none other ever has returned.
55 The threats of ocean I have borne, no storms
Could wreck my boat, wherever I have gone.
The empty ether cannot now suffice
The hatred of thy wife; earth fears to yield
Wild beasts for me to conquer, does not give
60 New monsters, none remain, and Hercules
Stands in their place. How many evil things

Have I, unarmed, destroyed. All dreadful forms
That rose against me, I, alone, o'erthrew,
Nor feared as babe or boy to meet wild beasts.
65 The toils commanded me seemed light, no day
Shone fruitless for me. Oh, how many ills
I vanquished, when no king commanded me,—
My valor drove me more than Juno's wrath.
What profit to have made the race secure?
70 Gods have not peace; the earth is free, but sees
All things it had to fear secure in heaven,
Juno translates the brutes: the crab, though slain,
Moves in a burning pathway, has been made
A Libyan constellation, ripening
75 The grain; the lion to Astraea gives
The flying year, he shakes his fiery mane,
Dries up the moist south wind, dispels the clouds,
Behold even now has each wild beast attained
The skies, and so outstripped me. From the earth
80 I still, though victor, must behold my foes.
To brutes and monsters Juno gives a star
That she may make the skies a dreaded place
For me. Aye, let her waste the earth and make
The heav'ns more terrible than earth or hell,
85 Yet still Alcides shall be given room.
If after war, if after conquered beasts
And Stygian dog, I still am deemed unmeet
For heavenly heights, Hesperia shall touch
Peloris, and the two lands be but one;
90 I'll put the seas to flight—or dost thou bid
That they be joined? Let Isthmus no more part
The waves, and on united seas let ships
Be borne by new-found paths to Attica.
Let earth be changed: the Ister flow along
95 Through channels new, the Tanais find new ways.
Grant, Jupiter, at least, that I may guard
The gods; thou needst not hurl thy thunderbolt
Where I shall be the guardian. Though thou bid
That I protect the realms of heat and cold,
100 Believe, the gods are safe in that abode.
The dragon slain, Apollo merited
A Delphian temple and a heavenly home,—
How many Pythons in the Hydra lay!
Bacchus and Perseus have attained the skies,
105 How small a region was the east he quelled!
How many monsters in the Gorgon lived?
What son of thine, of Juno born, deserved
A constellation by his glorious deeds?
The realm I on my shoulders bore I seek.

110 But thou, O Lichas, comrades of my toils,
Herald my triumph, of the conquered home
And fallen realm of great Eurytus tell.
[*To his servants.*] Drive ye the victims quickly to the fanes
Built to Cenæan Jove where wild with storms
115 The feared Eubæan ocean hurls its waves.

Scene II

Iole, Chorus of Œchalian Maidens.

Chorus. The equal of immortal gods is he
Whose life and fortune travel hand in hand;
But he who slowly drags his life along
With heavy groans, believes it worse than death.
120 He who beneath his feet put eager fates,
And steered the boat on the dark river's flood,
Shall never give to chains his captive arms,
Nor ever grace the tyrant's triumph car.
He to whom death is easy never finds
125 Life wretched: though his vessel in mid seas
Desert him, when old Boreas in his might
Drives back the south wind, or when Eurus strives
With Zephyr, when the waters seem to part,—
He may not gather up the broken beams
130 Of his wrecked ship that, in the waters' midst,
He may yet hope for land; he cannot know
Shipwreck, who freely can forgo his life.
   Base weakness, tears, locks sordid with the dust
Of my dear fatherland are mine, not flames
135 Nor crash of fortune strike me down. O Death,
Thou comest to the happy; wretched men
Thou fleest. Still I live; my fatherland,
Alas! shall lapse to wilderness and woods,
Its fallen temples yield to sordid huts,
140 The cold Dolopian thither lead his flock
Where yet Œchalia's growing ashes lie;
Thessalian shepherds, to the very town
Bringing their unskilled pipes, in doleful lays
Retell the mournful story of our times,
145 And ere a few more generations pass
The world shall seek in vain the place where stood
My country. Happy once, I made my home
By no unfruitful hearth nor dwelt among
Thessalia's barren acres; now I go
150 To Trachin, land of rocks and heavy brakes,
Parched mountain summits, groves the mountain goat
Scarce loves to haunt. But if a milder fate

Await the slave, if Inachus' swift stream
Shall bear him on its bosom, if he dwell
155 By Dirce's fountain where the languid stream
Ismenos flows, a slender thread—'twas there
The mother of proud Hercules was wed.
False is the fable of the double night,
When longer in the heavens shone the stars,
160 When Hesperus arose for Lucifer,
And slow Diana long delayed the sun.
What rocks or cliffs of Scythia nourished thee?
Did Rhodope's wild mountain bring thee forth
A Titan; or Mount Athos' rugged steeps;
165 Or the stern mountains by the Caspian shore?
What tiger's spotted breast has suckled thee?
He cannot feel a wound, the spear grows dull,
The steel is softened, shattered is the sword
That smites his naked body, and the stones
170 Fly back; he does not fear the fates, invites
With flesh unconquerable death itself;
Spears may not pierce him, nor the Scythian shafts
From the tense bowstring shot, nor any dart
The cold Sarmatians bear, nor can they wound
175 Who eastward, near the Habatæans, dwell,
Where arrows truer than the Cretan's fly—
The Parthian's. With his body he o'erthrew
Œchalia's walls, against him naught can stand.
What he prepares to conquer is o'ercome.
180 His hostile face brings death, to have but seen
The wrath of Hercules is woe enough.
Could vast Briareus, or could Gyas huge,
Who, standing on Thessalian mountains, stormed
The skies with snake-armed hands, make him afraid?
185 Beside great evils lie his great rewards,
No more of ill is left, we have beheld—
Unhappy we—great Hercules in wrath.
    Iole. Me miserable! Not that temples lie
With gods and homes o'erthrown, that in the flames
190 Fathers with sons, divinities with men,
The temple with the tombs, are burned to dust—
We mourn no common woe; my tears are caused
By other sorrows, fortune bids me weep
For other ruins. What first shall I mourn?
195 What most demands my tears? All equally!
Earth hath not breasts enough to sound with blows
Worthy these sorrows. O ye gods above,
Make me a mournful Sipylean rock;
Or place me by the banks of Po where sounds
200 The murmur of the trees, the sisters sad

        Of Phaethon, or on Sicilian rocks
        Where I, a siren, may lament the fate
        Of Thessaly or to the Thracian woods
        Bear me, where like a swallow Procne sits
205   Beneath Ismavian shade and mourns her son.
        Give me a form fit for my bitter tears,
        And let harsh Trachin echo with my woe.
        Still Cyprian Myrrha weeps, and Ceyx' wife
        Grieves for her husband, Niobe outlives
210   Herself, and Thracian Philomela flees
        And, a sad nightingale, laments her son.
        Oh, happy, happy were I, if my home
        Might be the woods, if I, a bird, might rest
        Within my country's meadows and bemoan
215   My fate with querulous murmur, and fame tell
        Of winged Iole. I saw, I saw
        My father's wretched fate, when smitten down
        By Hercules' death-dealing club, he lay
        Through all the courtyard scattered. If the fates
220   Had given thee a tomb, where had I sought,
        O father, for thy members? Have I borne
        To see thy death, O Toxeus, when not yet
        Thy tender cheeks with manly beard were decked,
        Nor yet man's blood was coursing through thy veins?
225   But why, my parents, should I mourn your fate
        Whom friendly death holds safe? My fate demands
        My tears. A captive, I am forced to drive
        The distaff and the spindle for my lord.
        Oh, cruel beauty, comeliness of form
230   That brought me death! My home for this alone
        Fell ruined, since my father would not give
        His daughter to Alcides, feared to be
        Akin by marriage to great Hercules.
        But I must seek my mistress' proud abode.
235   *Chorus.* Why foolishly recall thy father's realm
        And thy sad fate? Forget thy former lot,
        He only can be happy who has learned
        To keep, as king or slave, an equal mind,
        And suffer varying fortunes. He has snatched
240   The heaviness from ill, strength for himself,
        Who bears whate'er befalls with steadfast soul.

ACT II

Scene I

The Nurse, alone.

    What cruel raging seizes woman's heart
When one roof covers wife and concubine!
Charybdis, Scylla, in Sicilian straits,
245 Need less be feared; less wild the savage beast.
For when the beauty of the captive shone,
And Iole was bright as cloudless day,
Or like the stars that shine in nights serene,
The wife of Hercules like one insane,
250 With fierce look stood. As lying with her young
Within a cavern in Armenia's land,
The tigress, at an enemy's approach,
Springs forth, or as the mænad, god-inspired,
When bidden wave the thyrsus, for a time
255 Stands doubtful whither she shall turn her steps,
So rages through the house of Hercules
His wife, nor does the house give room enough;
She rushes up and down, roams to and fro,
Then pauses, in her cheeks all sorrows burn,
260 Naught is within her bosom hid; swift tears
Follow her threats, nor does one mood endure,
Nor is she with a single phase of wrath
Contented: now her cheeks are like a flame,
Now pallor drives away the red, her grief
265 Takes every form, she weeps, laments, implores.
The door creaks, see, with headlong steps she comes,
Telling with words confused her inmost thoughts.

Scene II

Dejanira, Nurse.

    Dejanira. O wife of Jove, wherever thou may'st be
Within thy airy home, send thence, I pray,
270 Against Alcides such a savage beast
As may suffice me. If a dragon lives
Unconquered, vaster, with more fruitful head;
If any beast exists so huge and dire,
So terrible, that Hercules himself
275 Averts his eyes, let this from some vast cave
Come forth; or if wild beasts must be denied,
I pray thee to some terror change this form—

With this mind I can do whatever ill
Thou wouldst. Oh, make my form express my woe!
280 My bosom will not hold the wrath I feel.
Why searchest thou the ends of earth? Why turn
The world about? Why seek for plagues in Dis?
Within this bosom wilt thou find all ills
Which need be feared, with this shaft arm thy hate;
285 I too may be a stepdame. Thou canst slay
Alcides, use this hand for what thou wilt.
Why pause? Use me, the mad one, what new crime
Dost thou command? Say on, why hesitate?
'Tis well that thou shouldst rest, this wrath does all.
290   *Nurse.* O foster-child, a little calm thyself.
Restrain thy plaints, control thy fiery rage,
And curb thy grief, now show thyself indeed
The wife of Hercules.
    Dejanira. Shall Iole,
The captive maid, give brothers to my sons,
295 The slave become the daughter of great Jove?
Not in one bed can flame and torrent flow,
The northern bear may not in ocean's blue
Be wet—not unavenged will I remain.
What though thy shoulders bore the sky, though earth
300 Must thank thee for its peace? There yet remains
A greater terror than the Hydra's rage:
The anger of an injured wife. Burn thus
The flames of glowing Etna? This my wrath
Can conquer all thy conquests, shall a slave
305 Seize on my marriage-bed? Till now I feared.
Dread monsters, none remain, those plagues are gone,
In place of beasts there comes the hated slave.
By Titan, by the ruler of the gods,
I was Alcides' wife but while he feared!
310 The prayers I made the gods, they grant the slave,
I was successful for the concubine!
Ye heard my prayers, ye gods, but for her sake,
And for her sake he came again unharmed.
O anguish that no vengeance can assuage,
315 Seek some revenge unthought, unspeakable,
And dreadful, teach great Juno how to hate;
She knows not how to rage. For me he warred,
For me made red the Acheloüs' waves
With his own blood, he overcame the snake,
320 He turned his threats against the bull, and slew
A thousand foes in one. But now no more
He finds me pleasing, and a captive maid
Has been preferred to me—but shall not be!
The day that ends our marriage ends his life.

325 Yet what is this? My courage fails, my wrath
Declines, my anger ceases, wretched one,
Why languid? Wherefore lose thy rage? Wouldst keep
A woman's patient constancy? What law
Forbids add fuel to the flame? What force
330 Subdues the fire? O strength of wrath, abide!
Peers shall we be, I have no need of vows,
A stepdame will be with me who will guide
My hands aright, though she be uninvoked.
  Nurse. What crime preparest thou, O heart insane?
335 Wouldst slay thy husband, him whose glory spreads
From east to west, his fame from earth to heaven?
The land of Greece would rise 'gainst such a deed,
His father's house, the whole Ætolian race
Would grieve, and all the earth avenge his death.
340 What canst thou do alone? Though thou shouldst think
T' escape the vengeance of the earth and man,
The father of Alcides wields his bolts.
See, see his threatening torches in the sky,
The thunder-riven heavens! Fear death itself,
345 In which thou hop'st thou yet mayst safety find.
There rules the uncle of thy Hercules;
Wherever thou wouldst turn, unhappy one,
Thou findest there thy husband's kindred gods.
  Dejanira. The crime is great, I own, but grief impels,
  Nurse. Thou'lt die.
350   *Dejanira.* But yet the wife of Hercules.
No day shall rise to find me widowed wife,
No captive concubine enjoy my couch.
The day shall sooner rise from out the west,
The Indian beneath the northern sky
355 Shall sooner pale, and sooner Phœbus' rays
Make dark the Scythian than Thessalian maids
See me deserted; with my blood I'll quench
Their marriage torches. He shall die or I;
To savage beings slain he yet may add
360 A wife, and I among his mighty deeds
Be numbered. Yet in death I'll still embrace
The couch of Hercules. Alcides' wife
May freely pass among the shades, but goes
Not unavenged; should Iole conceive
365 A child by Hercules, these hands of mine
Shall tear it from her womb, yea through the blaze
Of marriage torches I will seize the maid.
What though in anger, on his wedding day,
He make of me the victim, if I fall
370 Above the lifeless form of Iole?
Who falls upon the forms of those he hates dies happy.

Nurse. Why add fuel to the flame?
Why feed thy boundless sorrow? Wretched one,
Why needlessly afraid? He chose the maid
375 While yet her father reigned; he sought in her
The daughter of a king, but when the queen
Declined into a slave, love lost its force
And her misfortune took away her charm:
Forbidden things are loved, what one may have
One willingly foregoes.
380   *Dejanira.* Her lowered state
Inflames a greater love; he loves her still.
Although she lacks a home, although her hair
Hangs unadorned with gold or precious gems.
Perchance his pity loves her very grief.
385 This is his wont, to love his captive ones.
    Nurse. Dardanian Priam's sister, whom he loved,
He gave away; recall how many wives,
How many virgins he has loved before,
Inconstant ever. While she wove the dance
390 In Pallas' honor, the Arcadian maid,
Augeia, suffered from Alcides' lust—
She died and Hercules remembered not
His former love. Need I of others speak?
The muses have no lover, brief the flame
395 Which burned for them within Alcides' breast.
A guest upon Timolus, he caressed
The Lydian maid, and, still the slave of love,
He sat beside the wheel and lightly turned
With unaccustomed hand the moistened thread;
400 He laid from off his neck the lion's spoil,
The Lydian fillet bound his shaggy locks
That dripped with myrrh from Saba. Everywhere
He feels the heat of love, but brief the flame.
    Dejanira. A gallant ever follows wandering flames.
405   *Nurse.* Could he prefer a slave, a foeman's child, to thee?
    Dejanira. As when the early sunshine clothes
The grove's bare boughs, the joyous woods put forth
New buds, but when the cold north wind drives back
The south wind and harsh winter cuts away
410 The leaves, and one beholds the bare brown trunks,
So we in running life's long journey lose
Some beauty ever and less lovely grow.
That way has love departed, what in us
He loved is gone, and pain and motherhood
415 Have robbed me of him. Seest thou not the slave
Has not yet lost her pristine comeliness?
Rich ornaments indeed she lacks, and sits
In squalor, yet her beauty shines through all,

And time and chance have taken from her naught
420 Except her kingdom. Therefore grief slays sleep.
I was the wife most honored everywhere,
And every woman looked with envious eyes
Upon my marriage; when Argolic maids
Made prayers for aught to any of the gods,
425 I was the measure of the good they asked.
What father shall I have that equals Jove?
What husband under heaven equals mine?
Should he who gave Alcides his commands,
Eurystheus' self, espouse me, he is less.
430 To have been severed from a prince's bed
Were little; she indeed is sorely reft
Who feels herself bereft of Hercules.
  Nurse. The children oft win back the husband's love.
  Dejanira. Her child, perchance, will draw him from my couch
435   *Nurse.* Perchance he brought her to thee for a gift.
  Dejanira. The man thou seest pass among the towns,
Illustrious, and bearing on his back
The tawny lion's skin, who from the proud
Takes realms and gives them to the sore distressed,
440 Who in his dread hand bears a mighty club,
Whose triumphs by the farthest lands are sung,
Are sung by all the peoples of the earth,
Is most inconstant; nor does glory's grace
Incite him, through the world he wanders still,
445 Not as the peer of Jove, nor as the great
Should pass through Argive cities, but he seeks
One he may love, would gain a virgin's bed.
He ravishes whatever is denied,
Against the people's anger, from their wreck,
450 Procures his brides, and raging passion gains
The name of courage. Famed Œchalia fell;
One day, one sun beheld the city safe
And ruined, Love the only cause of war.
As often as a father shall refuse
455 To give his daughter to great Hercules,
So oft he needs to fear. Who will not be
Alcides' father is Alcides' foe,
And if he be not made a son, he slays.
Why keep I then my hands in innocence,
460 Till, feigning madness, with his savage hands
He bends his bow and slays his son and me?
So Hercules is wont to cast aside
His wives, so wont to break his marriage bond.
Nor can one count him guilty; to the world
465 Juno appears the cause of all his crimes.
Why should inactive anger pause amazed?

Anticipate his crime—up, hands, and smite,
While yet my wrath burns hot within my breast.
    Nurse. Wouldst slay a husband?
    Dejanira. Yes, of concubines!
    Nurse. The Jove-begotten?
470   *Dejanira.* Of Alcmena's race.
    Nurse. Not with the sword?
    Dejanira. The sword.
    Nurse. But if too weak?
    Dejanira. By guile I'll kill him.
    Nurse. Oh, what madness this!
    Dejanira. My husband was the teacher.
    Nurse. Wilt thou slay
The man whom Juno could not?
    Dejanira. Whom the gods
475 Most hate they render wretched, whom men hate they bring to nothing.
    Nurse. Spare him, wretched one, and fear.
    Dejanira. Who does not stand in fear of death
Fears nothing. I rejoice to meet his sword.
    Nurse. O foster-child, thy grief is heavier
480 Than's meet, the fault demands an equal hate
Oh, why so harshly judge his light offence?
Measure thy grieving by thy injury.
    Dejanira. And is a mistress then a slight offence
Against a wife? Whatever else she bears, this is indeed too heavy.
485   Nurse. Has thy love for great Alcides fled?
    Dejanira. Nay, nurse, not fled
Believe, it lives deep fixed within my heart,
But angered love is anguish infinite.
    Nurse. By magic arts and prayers have wives oft bound
490 Their husbands. I have made the winter groves
Grow green, the hurtling thunderbolt stand still,
Have made the dry earth glad; the rocks gave place,
The gates of hell flew back, the dead stood still,
The gods infernal spoke at my command,
495 The dog of hell was silent, midnight saw
The sun, and day was overwhelmed in night,
The earth and sea, the sky and Tartarus,
Obeyed me, nothing kept its ancient seat
Before my incantations. Let us seek
500 To bend his will, my songs will find a way.
    Dejanira. What plants does Pontus nourish, or what grows
On Pindus underneath Thessalian rocks?
Where shall I find a charm to conquer him?
Though Luna at the magic of thy songs
505 Should leave the stars and hide within the earth,
And winter see the harvest; though the flash
Of Jove's swift lightning pause at thy command;

    Though nature's order be reversed, and day
Should shine with many stars, he will not bend.
510   *Nurse.* Love conquers even the immortal gods.
        Dejanira. This too, perchance, he'll conquer, gain this spoil,
And love may be Alcides' last great task.
By the divinity of all the gods,
By this my fear, I pray thee: keep concealed
515 Whate'er I do in secret, hide it well.
      Nurse. What is it thou wouldst hide?
      Dejanira. Not spears, nor swords,
Nor yet avenging fires.
      Nurse. I can and will
Keep silence, if such silence be not sin.
      Dejanira. I pray thee look around, lest any hear
520 And keep a watchful eye on every side.
      Nurse. The place is safe from any prying one.
      Dejanira. In a far corner of this realm there lies
A hidden cave that keeps our secret well.
That place sees not the sun at morning's prime
525 Nor yet when Titan, bringer of the light,
Sinks with the spent day in the crimson sea.
There lies assurance of Alcides' love,
The charm from Nessus comes, whom Nephele
Conceived by the Thessalian king and bore
530 Where Pindus lifts its head among the stars,
Where rising o'er the clouds bald Othrys stands.
For when, exposed to dread Alcides' club,
Acheloüs took lightly every form,
But, having passed through all, stood forth at last
535 Subdued, with broken horns and wounded head,
The victor Hercules to Argos went
With me, his wife. Evenus' wandering stream
Swift through the meadows to the ocean bore
Its flood of waters, its impetuous waves
540 Already almost reached the line of woods.
The centaur Nessus, used to crossing floods,
Was eager for a prize, and bearing me
Upon his back where join the horse and man,
He stemmed the swelling water's threatening waves.
545 Alcides still was wandering in their midst
Cutting the eager depths with mighty strides.
Then when he saw Alcides still afar:
'My spoil art thou,' he said, 'my wife shalt be,
The waves are passed.' Then holding me embraced,
550 His steps he hastened. But the waves no more
Detained great Hercules. 'Base ferryman,'
He said, 'though Ister and the Ganges flow
With mingled currents, I will conquer both,

My shafts will speed thy flight.' More swift his bow
555 Than words; the arrow, flying to the wound,
Transfixed the centaur, ending flight in death.
Already searching blindly for the light
He caught the poison flowing from the wound,
And in his hoof, which with his savage hand
560 He boldly tore away, he gave it me.
Then spake he dying words: 'This charm,' he said,
'Can fix a wavering lover, so the brides
Of Thessaly were by Mycale taught—
She was the mage at whose command the moon
565 Deserted starry heaven to follow her,
A garment smeared with this, this very blood,'
He said, 'give thou to fickle Hercules,
If e'er a hated mistress should usurp
Thy marriage rights, and he should give great Jove
570 Another daughter. It must see no light,
In darkness most remote lie things like this.
So only shall this blood retain its strength.'
Then did the sleep of death cut short his words,
And brought his weary members long repose.
575 O thou, to whom I trust, with whom I share
This secret, quickly go and bring the charm,
That, smeared upon his shining robe, its force
May enter through his heart and limbs, and pierce his inmost marrow.
    Nurse. Quickly I obey
580 Thy will, dear foster-child; do thou invoke
With earnest prayer the god invincible
Who shoots with youthful hand his certain shafts.

Scene III

Dejanira, alone.

O thou whom earth and sea and heavenly powers
Adore in fear, who shakest Etna's fires,
585 I make my prayer to thee, O winged child,
Feared of thy ruthless mother; with true aim
Make ready thy swift dart, no common shafts;
I pray thee, choose the keenest, which not yet
Thy hands have aimed at any, there is need
590 Of such that Hercules may learn to love.
With firm hand draw the bow till both horns meet,
Shoot now the shaft that wounded once dread Jove
When casting down his thunderbolt, the god
Put on a horned and swelling front, and cleft
595 The raging seas, and as a bull bore off
The fair Assyrian maid. Oh, pierce with love,

A love more keen than any yet have felt!
Let Hercules learn love for me his wife.
And if the charms of Iole should set
600 The fire of love aflame within his heart,
Oh, let it drink the love of me and die.
Thou oft hast conquered thunder-bearing Jove,
And him who in the land of shadows wields
The dusky scepter, ruler of the Styx
605 And leader of the great majority.
More strong than angered stepdame, take, O god,
This triumph—thou alone—quell Hercules.

Scene IV

Dejanira, Nurse.

Nurse. The charm is ready, and the shining web
That wearied all thy damsels' hands to weave.
610 Smear now the poison, let Alcides' robe
Drink in the blood, I'll strengthen with my prayers
Its magic power. But see where Lichas comes,
The charm must be concealed, nor our device
Be known.

Scene V

Dejanira, Nurse, Lichas.

615   *Dejanira.* In palaces of kings is rarely found
A faithful servant; faithful Lichas, take
This garment which with my own hands I spun
While Hercules was wandering through the world,
Or drunk with wine was holding on his breast
620 The Lydian maid, or seeking Iole.
Yet peradventure, having well deserved,
I may win back the rugged hero's heart,
For merit often overcometh ill.
Command my husband not to wear the robe
625 Until with incense he has fed the flames,
And reconciled the gods, and on wet locks
Has bound a wreath of silver poplar leaves.
Within the palace I will make my prayers
To Venus, mother of unconquered love.
630 Ye Calydonian women, friends who came
From home with me, lament my mournful fate.

Scene VI

Chorus of Ætolian Women.

    O daughter of Oineus, thy childhood's friends,
    We weep thy hapless marriage, honored one.
    We, who with thee were wont to wade the shoals
635 Of Acheloüs, when with passing spring
    Its swollen waters ebbed, and with slow sweep
    Its slender current wound, and when no more
    The yellow waters of Lycormas rolled,
    A headlong, turgid river; we were wont
640 To seek Minerva's altars, and to join
    The virgin chorus; we with thee were wont
    To bear the holy emblems treasured up
    Within the Theban ark, when winter's cold
    Had passed, and thrice the sun called summer forth,
645 When the grain-giver Ceres' sacred seat
    Eleusis shut the priest within her shrines.
    Whatever fate thou fearest, let us still
    Remain the faithful sharers of thy lot.
    When happier fortune smiles, fidelity
650 Is rare. Though all the people throng thy courts,
    Though hundreds cross thy threshold, though thou pass
    Surrounded by a crowd of followers,
    Yet hardly shalt thou find among them all
    One faithful friend; the dread Erinnyes hold
655 The gilded portals, and when great men's gates
    Are opened fraud and craft and treachery
    And lurking murder enter, and abroad
    Thou goest among the people companied
    By envy. Oft as morning drives out night,
660 Believe, so often is a monarch born.
    Few serve the king and not his kingly power,
    The glory of the court is dear to most:
    One seeks to be the nearest to the king
    And pass illustrious through the city streets;
665 And one with glory's lust is burnt, and one
    Would sate his thirst with gold—nor all the tracts
    Of Ister, rich in gems, suffice his greed,
    Nor Lydia quench his thirst, nor all the land
    Where Zephyr sighs and golden Tagus flows;
670 Nor were the Hebrus his, flowed through his fields
    The rich Hydaspes, if the Ganges' flood
    Within his borders ran; the world itself
    Is all too small to serve the covetous.
    Kings and kings' palaces one cultivates,

675 Not that to drive the plough with bended back
The ploughmen never cease, or thousands till
The fields—he only longs for heaped-up wealth.
One serves the king that he may trample all,
May ruin many and may strengthen none;
680 He longs for power but to use it ill.
How few death finds at fulness of their fame;
Whom Cynthia beholds in happiness,
The new-born day sees wretched; rare it is
To grow old happy. Softer is the sod
685 Than Tyrian robe and brings a fearless sleep,
But golden roofs disturb repose, and kings
Must lengthen out the watches of the night.
Oh, if the rich man's heart were visible,
How many fears fair fortune stirs within!
690 The Bruttian waters, tossed by northwest winds,
Are port more peaceful. With untroubled heart
The poor may rest, his cup and plate, indeed,
Are only birchwood, but with fearless hand
He holds them; easily his simple food
695 Is gathered, and he fears no waiting sword:
In cup of gold the drink is mixed with blood.
The wife who weds a man of humble means
May wear no costly necklace nor be decked
With Red Sea's gift, nor carry in her ears
700 The choicest gems of eastern waves, nor wear
Soft wool twice dipped in rich Sidonian dyes,
Nor with Mæonian needle broider it—
The Seres, dwelling near the rising sun,
To eastward, made the needle from the trees.
705 What though with common plants she dye the weft
Her unskilled hands have woven, she enjoys
Untroubled marriage. Whom the people praise
The dread Erinnys follows with her scourge,
And poverty itself is scarcely glad
710 Until it sees the fortunate o'erthrown.
The man who will not keep the middle course
Ne'er finds his pathway safe. When once he sought
To drive his father's car and bring the day,
The boy kept not the wonted road, but found
715 With wandering wheel a way among the stars
Unknown to flaming Phœbus—in his fall
The world was ruined. While he ploughed through heaven
A middle course, bold Dædalus steered safe
Through peaceful climes, nor gave the sea a name,
720 But Icarus despised his father's flight
And dared to fly beyond the birds themselves,
Close to the sun. He gave an unknown sea

His name. Great deeds are recompensed by ill.
Be others known as fortunate and great,
725 But let no crowd hail me as powerful,
Let no great gale compel my slender ships
To sail broad seas, small boats should keep near shore;
Misfortune passes by the quiet ports
And seeks the ships that ride the deep, whose sails
730 Knock at the clouds. But why with pallid face,
Like mænad drunk with Bacchus, stands the queen?
Speak, wretched one, what grief does Fortune's wheel
Roll round for thee? Though thou refuse to speak
Thy face would tell the sorrows thou wouldst hide.

ACT III

Scene I

Dejanira, Nurse, Chorus.

735   *Dejanira.* A trembling shakes my terror-smitten limbs,
My hair with horror stands erect, and fear
Benumbs the soul till now so madly tossed;
Aghast and terrified, my heart leaps up,
With throbbing veins my liver palpitates;
740 As when the storm-blown sea still tosses high,
Although the day has calmed and languid airs
Breathe softly, so my mind that hitherto
Has swelled with fear is still with dread oppressed;
When once god turns against the fortunate
745 Misfortune follows fast. Such end awaits
Performance of great deeds.
    Nurse. What cruel fate turns now the wheel for thee, O wretched one?
    Dejanira. When I had smeared the robe with Nessus' blood
And sent it, and had sadly turned to seek
750 My chamber, sudden fear, I know not why,
Assailed me—fear of fraud. I'll test the charm.
Fierce Nessus bade me keep the charmed blood
From flame or sun, this artifice itself
Foreboded treachery. Undimmed by cloud,
755 The glowing sun was ushering in bright day;
Fear hardly yet permits me speak! I cast
Within the fiery beams of Titan's light
The blood with which the palla had been wet,
The vestments smeared. The blood I threw away
760 Quivered, and, hardly yet by Phœbus' beams
Made warm, blazed up. I scarce can tell the tale!
As Eurus or warm Notus melts the snow
That slips from sparkling Mimas in the spring;

As the Leucadian headland breaks the waves
765 That roll against it from the Ionian sea,
And all the wearied surf breaks into foam;
Or as the bitter incense melts away
Upon the glowing altar of the gods,
So all the wool was withered and destroyed,
770 And while I wondered, that which gave me cause
For wonder vanished, but the earth was moved
Like foam, and everything the poison touched
Shrank into nothingness. But swift of foot
And terrified, I see my son approach.

Scene II

Hyllus, Dejanira, Nurse, Chorus.

775   *Dejanira.* What tidings dost thou bring me? Speak, I pray.
    Hyllus. Fly, fly, if any hiding-place remains
On earth, or sea, or ocean, in the skies
Or Hades, mother, fly beyond the hand of Hercules.
    Dejanira. 'Tis what my soul presaged!
780   *Hyllus.* Oh, seek the realm of the victorious one,
Seek Juno's shrine, this still is free to thee,
All sanctuaries else are snatched away.
    Dejanira. Oh, speak, what fate awaits me innocent?
    Hyllus. That glory of the earth, the only guard
785 The fates have given to a stricken world
In place of Jove himself, is gone; there burns
Within the trunk and limbs of Hercules
Some plague, I know not what. Who ruled the beasts,
That victor now is conquered, moans, laments.
What further wouldst thou ask?
790   *Dejanira.* The wretched seek
To know their misery; speak, what the fate
That presses on our home? O household gods!
Unhappy household gods! I am indeed
Now widowed, exiled, overwhelmed by fate!
795   *Hyllus.* Thou weepest not alone for Hercules,
The world must mourn him with thee, do not deem,
O mother, that the grief is thine alone;
Already all the race lifts up its voice.
Lo, all the world laments with heavy grief
800 The man thou mournest; thou but sufferest
A sorrow that the whole earth shares with thee,
Thou mourn'st Alcides first, O wretched one, but not alone.
    Dejanira. Yet tell me, tell, I pray,
How near to death lies now my Hercules.
805   *Hyllus.* Death, whom in his own realm he conquered once,

Flies from him, nor dares fate permit the wrong.
Dread Clotho throws aside the threads, perchance,
And fears to end the fates of Hercules.
O fatal day! O day calamitous! Shall great
810 Alcides see no other day?
    Dejanira. What? Dost thou say that he has gone before
To death, the shadow realm, the dark abode?
May I not be the first to die? Oh, speak, if he not yet has fall'n.
    Hyllus. Euboea's land,
815 That swells with mighty headlands, on all sides
Is beaten by the sea; the Hellespont
Smites Cephereus; this side the south wind blows,
But there Aquilo's snowy storm-winds threat,
Euripus turns the restless, wandering tides
820 That seven times roll up and seven times
Drop back ere Titan in the ocean's flood
Merges his weary head. Upon the isle,
High on a cliff which many clouds surround,
An ancient temple of Cenæan Jove
825 Shines forth. When on the altars he had placed
The votive offering and all the grove
Was filled with lowing of the gilded bulls,
He threw aside his tawny lion's skin
All foul with putrid-gore, laid down his club
830 And freed his shoulder from the quiver's weight,
Then shining in thy robe, his shaggy locks
With silver poplar bound, he lit the fire
Upon the altar. 'Take,' he said, 'this gift,
O father, let thy sacred fires shine bright
835 With plenteous incense, which from Saba's trees
The Arabs, wealthy servants of the sun,
Collect. The earth,' he said, 'the sky, the sea,
Are all at peace; all savage beasts subdued,
And I have come a victor. Lay aside
840 Thy thunderbolt.' But even as he prayed,
He groaned, and wondering at himself fell prone.
A horrid clamor filled the air, such noise
As when the bull attempts to fly the wound
Inflicted by the two-edged ax, and feels
845 The sting of steel, and with his mighty roar
Fills all the holy place; or, as Jove's bolt
From heaven thunders, so this groaning rolled
Skyward and seaward; Chalcis heard the sound,
It woke the echoes of the Cyclades,
850 The crags of Cephereus and all the groves
Gave back Alcides' voice. I saw him weep;
The people thought him mad as once he was;
His servants fled; he turned with fiery glance

And sought for one alone among them all—
855 Sought Lichas. He with trembling fingers grasped
The altars, died of fear, and left small room
For vengeance. With his hand the hero grasped
The quivering corpse. 'By this hand, this,' he cried,
'O fates, have I at last been overcome?
860 Has Lichas conquered Hercules? Behold
Another conquest: Lichas overwhelmed
By Hercules. My deeds grow poor and mean.
Be this my latest labor.' 'Mid the stars
He flung him, sprinkled with his blood the clouds.
865 So flies the Getic arrow from the bow
Toward heaven, so the Cretan archer shoots
His shaft, but not so far the arrow flies.
The head was shattered on the cliffs, the trunk
Fell into ocean, there they both abide.
870 'Stay, madness has not seized my mind,' he said,
'This ill is worse than madness or than wrath,
I rage against myself.' He spoke and raged.
He rent apart his joints, with cruel hand
He tore his giant limbs and wounded them;
875 He sought in vain to pluck away the robe.
In this alone I saw Alcides fail,
Yet striving still to tear it off he tore
His limbs themselves, the robe had grown a part
Of Hercules' dread body, with the flesh
880 The garment mingled, nor could one detect
The dread disaster's cause, though cause there is.
Now hardly able to endure his pain,
Wearied he lies and presses with his face
The earth, then longs for ocean, his distress
885 The waves soothe not; he seeks the sounding shore
And leaps into the deep, his servants' hands
Hold back the wandering one. O bitter fate!
We were the equal of great Hercules!
Now to Euboea's shore a vessel bears
890 The hero back, a gentle south wind wafts
Alcides' giant weight; life leaves his limbs,
Night sits upon his eyes.
   Dejanira. Why faint, my soul?
Why art thou so amazed? The crime is done.
Can Jove demand again his son of thee,
895 Or Juno ask her rival? To the world
Thou must atone, render then what thou canst.
The sword shall smite me. Thus it shall be done.
Suits such light punishment such heavy guilt?
O father, with thy thunderbolts destroy
900 Thy sinful child, nor let thy hand be armed

With common weapons. Send that thunderbolt
With which, had not Alcides been thy son,
Thou wouldst have burned the Hydra: as a scourge
Destroy me, as an evil dreaded more
905 Than angry stepdame. Such a bolt send forth
As once at wandering Phaethon was hurled.
I ruined, in Alcides, all the world.
Why ask a weapon of the gods? Now spare
Thy son, O Jove; the wife of Hercules
910 Should be ashamed to beg for death, this hand
Shall give the gift I ask for. Seize the sword:
Yet why a sword? Whatever drags to death
Is sword sufficient. From some soaring cliff
I'll cast me down. This Œta will I choose,
915 This Œta where first shines the newborn day;
From this I'll fling myself, the rugged rocks
Shall cut me into pieces, every stone
Shall take a part of me, my wounded hands
Shall hang upon them, all the mountain side
920 Be crimsoned with my blood. A single death
Is nothing.—Nothing? Can I make it more?
Canst thou not choose the weapon, O my soul,
On which to fall? Oh, might Alcides' sword
Become my couch! 'Twere well to die on this.
925 Is it enough that by my own right hand
I die? Assemble nations of the earth,
Hurl rocks and flaming brands, let no hand fail,
So have I found at last my punishment.
Already cruel kings bear rule unchecked;
930 Now unrestrained, are savage monsters born;
Again the accustomed altars seek to take
A brother's blood for sacrificial gift.
My hand has opened up a path for crime,
Has snatched away the punisher of kings,
935 Of tyrants, beasts, and monsters, 'gainst the gods
I set myself. O wife of thundering Jove,
Dost stay thy hand? Why spare thy lightning's shaft,
Nor imitate thy brother, sending forth
The thunder snatched from Jove? Why slay me not?
940 From thee great glory, honor infinite,
I snatched, O Juno, in thy rival slain.
    Hyllus. Why wouldst thou overthrow a tottering house?
If crime is here it is of error sprung;
And he who sins unwittingly scarce sins.
945   *Dejanira.* Who would remit his fate and spare himself
Deserves to err. 'Tis well that I should die.
    Hyllus. Who longs for death seems guilty.
    Dejanira. Death alone makes guiltless those deceived.

Hyllus. From Titan's beams first fleeing—
Dejanira. Titan flees, himself, from me,
Hyllus. Wouldst part with life?
Dejanira. Alcides would I seek.
Hyllus. He breathes, he yet takes in the vital air.
Dejanira. When Hercules was conquered, he was dead!
Hyllus. Wouldst leave thy son? Thyself cut short thy life?
Dejanira. She lives too long whose son must bury her.
Hyllus. Follow thy husband.
Dejanira. Ah, the faithful wife
Is wont to go before.
Hyllus. Unhappy one,
If thou condemn thyself, thou seemst indeed
To prove thyself the guilty.
Dejanira. He who sins
May not himself annul the punishment.
Hyllus. The life of many a one is spared whose sin
Was done in error, not by his own hand. Who blames his lot?
Dejanira. Whoever draws a lot unfavoring.
Hyllus. The man, forsooth, whose darts
Pierced Megara, whose fiercely raging hand
Sent the Lernæan shaft that slew his sons,
Though thrice a murderer, yet forgives himself.
In Cinyphs' stream, beneath the Libyan skies,
He bathed his hands and washed away his guilt.
Oh, whither art thou driven, wretched one?
Why blame thy hands?
Dejanira. The conquered Hercules
Himself condemns them—one should punish crime.
Hyllus. If I have known Alcides, he will be
Again the victor; treachery, o'erwhelmed,
Will bow before thy Hercules.
Dejanira. His joints are wasted by the Hydra's venomed gore,
The poison eats my husband's giant limbs.
Hyllus. Thou deemst the poison of the strangled snake
Can slay the one who took its evil life?
He killed the dragon, though its teeth were fixed
Within his flesh; and, though his limbs were wet
With flowing venom, as a victor stood.
Can Nessus' blood destroy the one who slew dread Nessus' self?
Dejanira. In vain wouldst thou detain
One doomed to die. The sentence has gone forth
That I must leave the light, enough of life
Has he who meets his death with Hercules.
Nurse. By these white hairs, I ask thee; by this breast
That like a mother's nourished thee, I pray,
Put by thy wounded spirit's heavy threats;
Thrust out the fearful thoughts of dreaded death.

Dejanira. He who persuades the wretched not to die
Is cruel; death is sometimes punishment,
But, oft a blessing, has to many brought forgiveness.
    Nurse. Yet unhappy one, restrain
995 Thy hand, that he may know the crime to be not thine, but error's.
    Dejanira. There I'm free indeed!
I think the gods infernal will absolve.
I am by my own self condemned; these hands
Let Pluto purge. Forgetful, by thy banks,
1000 O Lethe, let me stand, a mournful shade,
Receive my husband! Whosoe'er was bold
For crime, his sin was less than my mistake:
Not Juno's self had dared to snatch from earth
Great Hercules. Some worthy penalty
1005 Prepare; let Sisyphus desert his stone
And let my shoulders roll its heavy weight.
Me let the wandering waters fly, my thirst
The faithless waves delude; I have deserved
That thou shouldst roll me round, O flying wheel
1010 Whereon the king of Thessaly is racked.
Let eager vultures on my entrails feed;
One child of Danaus there lacks—the tale
Of fifty I will fill; O Theban wife,
Take me as thy companion, with worse crime
1015 Than thine this hand is stained, though thou didst slay
Thy children and thy brothers; take thy child,
Mother Althea, take thy child indeed!
Yet no such deed was thine! Ye faithful wives,
Who in the sacred woodland stretches dwell,
1020 Shut me from fields Elysian. If one there
Has sprinkled with her husband's blood her hands,
Unmindful of chaste marriage torch has stood,
A bloody child of Belus, with drawn sword,
She as her own will know me, praise my deed;
1025 That company of wives I well may join;
But they, too, shun my hands so basely stained.
O husband, strong, invincible, my soul
Is innocent, my hands alone are stained.
O mind too credulous! O Nessus false
1030 And of half beastly guile! A concubine
I sought to ruin, but destroyed myself!
Bright Titan, life, that flattering still dost hold
The wretched in the light of day, depart!
Where Hercules is not the light is vile.
1035 I will discharge the penalty for thee,
Will give my life. Shall I prolong that life
Till at thy hand, O husband, I meet death?
Hast any strength? Can thy right hand make tense

>   The bowstring for the sending of the shaft?
> 1040 Or do the weapons fall, thy languid hands
>   No longer draw the bow? O husband brave,
>   If thou art able still to slay, I wait
>   Thy hand, I wait for death; as thou didst dash
>   In pieces guiltless Lichas, slay me now,
> 1045 In other cities scatter me, in worlds
>   To thee unknown; that monstrous things may cease
>   In Arcady, destroy me. Yet from those
>   Thou didst return, O husband!
>   *Hyllus.* Mother cease. Excuse thy deed, an error is not crime.
> 1050   *Dejanira.* If filial piety be truly thine,
>   O Hyllus, smite thy mother. Wherefore now
>   Trembles thy hand? Why turn away thy face?
>   This crime were filial piety indeed.
>   O dastard, dost thou hesitate? This hand
> 1055 Snatched from thee Hercules, destroyed the one
>   Who gave thee for a grandsire thundering Jove;
>   I snatched from thee a glory far more great
>   Than e'er I gave thee when I gave thee light.
>   If crime is new to thee, then learn of me,
> 1060 Hew with the sword my throat, let iron pierce
>   The womb that bore thee, an intrepid soul
>   Thy mother gave thee. Such deed were not crime
>   For thee; by my will, though by thy right hand,
>   I die. Dost fear, O son of Hercules?
> 1065 Wilt thou not, like thy father, crush out ill,
>   Perform great deeds? Prepare thy good right hand!
>   Behold a bosom full of misery
>   Lies bared: strike, I proclaim thee free from crime:
>   The dread Eumenides themselves will spare,
> 1070 I hear their scourges singing. Who is that
>   Whose viperous locks upon her forehead writhe,
>   Who brandishes her sword and shakes her wings?
>   Why dost thou follow me with flaming torch,
>   Megæra? Dost demand the vengeance due
> 1075 For Hercules? I give it. Awful one,
>   Have hell's dread arbiters judged yet my cause?
>   Behold I see the dreadful prison doors.
>   What aged one is he who strives to lift
>   The giant rock upon his wounded back?
> 1080 Behold already does the conquered stone
>   Roll back! Whose members tremble on the wheel?
>   Lo, pallid, dread Tisiphone appears,
>   She charges murder; spare thy blows, I pray!
>   Megæra, spare! Thy Stygian torches stay!
> 1085 The crime was caused by love. But what is this?
>   Earth shakes, the smitten roofs crack, whence these threats?

The whole world falls upon me, everywhere
The nations groan, the universe demands
Its great defender. O ye cities spare!
1090 Ah, whither can I fly? In death alone
I find a harbor for my shipwrecked soul.
I call to witness shining Phœbus' wheel
Of flame, the heavenly ones to witness call:
I die and leave great Hercules on earth.
1095   *Hyllus.* Ah me, she flies amazed; the mother's part
Is finished, she resolved to die, my part
Remains—to snatch her from the shock of death.
O pitiable filial piety!
If I should stay my mother's death, my crime
1100 Is great against my father; yet I sin
Against my mother, suffering her death;
Crime presses either way, yet she must be
Prevented—I must snatch her from this crime.

                    Scene III

                    Chorus.

What Orpheus sang, Calliope's blest son,
1105 When 'neath the heights of Thracian Rhodope
He struck his lute Pierian, is true:
Nothing abides. The rushing waterfall
Silenced its thunder at his music's sound,
The waters ceased their flow, forgot their haste,
1110 And while the rivers thus delayed their course,
The far-off Thracian thought the Hebrus failed.
The woodland brought the winged kind, they came
Resting within the groves, or if a wing
That, roaming, flew through upper air the while,
1115 Was wanting, when it heard the song it dropped.
Mount Athos tore away its crags and came,
Bearing the Centaurs as it moved along,
And stood by Rhodope; its snowy crown
Was melted by the song; the dryad fled
1120 Her oak and hasted to the prophet's side;
The wild beasts at thy singing with their dens
Drew near; the Afric lion sat beside
The fearless flock, nor did the timid does
Tremble before the wolves; the serpent came
1125 From gloomy den, its poisoned sting forgot.
    Nay more, he passed the gates of Tænarus
Among the silent manes, bearing there
His mournful lute, and with his doleful song
He overcame the melancholy gods

1130 Of Erebus, nor feared the Stygian lake
By which the gods make oath; the restless wheel
Stood still, its languid whirling forced to cease;
The heart of Tityus began to grow
The while the vultures listened to the song;
1135 Thou also heardst, O oarsman, and thy boat
Came oarless over the infernal stream;
Then first the aged Phrygian forgot
His raging thirst although the waves stood still,
Nor did he stretch a hand to reach the fruit.
1140 When Orpheus seeking thus the lower world
Poured forth his singing and the restless stone
Was conquered, following the prophet's song,
The Goddesses restored the severed thread
Of fair Eurydice. But Orpheus looked
1145 Behind, forgetful or not deeming true
Restored Eurydice was following him.
He lost the song's reward, she died again
Who hardly had been given back to life.
Then seeking comfort in his song, he sang
1150 These words to Getan folk in mournful strains:
Unchanging laws are given by the gods,
And he who rules the seasons ordereth
Four fleeting changes for the changing year.
Dead Hercules compels us to believe
1155 The Thracian Seer. The Parcæ tie again
The thread of life for none, however much
He may desire; all that has been born
Or shall be dies. When to the world shall come
The time when law is not, the southern sky
1160 Shall bury Libya, and on Afric's sands
Shall fallen lie; the northern sky o'erwhelm
Whatever lies beneath the poles, whate'er
Cold Boreas smites; pale Titan blot the day
From heaven; the royal palace of the sky
1165 In its own ruin drag the rising sun
And setting; death and chaos overtake
The gods; death find at last within itself
Its end. What place will then receive the world?
Shall Tartarus spread wide her doors to take
1170 The shattered heavens? Or is there space enough
Between the earth and heaven—perchance too much?
What place can hold such crime? A single place
Will hold the three realms—earth, and sea, and sky.
    But what great clangor moves the wondering air?
1175 It is the sounding voice of Hercules.

ACT IV

Scene I

Hercules, Chorus.

    Hercules. Bright Titan, turn again thy wearied steeds,
Send night, let perish to the world that day
Whereon I fell, let black cloud shadow day,
So thwart my stepdame. Father, now command
1180 Black chaos to return; their union rent,
The poles should here and there be torn apart;
Why spare the stars? O father, thou hast left
Thy Hercules! Scan well on every side
The sky, O Jove, lest any Gyas hurl
1185 Thessalian crags, and Othrys' weight be made
Too light for great Enceladus. The gates
Of Hell's black prison now are opened wide
By haughty Pluto, and his father's chains
Are broken—to the sky he leads him back.
1190 That son who stood in place of thy dread torch
And thunder, as avenger of the world,
Returns to Styx; and fierce Enceladus
Shall rise and hurl against the gods the weight
With which he now is held to earth. My death
1195 Shall make thy heavenly throne, O father, shake.
Before the giants make thy heavens their spoil,
Beneath the ruins of the universe,
O father, bury me in whom thou losest
The firmament itself.
1200   *Chorus.* Not empty are thy threats, O son of Jove.
Now on Thessalian Ossa Pelion stands,
And Athos piled on Pindus lifts its groves
Amid the starry ether, Typhœus thence
Shall overcome the cliffs and raise on high
1205 From out the Tuscan sea Inarime.
Enceladus, by lightning not yet slain
Shall rend his chimneys in the mountain side
And lift aloft great Etna. Even now
The realm of heaven is in thee destroyed.
1210   *Hercules.* I, I, who conquered death and scorned the Styx
And came again through stagnant Lethe's midst,
With spoil at sight of which bright Titan shrank
And from his fleeing horses almost fell;
Yes, I, whose power the gods' three realms have felt,
1215 I die although no sword has pierced my side,
Although Mount Othrys did not bring my death,

Although no giant form with fierce wide jaws
Has overwhelmed me with all Pindus' ridge.
I fell without a foe and worst of all—
1220 O wretched valor!—Hercules' last day
Shall see no monster prostrate! Woe is me,
I lost my life, but not in noble deeds!
O judge of earth, ye gods who oft have seen
My labors, and thou earth, is it your will
1225 To smite your Hercules with death? O shame
Unmatched! O bitter fate! A woman's hand
To be the author of Alcides' death!
If fate unchanging willed my fate should be
By woman's hand, if such base threads run out
1230 My last of life, ah me, why might I not
By Juno's hatred fall? By woman's hand
I should have fallen, but by one divine.
If this had been too much to ask, ye gods,
An Amazon brought forth 'neath Scythian skies
Might well have vanquished me. What woman's hand
1235 Could conquer me, great Juno's foe? Ah, worse
Thy shame in this, my stepdame! Wherefore call
This day a glad one? What has earth brought forth
To satisfy thy wrath? A woman's hate,
1240 A mortal's, was more powerful than thine.
Till now thou hadst to tolerate the shame
Of finding thou wast not Alcides' peer,
Now thou art by two mortals overcome,
The gods should be ashamed of such revenge!
1245 Would the Nemæan lion with my blood
Had satisfied his thirst, or I, brought low,
Surrounded by the hundred-headed snake,
Had trembled; would that I, had been the prey
Of Nessus, or that I might wretched sit
1250 Forever on an everlasting rock
Conquered among the shades. Fate stood amazed,
While I dragged forth my latest prey and came
From Stygian depths again to light, and broke
The chains of Dis: Death fled me everywhere
1255 That I might lack in death a glorious fate.
O monsters, conquered monsters! Not the dog
Of hell, at sight of day, has dragged me back
To Styx, not underneath the western sky
Has the Iberian Geryon's savage rout
1260 O'ercome me, not twin dragons; woe is me,
How often have I lost a noble death!
What fame shall be my last?

    Chorus. Dost see how courage, conscious of itself,
Shrinks not at Lethe's stream? He does not grieve

1265 At death, but feels ashamed before its cause,
He fain would end his final day of life
Beneath some swelling giant's mighty form,
Of mountain-bearing Titan feel the weight,
Or owe his death to ravening wild beast.
1270 O wretched one, thy hand itself the cause
Why no wild beast or savage monster lives;
What worthy author of Alcides' death
Remains, unless it be thy own right hand?
      Hercules. Alas, what scorpion within my breast,
1275 What cancer from the burning plains turned back
And fixed within my bosom, burns my reins?
My lungs once full of swelling blood are dry,
With burning venom is my heart aflame,
Slow fever dries my blood. The pest first eats
1280 My skin, thence makes an entrance to my limbs;
The poison takes away my sides, it gnaws
My joints and ribs, my very marrow wastes;
Within my empty bones the venom stays,
The bones themselves may not for long endure,
1285 Torn from the ruptured joints the mighty mass
To ruin falls, my giant body fails,
The limbs of Hercules are not enough
To satisfy the pest. How great the ill
That I own great. O dreadful infamy!
1290 Behold, ye cities, see what now remains,
See what remains of that great Hercules!
O father, dost thou recognize thy son?
Did these arms hold to earth the conquered neck
Of the dread lion? Did the mighty bow,
1295 By this hand strung, bring down Stymphalian birds
From out the very stars? Did I o'ertake
With steps of mine the fleet-foot stag that bore
The branching gold upon his radiant front?
Did Calpe, dashed to pieces by these hands,
1300 Let out the sea? By these hands overcome,
Lie low so many beasts, so many crimes,
So many kings? Sat once the dome of heaven
Upon these shoulders? Is this body mine?
This neck? Have I against a falling sky
1305 Stretched forth these hands? Or was the Stygian dog
Dragged by my hand beyond the river Styx?
What sepulcher contains my early strength?
Why call I Jove my father? Why through him
Claim I, unhappy one, my right to heaven?
1310 Already is Amphitryon deemed my sire.
Whatever venom lurks within my veins,
Come forth! Why seek me with a secret wound?

Wast thou within the Scythian sea brought forth,
Beneath the frozen sky? Was Tethys slow,
1315 Or Spanish Calpe on the Moorish shore
Thy author? O dread ill, didst thou come forth
As serpent lifting up thy crested head?
Or something evil, yet unknown to me?
Wast thou from blood of the Lernæan snake
1320 Produced, or wast thou left upon the earth
By Stygian dog? Thou art all ills and none.
What face is thine? Grant me at least to know
By what I die; whatever evil thing
Or savage beast thou art, fight openly.
1325 Who makes for thee a place within my bones?
Lo, from my mangled flesh my hand draws forth
My entrails; deeper yet the way is found
Within the seat of life. O malady,
Alcides' peer! Whence come these bitter groans?
1330 Whence come these tears I feel upon my cheeks?
My eyes unconquerable once, nor wont
To show a tear before my enemies,
At last have learned to weep. O bitter shame!
What day, what land e'er saw Alcides' tears?
1335 How many evils have I borne dry-eyed,
To thee alone what courage yields which slew
So many monsters, thou alone, thou first,
Hast made me weep! More hard than frowning rock,
Or Chalybean steel, or wandering isles,
1340 The stern Symplegades, thy might has crushed
My power, has forced my eyes at last to weep.
O mighty ruler of the skies, the earth
Beholds me weeping, groaning, worst of all,
My stepdame sees me. Ah, once more it burns
1345 My fibers; lo, the fever glows again.
Where now is found for me a thunderbolt?

  Chorus. What cannot suffering conquer? Once more firm
Than Getic Hæmus, than Parrhasian skies
Not milder, to the bitter pain he yields;
1350 He bows his wearied head upon his breast,
From side to side he moves his ponderous weight,
His valor often overcomes his tears.
So with however warm a beam he shine;
Titan can never melt the arctic snows;
1355 The radiance of the ice outshines the torch of blazing Phœbus.

  Hercules. Father, turn thy face
To my complaint, Alcides ne'er before
Asked aid; not when the fruitful Hydra wound
Its fold about my limbs; between hell's lakes
1360 Where black night reigns I stood with death, nor sought

Thy aid; dread monsters, tyrants, kings, I slew,
Nor skyward turned my face. This hand of mine
Was still my pledge, for me no thunderbolt
E'er flashed from out Jove's heaven. This day compels
1365 A prayer from me; it is the first, last time
That he shall hear me pray: one thunderbolt
I ask, one only, but a giant one.
I might have stormed the heavens, but since I deemed
Thou wert my father, I have spared the skies.
1370 O father, whether thou art merciful
Or cruel, to thy son stretch forth thy hand,
Speed now his death and give thyself this fame.
Or if it grieve thee, and thy hand refuse
To do the deed, from the Sicilian peak
1375 Send for the Titans, bearing in their hands
Mount Pindus, or let Ossa with its weight
O'erwhelm me; burst the doors of Erebus
And let Bellona with drawn sword attack:
Send forth fierce, rushing Mars, against me arm
1380 That terrible swift one; he is indeed
My brother, yet my stepdame Juno's son.
Thou too, Athena, by one parent born
The sister of Alcides, hurl thy spear
Against thy brother; supplicating hands
1385 I stretch toward thee, my stepdame, hurl at length
A dart, I pray, against me, I would still
By woman's hand be slain; already calmed,
Already satisfied, why nourish wrath,
Why seek for further vengeance? Suppliant here
1390 Thou seest Hercules; no savage beast,
No land, e'er saw me praying thus to thee.
Now that I need indeed a stepdame's wrath,
Now, does thy anger cease? Dost put aside
Thy hatred? Since I wish for death, thou sparest.
1395 O earth, O cities of the earth, does none
Yield torch or weapon now for Hercules?
Ye rob me of my arms? When I am gone
May no land bring forth monsters wild, the world
Long never for my hand if evil rise,
1400 Or hate be born. Cast at my hapless head
Great stones, and end at last my misery.
O world ungrateful, dost thou now desert?
Hast thou forgot? Thou wouldst have been the prey
Of beasts and monsters hadst thou not borne me.
1405 Ye nations, now snatch hence the rescuer;
This time is given you to recompense
My benefits, death be their great reward.

Scene II

Hercules, Alcmena.

Alcmena. Where shall Alcides' wretched mother go?
Where seek her son? If sure my sight, lo, there
1410 With throbbing heart he lies and passion-tossed.
He groans, 'tis finished. Let me, O my son,
For the last time embrace thee, let me take
Thy fleeting breath. Receive my last embrace.
But where are now thy limbs? where now that neck
1415 That bore the firmament with all its stars?
Who is it leaves to thee so small a part of all thy powers?
  Hercules. O mother, thou indeed
Dost look on Hercules, but on his shade.
O mother, recognize thy son. Why weep,
1420 With eyes turned from me? Wherefore veil thy face?
Dost blush that Hercules is called thy son?
  Alcmena. What land brought forth this new calamity?
What fearful thing has triumphed over thee?
Who is the conqueror of great Hercules?
1425 *Hercules.* Thou seest Alcides slain by woman's guile.
  Alcmena. What guile is great enough to conquer him?
  Hercules. A woman's anger, mother, is enough, Alcmena.
Whence flowed the poison in thy bones and joints?
  Hercules. Her venom found its way through poisoned robe.
1430 *Alcmena.* But where the robe? I see thy naked limbs.
  Hercules. With me it is consumed.
  Alcmena. Can such things be?
  Hercules. Mother, the Hydra and a thousand beasts
Invade my vitals. What flame like to these
Divides Sicilian skies or Lemnos' isles,
1435 Or heaven's burning plain whose fiery zone
Forbids the day to move? Oh, cast me, friends,
Into the channel or the river's midst.
The Ister is not deep enough for me,
Nor mighty ocean's self could quench my flames;
1440 All water fails me, every stream dries up.
Why didst thou send me back again to Jove,
O lord of Erebus? 'Twas right to keep.
Give back thy darkness, show to conquered hell
Alcides; nothing will I carry thence,
1445 Why be afraid again of Hercules?
Death, fear not, come; now Hercules can die.
  Alcmena. Restrain thy tears; at least control thy woe,
Be still invincible before such ills.
As thou art wont, smite death and conquer hell.

1450 *Hercules.* If rugged Caucasus should offer me,
Bound by his chains, a feast for eager birds,
In Scythia that echoes with their cries,
No lamentations would be heard from me;
Or if the wandering Symplegades
1455 Returning crush me 'midst their cliffs, I'd wait
Unmoved their threatened ruin. Should the weight
Of Pindus lie upon me, Hæmus too,
And Athos, where the Thracian seas break high,
And Mimas smitten by Jove's thunderbolts;
1460 My mother, should this universe itself
Fall on me, and above my body blaze
The burning wheel of Phœbus' flaming car,
Ignoble clamor should not overcome
Alcides' courage. Should a thousand beasts
1465 Attack and tear me—here Stymphalian birds
With clangor wild fly at me from the air,
And there the threatening bull with all his force;
All monsters that have been! Or should the groves
Rise everywhere, and cruel Sinis hurl
1470 His mighty limbs against me, scattering me,
I still were silent; savage beasts, nor crimes,
Nor aught that I could meet in open fight
Could force from me a groan.
    Alcmena. Perchance, my son,
No woman's poison scorches now thy limbs,
1475 But all thy heavy tasks, thy labors long,
Now make thee tremble with some dread disease.
    Hercules. Where is the sickness, where? Does any ill
Exist upon the earth with me till now?
Let it come hither, hand me now a bow.
1480 These naked hands suffice. Come on! Come on!
    Alcmena. Ah me, his overwhelming pain destroys
His senses. Take away his darts, I pray,
Snatch hence his murderous arrows, I beseech.
His cheeks suffused with fire threat dreadful crime.
1485 What place of hiding can I, aged one,
Seek out? This rage is madness. Hercules
Alone can rule himself. Why, foolish one,
Seek flight or hiding? By a hero's hand
Alcmena merits death; so let me die,
1490 E'er anything ignoble bids me fall,
E'er evil hands may triumph over me.
But see, by troubles weakened, pain binds up
His wearied limbs with sleep, his bosom heaves
With heavy sighs. Be merciful, ye gods!
1495 If ye refuse me my illustrious son,
At least preserve its savior to the world.

Drive out his bitter pain, let Hercules
Renew his ancient strength.

Scene III

Hercules, Hyllus, Alcmena.

Hyllus. O cruel light! O day so full of crime!
1500 The thunderer's daughter dies, his son lies low,
The grandchild only lives. He lost his life,
Slain by my mother's hand, by treachery
Was she deceived. Alas, what man grown old
Through all the changes of the years has known
1505 In all his life such sorrows? One day snatched
Both parents from me. But of other ills
I will not speak: great Hercules is dead.
  Alcmena. Be silent, noble son of Hercules,
Grandson of sad Alcmena—for perchance
1510 Long sleep will overcome Alcides' ills.
But see, repose deserts his wearied mind,
He is recalled to sickness, I to grief.
  Hercules. What see I? Trachin with its rugged cliffs?
Or, placed among the stars, have I at length
1515 Escaped mortality? Who opens heaven?
I see thee, father; thee behold I too,
My stepdame, reconciled. What heavenly sound
Strikes on my ear? Great Juno calls me son.
I see bright heaven's shining realm, I see
1520 The sun's encircling road with Phœbus' car.
But what is this? Who closes heaven to me?
Who drives me from the stars? But now I felt
The breath of Phœbus' car, almost I stood
In heaven itself. 'Tis Trachin that I see,
1525 Who brings me back to earth? I see night's couch,
The shadows call me hither. Only now
Mount Œta stood below me; all the world
Was spread beneath. How happily, O pain,
Thou wast forgot! Thou forcest me to speak,
1530 Oh, spare me! take away this voice from me!
This gift, this benefit, thy mother gave,
Hyllus. Would that with my lifted club
I might have beaten out her wicked life,
As once beside the snowy Caucasus
1535 I tamed the Amazon. O Megara,
Much loved, wast thou my wife when I was mad?
Give back my bow and club; my hand is stained,
I will with glory wipe away the spot,
And Hercules' last toil shall by his wife be given.

1540 *Hyllus.* Father, curb thy wrathful threats;
Tis finished, she has suffered, she has paid
The penalty thou fain wouldst from her claim.
Dead lies my mother, by her own hand dead.
  Hercules. Thou, trouble, still abidest at my side;
1545 She by the hand of wrathful Hercules
Deserved to perish, Lichas is bereft
Of fitting comrade; wrath compels me rage
Against her lifeless body. Why should that
Escape my vengeance? Let the wild beasts take their food.
1550 *Hyllus.* She suffered most, thou wouldst have wished
Somewhat to lighten that her load of woe;
Grieving for thee, she died by her own hand.
A heavier penalty than thou wouldst ask,
She suffered. But thou liest overcome
1555 Not by the baseness of thy cruel wife,
Not by my mother's treachery; thy pain
Was heaped on thee by Nessus whom thy shaft
Deprived of life; the robe was dipped in blood
Of that half beast, half man, and Nessus now demands revenge.
1560 *Hercules.* He has it, 'tis complete.
My life is finished, this day is my last,
The prophet oak foretold this fate to me,
And the Parnassian grot that with its groans
Shook the Cirrhean temple: 'Thou shalt fall,
1565 Alcides, conquered by the hand of one
Whom thou hast conquered; this shall come to pass
When earth and sea and hell are overcome.'
I make no plaint, 'twas right this end be given
Lest any one should live to boast himself
1570 Alcides' conqueror. Now comes at length
A noble death, of great and wide renown,
And worthy me. This day shall I see feared.
Let all the woods be cut, let Œta's groves
Be dragged together that a mighty pyre
1575 Receive me; but before I come to die,
Thou, Pœan's son, perform for me, dear youth,
The melancholy office, let the day
Be set ablaze with the Herculean flames.
To thee, I make, O Hyllus, my last prayer:
1580 There is, within, a noble captive maid,
She bears her kingly lineage in her face,
The virgin Iole, Eurytis' child;
Receive her for thy bride. I, stained with blood,
Victorious, bore her from her home and land.
1585 To the unhappy maid I've given naught
But Hercules, and he is snatched away.
Jove's grandchild she shall wed, Alcides' son,

And find a recompense for all her woes.
Whatever seed she has conceived by me
¹⁵⁹⁰ To thee she shall bring forth. O mother dear,
Forbear thy grief, Alcides lives for thee.
My courage makes thy rival to be deemed
A stepdame; either certainly is known
The night on which Alcides was begot,
¹⁵⁹⁵ Or else my father was a mortal man.
Yet though, perchance, my lineage be feigned,
I have deserved such noble parentage,
My glorious deeds brought honor to the skies,
My mother to Jove's glory brought me forth.
¹⁶⁰⁰ And if my father, though great Jove himself,
Rejoices in his fatherhood, restrain
Thy tears, O mother, proudest shalt thou be
Among Argolic mothers; no such son
Has she who wields the scepter of the skies,
¹⁶⁰⁵ Great Juno, wife of thundering Jove, brought forth;
She envied mortal though the heaven was hers,
She longed to call great Hercules her son.
Now Titan, thou must run alone thy course,
I who have been thy comrade everywhere
¹⁶¹⁰ Seek now the manes and Tartarean shades;
Yet to the depths of hell I bear this fame:
No evil slew Alcides openly
Alcides conquered openly all ill.

Scene IV

Chorus.

O radiant Titan, glory of the world,
¹⁶¹⁵ At whose first shining wearied Hecate leaves
Her night-dark car, say to the Sabean lands
That lie beneath thy dawning, say to Spain
That lies beneath thy setting, say to all
That suffer underneath the Greater Bear,
¹⁶²⁰ Or palpitate beneath the burning wheel:
Alcides hastes to everlasting shades
And to the kingdom of the sleepless dog
Whence he has once returned. Let clouds surround
Thy brightness, look upon the mourning lands
¹⁶²⁵ With pallid face and veil thy head with mists;
When, where, beneath what sky, mayst thou behold
Another Hercules? Whose hand shall earth
Invoke, if e'er in Lerna should arise
A hundred-headed Hydra scattering bane,
¹⁶³⁰ Or any Erymanthian boar disturb

The quiet of Arcadia's ancient race;
Or any child of Thracian Rhodope,
More harsh than snowy Helice, make wet
With human blood its stables? Who will give
₁₆₃₅ Peace to a timorous people if the gods
Be angry and command new monsters rise?
Like other mortals now he lies whom earth
Produced the equal of the Thunderer.
Let all the world reecho sounds of woe;
₁₆₄₀ Your bare arms beat, ye women, let your hair
Fall loose; and let the temples of the gods
Shut fast their portals, open not their gates
But for my fearless stepdame; to the shores
Of Styx and Lethe goest thou, from whence
₁₆₄₅ No keel shall bring thee back; unhappy one,
Thyself a shade, thou goest with fleshless arms,
Pale face, and drooping shoulders, to the shades
From whence thou camest once victorious,
When thou hadst conquered death. Nor thee alone
₁₆₅₀ Shall that ship bear. Yet not with common shades,
With the twin Cretan kings and Æacus
Shalt thou be judge of men, smite tyrants down.
Spare, O ye mighty ones, refrain your hands;
'Tis great indeed to keep your swords unstained,
₁₆₅₅ And while you reign to keep the realm in peace.
But valor has a place among the stars.
Wilt thou thy seat to northward find, be placed
Where Titan carries fervid heat? Wilt shine
Within the mild west whence thou mayest hear
₁₆₆₀ Calpe reëcho with the sounding waves?
Where in the heavens serene wilt thou be set?
What place will be secure among the stars
When Hercules has come? O father, grant,
A seat from the dread lion far removed
₁₆₆₅ And from the burning cancer, lest the stars
Should tremble at thy coming and forsake
Their ancient laws, and Titan be afraid.
While flowers blossom with the spring's warm days,
While winter cuts the foliage from the groves,
₁₆₇₀ Or warmth calls back the foliage to the groves;
While with the flying autumn falls the fruit,
No flight of time shall snatch thee from the world:
Thou shalt be mate to Phœbus and the stars.
Sooner shall cornfields flourish in the deep,
₁₆₇₅ The straits shall sooner whisper with soft waves,
The constellation of the icy bear
Shall sooner leave the heavens and enjoy
Forbidden seas than nations shall forget

　　　　　To sing thy praises. Father of the world,
1680　We wretched ones entreat thee, let no beasts
　　　　　Be born, no monsters, nor the troubled world
　　　　　Fear cruel leaders, let us not be ruled
　　　　　By any court that deems the dignity
　　　　　Of empire lies in ever-threatening sword.
1685　If any monster rise again on earth,
　　　　　We seek a savior for the orphaned world.
　　　　　Ah, hear! heaven thunders, does his father mourn
　　　　　Alcides? Is the cry the voice of gods,
　　　　　Or timid stepdame? Does great Juno flee
1690　At sight of Hercules? Or 'neath his load
　　　　　Does Atlas tremble? Are the dreaded shades
　　　　　Now shaken by the sight of Hercules?
　　　　　Or does the hell-hound rend away his chains
　　　　　And fly in fear that face? We are deceived,
1695　Behold with joyous look comes Pœan's son
　　　　　Alcides' follower; on his shoulder clangs
　　　　　The well-known shafts and quiver.

ACT V

Scene I

Philoctetes, Nurse, Chorus.

　　　　　Nurse. Tell, youth, I pray, the fate of Hercules,
　　　　　Say with what mien Alcides met his death.
1700　　　*Philoctetes.* With such a mien as no one e'er met life.
　　　　　Chorus. So gladly did he mount his funeral pyre?
　　　　　Philoctetes. He showed that flames are naught, what is there left
　　　　　On earth which Hercules has not o'ercome? Lo, all is conquered.
　　　　　Chorus. 'Midst the flames what place for mighty deeds?
1705　　　*Philoctetes.* One evil in the world
　　　　　He had not yet o'ercome, but he has ruled
　　　　　The fire, this also to the savage beasts
　　　　　He adds, among the tasks of Hercules shall fire be placed.
　　　　　Chorus. I pray thee, now unfold
1710　The way in which the flames were overcome.
　　　　　Philoctetes. Each sorrowing hand cut Œta's forests down,
　　　　　The beech-tree lost its wealth of shade, and lay
　　　　　Hewn from its base; one strong hand felled the pine
　　　　　Whose top reached heaven, and called it from the clouds,
1715　Falling it moved the rocks and with it bore
　　　　　The lesser trees. An oak with spreading top,
　　　　　Like that which whispers in Chaonia,
　　　　　Shut out the sun and stretched on either side
　　　　　Its boughs; the great tree, pierced by many wounds,

1720 Cried out and broke the wedges, the dulled steel
Recoiled, the ax was injured, nor was found
Inflexible enough; but, stirred at length,
The oak bore ruin with it in its fall,
And everywhere the place admits the sun.
1725 The birds are driven from their resting-place
And eddying through the sunlight where the grove
Has fallen, querulous, on wearied wing
They seek their homes. Already every tree
Resounds, the sacred oak-trees even feel
1730 The hand that holds the dreaded ax, the grove
Is no avail to save the holy place.
The forest forms a mound, alternate beams
Raise to the skies a pyre all too small
For Hercules. The pine and hardy oak
1735 And shorter ilex carry up the flames,
And poplars wont to ornament the brow
Of Hercules fill up the funeral pyre.
As roars a mighty lion lying sick
In Afric forests, he is borne along;
1740 Who will believe him carried to the flames?
His glance was seeking for the stars, not fires.
As Œta's soil he pressed and with his glance
Scanned all the pyre, mounting upon the beams
He broke them. For his bow he asked, then said:
1745 'Take this, O son of Pœas, take the gift
Of Hercules; the Hydra felt these shafts,
By these were slain the foul Stymphalian birds,
And every evil that from far I slew.
O youth, be happily victorious,
1750 Nor ever send without avail these shafts
Against a foe. Or, shouldst thou wish to bring
The birds from out the clouds, let birds descend,
Let slaughter always follow thy sure shaft,
Nor ever let this bow thy right hand fail;
1755 Well has it learned to free the shaft and give
A sure direction to the arrow's flight,
Sent from the string the dart shall never fail
To find the way. I pray thee, bring the fire,
And light for me the funeral torch. This club,'
1760 He said, 'which never hand but mine shall bear,
Shall burn with me; this mighty weapon go
With Hercules. This too thou mightest have,'
He said, 'if thou couldst wield it; it may aid
Its master's funeral pyre.' And then he asked
1765 That with him might be burned the shaggy spoil
Of the Nemæan lion; with the spoil
The pyre was hid. The throng about him groaned,

       And sorrow filled the eyes of all with tears.
       His mother, raging with her grief, laid bare
1770   Her ample bosom, even to the womb,
       And smote with heavy blows her naked breasts,
       And, moving with her cries the gods themselves
       And Jove, with woman's shrieks the place she filled.
       'O mother, thou mak'st base Alcides' death,
1775   Restrain thy tears, and let thy woman's grief
       Turn inward. Why shall Juno know one day
       Of joy because thou weepest? She is glad
       To see her rival's tears. Thy feeble heart
       Control, O mother, it is sin that thou
1780   Shouldst tear the womb and breast that nourished me.'
       Then roaring mightily, as when he led
       The dreaded hell-hound through Argolic streets,
       What time he came again from conquered Dis
       And trembling death, a victor over hell,
1785   Upon his funeral pyre he laid him down.
       What conqueror at his triumph ever stood
       So joyous in his car? What tyrant prince
       With such a glance e'er gave the nations laws?
       How calmly did he bear his fate! Our tears
1790   Were dried, our sorrow, smitten, fell away;
       None raised lament for him who was to die.
       'Twere shame to weep. Although sex bade her mourn,
       Alcmena stood with cheeks unwet with tears,
       A mother almost equal to her son.
1795   *Chorus.* And did he, on the point of death, lift up
       To heaven no invocation to the gods,
       Nor look toward Jove in prayer?
           Philoctetes. Secure he lay
       And, scanning heaven with his eyes, he sought
       The part from whence his father should look down.
1800   Then stretching forth his hand he said; 'That one
       For whom the night was joined to night, and day
       Deferred, is father to me. Whencesoe'er,
       O father, thou dost look upon thy son,
       Since either mete of Phœbus, and the race
1805   Of Scythians, and every burning strand
       Where glows the day now praise me; since the earth
       Has peace, no lands cry out, and none pollute
       The altars, since no evil thing remains,
       I pray thee, take this spirit to the stars.
1810   Not death, nor hell, nor mournful realm of Dis
       Could fright me; but to be a shade and pass
       To those divinities that I o'ercame,
       O father, makes me blush. Divide the clouds,
       Lay wide the day that eyes of gods may see

1815 Alcides burning. Thou canst close to him
The stars and heaven: vainly would one seek
To force thy will, O father, but if grief
May lift one prayer, then ope the Stygian lake
And give me back to death; but prove me first
1820 Thy son, let this day make it evident
That I am worthy of the stars. All deeds
Till now are poor, this day shall bring to light
Alcides, or reject him.' Having said,
He asked for fire. 'Up, friend of Hercules,'
1825 He said, 'be swift, snatch the Œtæan torch.
Why trembles thy right hand? What, timorous one,
Dost shrink before the dreaded infamy?
Give back the quiver, coward, slow, and weak!
That hand bend bow of mine? Why pales thy cheek?
1830 With face and courage such as thou dost see
Alcides wear, apply the torch; base one,
Consider him who is about to die.
Lo, now my father calls, he opens heaven.
I come!' His face was changed; with trembling hand
1835 I placed the glowing torch, the flames fled back,
The torches shrank away and shunned his limbs,
But Hercules pursued the flying flames.
Thou wouldst have thought that Athos, Caucasus,
Or Pindus was ablaze; no groan was heard,
1840 But loudly roared the flames. O iron heart!
Huge Typhon placed upon that funeral pyre
Had groaned, and fierce Enceladus himself
Who tore from earth and on his shoulders bore
Mount Ossa. But from out the hot flames' midst
1845 He rose half burned and mangled, gazed unawed.
'Now, mother, thou dost show thyself indeed
Alcides' parent,' said he, I thus to stand
Beside his pyre; 'tis meet to mourn him thus.'
Amid the smoke and threatening flame he stood
1850 Unmoved and steadfast, shrinking not, but bright,
And spoke encouraging and warning words.
To every ministrant he gave new strength,
You would have thought himself informed the blaze.
The people stood amazed and hardly deemed
1855 The flames were flames indeed, so calm his front,
Such majesty was his. He did not seek
To speed his burning, but when he believed
Sufficient fortitude in death was shown,
Into the hottest blaze he dragged the beams
1860 That seemed the least afire, and where the flame
Was brightest there the fearless hero stood.
He veiled his face with flames, his heavy beard

Was bright with fire, the threatening blaze leaped up
And shone about his head; Alcmena groaned
And tore her loosened hair.

Scene II

Philoctetes, Alcmena, Chorus.

Alcmena. Ye gods, stand now in awe of death!
So few Alcides' ashes, to this little dust
Has shrunk that giant! Ah, how great a one
Has fallen, Titan, into nothingness!
Ah me, this aged bosom shall receive
Alcides, here his tomb. Lo, Hercules
Scarce fills his urn, how light for me the weight
Of him who lightly bore the vault of heaven.
O son, to that far realm and Tartarus
Once hast thou journeyed and returned from thence;
Wilt thou perchance again from Styx return?
Not that again with spoil thou mayst return,
And Theseus owe again the light to thee,
But yet, perchance, alone? Can all the world
Placed o'er thy shades suffice to hold thee down?
Or Cerberus be able to constrain?
Wilt thou smite down the gates of Tænarus?
Within what portals shall thy mother pass?
Which way shall death be found? Thou goest now
To Hades, never more to come again.
Why waste the day in tears? Why, wretched life,
Dost thou still bide with me? Why wish for light?
Can I bear Jove another Hercules?
Or will Alcmena by another son
Like him be mother called? O happy, thou,
My Theban husband, thou didst enter in
The realm of Tartarus while still thy son
Was flourishing; perchance the gods of hell
Fear'd when thou camest, since, though not indeed
Alcides' father, thou wast known as such.
What country can I seek in this my age—
I, whom harsh tyrants hate (if any such
Still live)? Me miserable! If a son
Laments a father, let him seek revenge
On me. Let all attack me; if a child
Of wild Busiris or Antæus lives
And terrifies the tropic zone, I stand
A ready prey; if any seek revenge
For cruel Diomedes' Thracian herd,
Upon my members let the dread flock feed.

Perchance an angered Juno seeks revenge.
All cause for wrath is gone, secure at last,
She shall be free from conquered Hercules.
Her rival yet remains. I cannot pay
1910 The penalty she seeks. My mighty son
Has made his mother terrible. What place
Is left? What land, what kingdom, or what zone
In all the universe will dare defend,
Or to what hiding can a mother go
1915 Who is through thee so famed? Shall I seek out
My land and fallen home? Eurystheus rules
In Argos. Shall I seek the Theban realm?
Ismenus' stream? The couch where chosen once
I once saw Jove? Oh, happy had I felt
1920 Jove's bolt! Oh, would Alcides had been torn
Untimely from my womb! Now comes the hour
To see my son Jove's son through glory gained.
Would that this too were given: to know what fate
Might snatch me hence. O son, what nation lives
1925 That thinks on thee? ungrateful every race!
Shall I seek Cleon? The Arcadian realm?
The lands ennobled by thy glorious deeds?
There fell the serpent, there the savage birds,
There fell the cruel king, there was o'ercome
1930 By thee the lion which, since thou art dead,
Now dwells in heaven. If earth had gratitude,
All would defend Alcmena for thy sake.
Shall I repair to Thrace and Hebrus' shores?
Those lands were also by thy merits saved,
1935 The stables and the realm were overcome,
The cruel king is prostrate, peace is there.
What land indeed enjoys not peace through thee?
Where shall I, old, unhappy, seek a tomb?
All worlds contended for thy funeral pyre,
1940 What people, or what temple, or what race
Seek now the ashes of great Hercules?
Who asks, who wishes this, Alcmena's load?
What sepulcher, O son, suffices thee?
What tomb? This whole round world to which thy fame
1945 Shall give thee title! Why afraid, my soul?
Thou hast Alcides' ashes, hast his bones.
Thy aid, thy all-sufficing aid, shall be
His ashes, and his death make kings afraid.
    Philoctetes. O mother of illustrious Hercules,
1950 Although thy sorrow for thy son is due,
Restrain thy tears; he must not be bewailed,
Nor deeply mourned, whose valor banished death;
His valor is eternal and forbids that Hercules be mourned.

   Alcmena. My savior lost,
1955 Shall I, his mother, cease to mourn for him?
    Philoctetes. Thou dost not mourn alone, the earth and sea,
  And every place where purple day looks down
  On either ocean from her shining car mourns too.
   Alcmena. O wretched mother! In one son
1960 How many have I lost! I lacked a realm,
  Yet might have given one. I had no prayer,
  I only of all mothers earth brought forth;
  I asked the gods for nothing while my son
  Still lived. What was there that Alcides' zeal
1965 Could not bestow? What god could aught deny?
  In that hand lay fulfillment of each wish;
  Whatever Jove refused Alcides gave.
  What mortal mother e'er bore such a child?
  One mother was transformed to stone who stood
1970 Cut off from all her offspring and bewailed
  Twice seven children. To how great a band
  My son was equal! Until now there lacked
  A great example of sad motherhood:
  Alcmena gives it. Mothers, mourn no more,
1975 Although persistent grief till now compelled
  Your tears; though heavy sorrow turn to stone,
  Give place to my misfortunes. Up, sad hand,
  Smite now the aged breast! Canst thou enough,
  Thou humbled, aged woman, mourn his loss
1980 Whom all the world laments? Yet beat thy breast,
  Although thy arms are weary. Though the gods
  Be jealous of thy mourning, call the race
  To mourn with thee.
  Go smite your bosoms for Alcmena's son
1985 And Jove's; for his conception one day died
  And Eos was delayed for two long nights.
  One greater than the light itself has died.
  All nations, smite your breasts; your tyrants harsh
  He forced to penetrate the Stygian realm
1990 And put aside the dripping sword; mourn now
  His merits, let the whole world cry aloud.
  Blue Crete, dear land of Thundering Jove, lament
  Alcides, let thy hundred people mourn.
  Curetes, Corybantes, in your hands
1995 Clash now Idæan weapons, it is right
  To mourn him thus; now beat your breasts indeed,
  For Hercules is dead; he is not less,
  O Crete, than is thy Thunderer himself.
  Weep ye Alcides' death, Arcadian race,
2000 A race ere Dian's birth. Reëcho blows,
  Parrhasian and Nemæan mountain tops,

Let Menala give back the heavy sound.
The bristles scattered on your field demand
Groans for the great Alcides, and the birds
2005 Whose feathers veiled the day, whom his shaft slew.
Argolic peoples weep; Cleonæ, weep—
There once my son's right hand the lion slew
That terrified your city. Beat your breasts,
Bistonian matrons, let cold Hebrus' stream
2010 Give back the sound, lament for Hercules;
Your children are no longer born to feed
The bloody stables, on your flesh no more
Shall feast the savage herd. Weep, all ye lands
From fierce Antæus freed, the region snatched
2015 From cruel Geryon. Beat with me your breasts,
Ye wretched nations, let the blows be heard
By either Tethys. Weep Alcides' death,
O company divine of heaven's swift vault;
My Hercules upon his shoulders bore
2020 Your sky, O gods, when from his load set free
The giant Atlas, who was wont to bear
Olympus and its shining stars, had rest.
Where now, O Jove, thy lofty seat, where now
Thy promised dwelling in the skies? Alas!
2025 Alcides as a mortal died; alas,
As mortal is consumed. How oft he spared
Thy fires, how oft he spared thy thunderbolt!
Ah, deem me Semele and hurl at me
Thy torch! Hast thou, O son, already found
2030 The fields Elysian whither nature calls
The nations? Or does black Styx close the way,
Because of captured Cerberus, and fate
Detain thee at the outer gate of Dis?
What tumult now possesses all the shades?
2035 Flees now the boatman with receding skiff?
Through all the wondering realm of death flees now
Thessalia's Centaur? Does the Hydra fear
And hide its serpents underneath the waves?
Do all thy labors fear thee, O my son?
2040 Ah, no; I am deceived, am mad, I rave;
Nor shades nor manes fear thee, thy left arm
No longer bears th' Argolic lion's spoil,
The fearful pelt with all its tawny mane,
Nor do the wild beast's teeth entrench thy brows;
2045 Thy quiver is another's and thy shafts
A weaker hand lets fly; unarmed thou goest,
O son, through Hades, never to return.

Scene III

Hercules, Philoctetes, Alcmena, Chorus.

Hercules. I hold a seat within the heavenly realm,
Why with thy mourning dost thou bid me feel
2050 Once more the pang of death? I pray thee, spare!
Already had my valor made a way
Up to the stars, yes, to the very gods.
  Alcmena. Whence, whence the sound that strikes our startled ear?
Whence comes the sound forbids my tears? I know
2055 That Chaos is o'ercome. Dost thou return,
O son, again from Styx? Not once alone
Is cruel death subdued? Hast thou again
Been conqueror over death, and Charon's boat,
And hell's sad pools? Does languid Acheron
2060 Afford a passage and permit return
To thee alone? Nor even after death
The fates constrain thee? Or does Pluto close
For thee the way, and tremble for his throne?
I surely saw thee on the blazing woods,
2065 When raged the giant flames against the sky,
Why does the far abode no longer hold
Thy shade? Why do the manes feel dread fear?
Art thou a shade too terrible for Dis?
  Hercules. The fear of dark Cocytus held me not,
2070 The dread boat has not borne my shade across;
Forbear thy mourning, mother; once indeed
I saw the land of death, whate'er of man
I may have had was purged away by fire,
The part my father gave is borne to heaven's
2075 Thy part was given to the flames. Weep not
As one who weeps a deedless son, 'tis meet
To mourn th' unworthy; valor starward tends,
But fear toward death. O mother, from the stars
Alcides speaks. To thee the cruel king,
2080 Borne in thy car thou shalt lift up proud head.
'Tis meet that I should seek celestial climes,
Alcides once again has conquered hell.
  Alcmena. Stay, but a moment stay!
He's passed from sight,
2085 He has departed, he is starward borne.
Am I deceived, or do I dream I saw
My son? My sad heart is incredulous.
Thou art a god, the heavens evermore
Shall hold thee; in thy triumph I believe.
2090 The Theban realm I'll seek and there will sing

The glory of the new divinity.
Chorus. Never shall glorious valor be borne down
To Stygian shades, the brave forever live,
Nor shall the cruel fates through Lethe's stream
2095 E'er drag them; but when comes the final hour
Of life's last day, then glory shall lay wide
The pathway to the gods. Be present still,
Thou mighty victor over savage beasts,
Thou who hast given peace to all the world;
2100 Now from whatever place, behold our land,
And if a monster with new face should shake
The world with terror, with thy three-forked bolts
Break him in pieces, hurl thy lightning shafts
More boldly then thy father Jove himself.

OCTAVIA

DRAMATIS PERSONÆ

Nero.
Seneca.
Prefect of the Palace.
Octavia.
Poppæa.
Ghost of Agrippina.
Nurse of Octavia.
Nurse of Poppæa.
Messenger.
Chorus of Roman Women.

Scene: *Nero's Palace.*

OCTAVIA

ACT I

Scene I

Octavia.

Now bright Aurora, shining in the heavens,
Has put the stars to flight; with radiant beams
The sun is rising, giving back to earth
Clear day. Sore burdened by thy many griefs,
5 Return again to thy accustomed plaints,
Let them exceed the watery Halcyon's tears
And sad Pandion's winged children's cries,
Thy fortunes are than theirs more hard to bear.

O mother, primal cause of all my woe,
10 Ever for thee thy daughter must lament;
Hear her sad cries, if in the land of shades
Thou yet mayst hear. Would Clotho's aged hand
Had cut my thread of life ere I had seen
With bitter grief thy wounds, had seen thy face
15 Defiled with loathsome blood. O light of day,
Ever to me calamitous, since then
Thou art, O light, more hated than the dark.
I must obey a cruel stepdame's laws,
Her hostile will, her glances full of hate.
20 That baleful fury to my marriage-bed
Bore Stygian torches, blotted out thy life;
My father, whom the whole round world obeyed,
Even beyond the ocean, before whom
The Britains, to our leaders else unknown,
25 Fled. Father, woe is me, thou liest now
O'erwhelmed by thy wife's craft. Thy house, thy child,
Are slaves—a tyrant's captives.

Scene II

Octavia, Nurse.

Nurse. Whoe'er thou art who by the novelty
And outward splendor of the treacherous court
30 Art captive led, in admiration lost,
Behold great Claudius' house and lineage
Wrecked by one blow of skulking Fortune's hand.
The world was subject to his rule, the sea
Obeyed him long and, though unwillingly,
35 Floated his vessels. Lo, the man who first
Subdued the Britains, covered unknown straits
With countless fleets, and moved 'mid barbarous tribes
And over cruel waters all unharmed;
He by his wife's crime fell, she by her son's,
40 Whose brother now lies dead by poison killed.
Deeply the wretched wife and sister mourns,
Nor can she hide her hate though urged by fear
Of that harsh man—with equal hate they glow.
Her husband (such the chaste have ever shunned)
45 Burns with an impious flame. In vain I strive
With love and loyalty to soothe her grief,
My counsel is by boundless woe made naught,
Nor can her generous spirit be controlled,
It only serves to give her grief new strength.
50 Alas, how base a crime my fear foresees,
May god avert it!

Octavia. Oh, my bitter fate,
Equalled by none! Would that I might endure
Thy woes, Electra; thou mightst weep the fall
Of thy dead father, and mightst see the crime
55 Punished by thy avenging brother's hand,
A brother whom thy love had snatched from harm,
Thy faithfulness concealed. But fear forbids
That I should mourn my parents snatched away
By cruel fate, forbids that I should weep
60 A brother's death—in him my only hope
Was found, brief solace of my crowding woes.
Now am I left the shadow of a name
Once great, spared but for sorrow!
    Nurse. Hark, the voice of my sad nursling strikes upon my ears.
65 What, do thy slow feet cease to bear thee on into the bridal chamber, aged one?
    Octavia. O nurse, behold my tears, my grief's sure sign.
    Nurse. Poor child, what day will free thee from thy care?
    Octavia. The day that sends me to the Stygian shades.
    Nurse. Far be the omen.
70   *Octavia.* Not thy prayers control my lot, but fate.
    Nurse. A milder god will give a happier time.
With soft compliance win thy husband's love.
    Octavia. Ah, sooner could I tame
The savage lion or the tiger fierce,
75 Than that wild tyrant's cruel heart, he hates
Those sprung of noble blood, he scorns alike
The gods and men. He knows not how to wield
The fortune his illustrious father gave
By means of basest crime. And though he blush,
80 Ungrateful, from his cursed mother's hands
To take the empire, though he has repaid
The gift with death, yet shall the woman bear
Her title ever, even after death.
    Nurse. Restrain the words that speak thy spirit's rage,
85 And let thy voice be silenced by thy fear.
    Octavia. Whatever may be borne I will endure.
Nothing but bitter death can end my woes.
A mother slain, a father basely killed,
Reft of my brother, sunk in misery,
90 Bowed down by sorrow, by my husband's hate
Oppressed, the servant of my slaves, no more
Can I enjoy the light. With throbbing heart
It is not death I fear but worse than death.
Be but my death unmingled with reproach
95 I would be glad to die; 'tis worse than death
To look upon the tyrant's swelling pride,
His face so terrible to wretched me,
To feel the hated kisses of my foe.

Since the great sorrow of my brother's death,
100 Murdered so basely, scarce can I endure
The author of that murder, him who holds
My brother's kingdom and enjoys the crown.
How oft my brother's spirit comes to me
When, worn with weeping, slumber seals my eyes
105 And holds my weary limbs: with fury's torch
He armed weak hands, and in his brother's face
He waved it; then again in fear he fled
Into my chamber, by the foe pursued,
And, clinging to me, through my side received
110 The sword. Then shuddering terror broke my sleep,
And fear and grief and misery returned.
Besides all this that haughty concubine,
Made glorious with the plunder of our house,
For whom the son placed on the Stygian boat
115 His mother—shipwrecked, from the ocean saved,
He, harsher than the billows, with the sword
Slew her—what hope of safety can be mine
After such crime? That hostile victress stands
And threats my marriage-bed, with hate of me
120 She burns, and for adultery's recompense
Asks that the husband give his true wife's head.
O father, come from Hades bringing help
To thy poor child who calls to thee for aid;
Or through the riven earth lay bare the Styx
And swiftly bear me thither.
125   *Nurse.* All in vain
Thou callest on thy father's ghost for aid.
In vain, O wretched one! Among the dead
No more for any child of his he cares,
Who could prefer a child of alien blood
130 To his own son, who took his brother's child
To wife—an impious marriage whence has sprung
Full many a crime, murder, and treachery,
Desire of rule, and thirst for noble blood.
The son-in-law was slain, a sacrifice
135 In honor of the father's marriage-bed,
Lest by thy marriage he should grow too strong.
O monstrous sin! Falsely accused of crime,
And to a woman made a sacrifice,
Silanus' blood pollutes the household gods.
140 The enemy has entered, woe is me,
The captured home! The stepdame's wiles have made
The emperor's son his son-in-law as well;
A youth of base soul, capable of crime,
For whom his mother lit the marriage torch,
145 And, though thou wert unwilling, yet through fear

Made thee his wife. By such success made bold,
She dared, victorious one, to lay her hand
Upon the sacred scepter of the world.
Who can relate the many forms of crime,
Base hopes, and flattering wiles whereby she sought,
Climbing through evil deeds, to gain the throne?
Then holy love withdrew with fearful feet,
The dread Erinnyes with destroying step
Entered the empty courts, with Stygian torch
Defiled the sacred altars of the home,
Trampled the laws of nature and of god
Wife for her husband mixed the poisonous draft,
And fell ere long a victim to her son.
Thou also liest dead, unhappy boy,
Ever by me to be lamented sore,
Star of the world, prop of a noble house,
Britannicus! Ah, me, thou art become
But ashes and a shadow 'mong the shades;
Even the cruel stepdame wept for thee
When on the funeral pyre thy form was laid
For burning, and the mournful flame destroyed
Thy face and form so like the winged god's.

Octavia. Let him slay also me, lest by my hand he fall.
Nurse. Thou wert not gifted with such strength by nature.
Octavia. Anguish, wrath, and grief, and pain,
Will give the wretched strength in time of need.
Nurse. Nay, conquer by submission that hard man.
Octavia. That he may give me back a brother slain?
Nurse. That, helpless as thou art, thou mayst restore
Thy father's tottering palace through thy sons.
Octavia. The royal house must look for other sons.
The dread fates drag me to my brother's side.
Nurse. The nation's love should make thy spirit strong.
Octavia. It comforts me, but cannot ease my pain.
Nurse. The people's power is great.
Octavia. The king's is more.
Nurse. He will with favor look upon his wife.
Octavia. His concubine forbids.
Nurse. She is, forsooth, hated of all.
Octavia. Yet to her husband dear.
Nurse. She is not yet his wife.
Octavia. She soon will be—A mother too.
Nurse. A young man's passion burns
Fiercely at first, but soon it languishes;
Not long will he be swayed by sinful love,
Which is as changing smoke to constant flame.
Ever abides the love for a chaste wife.
He who first dared to violate thy bed,

      The slave who long possessed thy husband's heart, already fears—
        Octavia. One placed above herself.
        Nurse. Subject she is and humbled, and she builds
      Memorials that testify her fear.
195 Her will winged Cupid; false and fickle god,
      Also forsake; though she be beautiful
      And proud of power, her joy will be but brief.
      Such griefs the queen of heaven herself has borne:
      The father of the gods and king of heaven
200 Took every form, the plumage of the swan
      He wore, the horns of the Sidonian bull,
      In golden showers he fell; now in the sky
      Shines Leda's constellation, Bacchus dwells
      In high Olympus, in his father's home
205 Alcides, now become a god, enjoys
      Hebe, nor longer Juno's anger fears,
      He is her son-in-law who was her foe.
      The wise obedience, jealousy suppressed,
      Of the high-hearted wife has overcome;
210 Juno alone, secure, all-powerful,
      In the celestial marriage chamber holds
      The Thunderer, nor by mortal beauty won
      Does Jupiter desert the heavenly halls.
      Thou also, earthly Juno, sister, wife
215 Of great Augustus, hide thy heavy grief.
        Octavia. Sooner the raging seas shall mate with stars,
      The flood with fire, the sky with Tartarus,
      Sweet light with darkness, day with dewy night,
      Than mine with my sin-burdened husband's soul.
220 Ever I think upon my brother's death.
      Would that the ruler of the skies would come
      And smite that impious tyrant's hated head
      With flames, he often with his thunderbolt
      Makes the earth tremble, terrifies our souls
225 With sacred fires, prodigies unknown.
      I saw a glittering meteor in the sky,
      A comet showed in heaven its dreaded torch,
      There where forever slow Boötes drives
      In the cold north his wagon through the night.
230 With the fierce leader's breath the very air
      Is heavy. Slaughter new the star forebodes
      To all the nations that this vile king rules.
      Typhœus whom the parent earth brought forth,
      Angered by Jupiter, was not so fierce;
235 This pest is worse, the foe of gods and men;
      He from their temples drives th' immortal gods,
      The citizens he exiles from their land,
      He took his brother's life, his mother's blood

He drank, he sees the light, enjoys his life,
240 Still draws his poisonous breath! Ah, why so oft,
Mighty creator, throwest thou in vain
Thy dart from royal hand that knows not fear?
Why sparest thou to slay so foul an one?
Would that Domitian's son, the tyrant harsh,
245 Who with his loathsome yoke weighs down the earth,
Who stains the name Augustus with his rimes,
The bastard Nero, might at last endure
The penalt of all his evil deeds.
  Nurse. I own him all unmeet to wed with thee,
250 But to the fates and to thy fortunes bow,
O foster child, nor, I beseech thee, stir
Thy passionate husband's rage. Some god, perhaps,
Will come avenging, happier days will rise.
  Octavia. Long since the bitter anger of the gods
255 Pursued our house. First wrathful Venus filled
My wretched mother's heart with sinful love,
Married already, madly she embraced
A new, incestuous union; of her child,
Her husband, and the holy marriage vows
260 Unmindful, serpent-girdled, with loose hair,
The avenging goddess visited that couch,
Snatched from the hellish marriage-bed the torch,
And quenched its light in blood. With passion's heat
The cruel emperor's bosom was inflamed
265 To hideous murders. With the sword he slew
My wretched mother! Me, alas, he whelmed
In everlasting mourning by her loss,
His wife and son he dragged away to death,
And faithlessly betrayed our tottering house.
270   *Nurse.* Do not renew thy filial laments,
Nor trouble with thy tears thy mother's soul,
She suffered grievously for all her sin.

Scene III

Chorus of Roman Women.

What tale is this we hear? Would it were false,
And might lose credit, told in vain, though oft.
275 May no new wife to our chiefs chamber pass,
And may his bride, the child of Claudius, keep
Her place within his home, and bear him sons,
Pledges of peace which an untroubled world
May long enjoy; may Rome forever know
280 Her ancient glory. Juno was and is
Her brother's wife, why from her father's court

Should Caesar's wife and sister be expelled?
Does not her loyalty, her father crowned
A god by death, her chaste virginity,
Her purity, avail her anything?
We, too, would be forgetful of our prince
After his death, should we desert his child
Because we were afraid of Caesar's wrath.
Right Roman valor had our ancestors,
Theirs was the very race and blood of Mars,
They from the city drove the tyrant kings,
And well avenged thy fate, unhappy maid,
Child of Lucretius, by thine own hand slain
Because by tyrant's lust thou hadst been stained.
Tullia and her husband Tarquin paid
The penalty for sins unspeakable—
Over her murdered husband's form she drove
Her cruel chariot, and the furious child
Refused her murdered father's corpse a grave.
This age has also seen a son's base crime,
When in the Tuscan seas, on that dread ship,
The emperor drowned his mother treacherously;
At his command the sailors swiftly left
The quiet harbor, with the sounding oars
The strait reechoed, and the ship moves on
Into deep waters; there with parted keel
Sinking, it swallowed through its yawning side
The ocean. Great the cry that to the stars
Is borne, and mingled with it is the sound
Of mourning, women beating on their breasts.
Grim death was there, each sought from death to flee;
Some, naked, clung to the wrecked vessel's planks,
And strove to float; some swimming sought the shore,
The fates drowned many in the ocean's depths.
Augusta rent her clothes and tore her hair,
Her face with tears of bitter grief was marred.
When there was left no hope of being saved,
Glowing with anger, conquered by her woes,
'Is this,' she said, 'thy recompense to me,
My son, for all I gave thee? I confess,
Full worthy am I of this sinking keel,
I brought thee forth, I gave thee light, ah fool!
I gave an empire and the Caesar's name!
O husband, lift thine eyes from Acheron
And feed upon my punishment, behold,
I who brought death to thee and to thy sons
Graveless am borne to thee as I deserve,
Drowned in the waters of the raging sea.'
While she yet spoke the water smote her face,

330 She sank into the sea, then on the wave
She rose again. She strove against the sea,
Impelled by fear, but wearied sank at last.
Faith that scorned death remained in silent hearts.
Many there were who, weakened by the floods,
335 Yet dared to bring their drowning mistress aid;
As with weak arms she swam they called to her,
Lifted her in their arms; but what availed
That thou wert rescued from the cruel sea?
By thy son's sword thou wert about to die.
340 Scarcely will future ages, slow of faith,
Credit such crime. The monster, conscienceless,
Rages to see his mother still alive,
Saved from the sea; and he repeats his crime.
He speeds her to her death, he cannot brook
345 Delay, at his command a soldier hastes,
Who pierces with his sword his mistress' heart.
Unhappy mother, in her death she prays
That in her womb the murderer sheathe his sword.
'This, this,' she cried, 'must with the sword be pierced;
350 This which has borne a monster such as he.
Then with a dying groan she rendered up
Through the deep wound her sorrow-burdened soul.

ACT II

Scene I

Seneca.

I was content, why hast thou flattered me,
O potent Fortune, with thy treacherous smiles?
355 Why hast thou carried me to such a height,
That lifted to the palace I might fall
The farther, look upon the greater crimes?
Ah, happier was I when I dwelt afar
From envy's stings, among the rugged cliffs
360 Of Corsica, where my free spirit knew
Leisure for study. Ah, how sweet it was
To look upon the sky, th' alternate change
Of day and night, the circuit of the earth,
The moon, the wandering stars that circle her,
365 And the far-shining glory of the sky,
Which when it has grown old shall fall again
Into the night of chaos—that last day
Has come, which 'neath the ruin of the skies
Shall bury this vile race. A brighter sun,
370 Newborn, shall bring to life another race,

      Like that the young world knew, when Saturn ruled
      In the high heavens. Then great among the gods
      The virgin goddess Justice, with fair Faith,
      Sent from the skies, ruled on the tranquil earth
375 The race of man. The nations knew not war,
      Nor the harsh trumpet's sound, nor clash of arms,
      They were not wont about their towns to raise
      Protecting ramparts, every path was free,
      All things were used in common, the glad earth
380 Bared willingly for man her fruitful breast,
      A happy mother, in her foster-sons'
      Untainted love secure. Another race
      Less peaceful rose, a third in new arts skilled,
      But law-abiding; then a restless one
385 That dared to hunt the wild beasts in the chase,
      To catch in nets the fish in stormy seas,
      Or with the fowler's rod beguile the birds,
      Or to the yoke subject the savage bull
      And hold him with the halter, they first turned
390 The free earth with the plough; she, wounded, hid
      Deeper within her sacred breast her fruits;
      But even to the heart of Mother Earth
      A more degenerate generation pressed,
      Brought gold and iron thence, and by-and-by
395 Armed their fierce hands with weapons; cities rose,
      Their own they kept from danger with the sword.
      The virgin goddess Justice was despised
      And fled from earth, from men of cruel ways,
      From hands by blood polluted, to the skies.
400 Longing for war and avarice for gold
      Grew through the world, and luxury arose,
      Greatest of ills, a flattering, noisome thing,
      To which through man's delusion time gave strength.
      The garnered vices of so many years
405 Abound in us, we live in a base age
      When crime is regnant, when wild lawlessness
      Reigns and imperious passion owns the sway
      Of shameless lust; the victress luxury
      Plundered long since the riches of the world
410 That she might in a moment squander them.
      But see, where Nero comes with hasty steps,
      What will he do?

Scene II

Seneca, Nero, Prefect of the Palace.

    Nero. Go, do my bidding; send a man to slay
Plautus and Sulla, let him bring their heads.
    Prefect. There shall be no delay, I go at once.
    Seneca. It is not right to causelessly destroy thy kindred.
    Nero. He whose heart is free from fear may easily be just.
    Seneca. Yet clemency
Is a most potent remedy for fear.
    Nero. A leader's highest virtue is to slay his foe.
    Seneca. The father of his country finds
A greater in the service of the state.
    Nero. 'Tis meet for boys to govern weak old age.
    Seneca. 'Tis rather needful ardent youth be ruled.
    Nero. I'm old enough, I think, to rule myself.
    Seneca. I pray the gods approve whate'er thou dost.
    Nero. I were a fool to reverence the gods,
Myself am made a god.
    Seneca. Fear thou the more because thy power is great.
    Nero. My fortune gives to me in all things freedom absolute.
    Seneca. Fortune's a fickle goddess, trust her not.
    Nero. Unskilled are they who know not their own power.
    Seneca. He who does right is worthy to be feared,
Not he who does whate'er his will may prompt.
    Nero. The people scorn the feeble.
    Seneca. They destroy one whom they hate.
    Nero. The sword protects the prince.
    Seneca. Good faith protects him better.
    Nero. They must fear.
    Seneca. Man finds oppressive what is forced on him.
    Nero. They shall obey my will.
    Seneca. Rule justly then.
    Nero. Myself shall be the judge.
    Seneca. The people's voice must ratify thy will.
    Nero. The sword thou scornest shall force them to it.
    Seneca. God forbid that crime.
    Nero. And shall I longer suffer them to seek
My death, that I, despised and unavenged,
May suddenly be slain? Removed far hence,
Sulla and Plautus have not been subdued
By exile, with persistent rage they arm
Their agents for my murder; still they find,
Though absent, many followers in the town,
This nourishes the exile's hopes. The sword
Shall overthrow suspected enemies.

       My hated wife shall die, with her shall go
       The brother whom she loves, the proud shall fall.
         Seneca. To shine among the great is beautiful,
455 To keep one's hands from blood, be slow to wrath,
       Give the world rest, his generation peace,
       This is the height of virtue, by this path
       May heaven be attained; this is the way
       The first Augustus, father of the land,
460 Gained 'mid the stars a place and as a god
       Is worshipped now in temples. Yet for long
       Fate tossed him here and there by land and sea,
       Through all war's changing fortunes, till he slew
       His father's foes. The goddess suffered thee
465 To take his scepter without shedding blood,
       Subjected land and ocean to thy nod;
       Envy was conquered and to loyalty
       Gave place; the senate's favor and the knights'
       Was thine, by senators' and people's will
470 Thou wert elected arbiter of peace,
       Judge of the human race; thou rulest now
       The world in sacred majesty, art called,
       In turn, the father of the fatherland.
       Rome asks that thou deserve the name she gives,
475 And to thy care commends her citizens.
         Nero. I thank the gods, Rome and her senate do
       My bidding, and reluctant lips are forced
       By fear of me to utter humble prayers.
       Were it not madness that those citizens
480 Who swell with pride in their illustrious race,
       Who are a menace to the king and state,
       Should live, when with a word I might command
       That those whom I suspect be put to death?
       A Brutus armed himself to slay the prince
485 To whom he owed his safety; Caesar's self,
       In war invincible, the nation's lord,
       By highest honors equal made with Jove,
       Died by the murderous hand of citizens.
       Then Rome, so often rent with civil war,
490 Saw her sons' blood poured forth abundantly.
       How many nobles, youths, or aged men,
       Driven about the world in fear of death,
       Fleeing from home and the triumvir's sword,
       Their names inscribed upon the fatal list
495 That to grim death delivered them, were slain
       By great Augustus, who deserved the skies
       For good and glorious deeds? The senators
       In sorrow saw the heads of many slain
       Exposed upon the rostrum, nor might weep

Their dead, nor groan to see the forum stained
With foul corruption, noble blood distilled
From putrid faces. Nor was this the end
Of blood and slaughter, Philippi long feared
In misery wild beasts and birds of prey,
Sicilian waters swallowed up her fleet
And oft-revolting citizens, the world
Was shaken by the mighty leader's strength.
Conquered in war, shortly about to die,
He sought the Nile in ships prepared for flight,
A Roman leader's blood again was drunk
By Egypt the incestuous, now he dwells
Among the dead. Then impious civil war,
Long waged, at last was ended and at length
The wearied victor might lay by his sword
Blunted by savage warfare. He maintained
His throne by fear and in the loyalty
And weapons of his soldiers was secure.
He by the duteous action of his son
Was made a god, was reverenced after death,
Was honored in the temples. Other stars
Remain for us if with relentless sword
We first destroy whate'er would do us harm,
And found our house on children worthy us.
    Seneca. A woman of celestial lineage,
The ornament of honored Claudius' race,
Chosen, like Juno, for her brother's wife,
With godlike sons will fill thy palace halls.
    Nero. The mother's incest takes away my faith
In true-born sons. Her heart was never mine.
    Seneca. Love does not show its radiance in youth,
Then it conceals its flame in modesty.
    Nero. Indeed, I vainly long believed this true;
Although her hate of me was evident
In her unfriendly mien and countenance,
I judged at last the smart must be avenged.
I found a woman meet to be my wife
By birth and beauty, to whose loveliness
Venus, Jove's wife, the war-fierce goddess, bowed.
    Seneca. The probity and honor of a wife,
Her modesty and gentleness should charm
Her husband; graces of the mind and soul
Alone abide forever, beauty's flower a single day destroys.
    Nero. Ah, every grace
God has united in a single form,
And fate has caused her to be born for me.
    Seneca. Oh, banish from thy heart the god of love,
And put not foolishly thy trust in him.

Nero. Him whom the wielder of the thunderbolt
May not compel, the tyrant of the skies,
550 Who penetrates the seas and Pluto's realm,
And draws the gods from heaven?
Seneca. Man's error paints
The cruel god of love as winged, and arms
His hand with bow and arrow, gives a torch,
Believes him Venus' son and Vulcan's seed.
555 Love is but passion's force within the soul,
A pleasing heat, 'tis born of youth and fed
By ease and luxury when fortune smiles.
Cease thou to feed and cherish it, it fails,
Loses its strength and dies.
Nero. This I believe
560 The greatest source of life, from this springs joy;
The human race will never be extinct,
'Tis ever generated by sweet love,
Love soothes the hearts of savage beasts. The god
Shall bear for me the marriage torch, his fire
565 Shall join Poppæa to me as my wife.
Seneca. This marriage scarcely will the people brook,
And holy Justice scarce will sanction it.
Nero. Am I alone forbid what all may do?
Seneca. More is demanded of the powerful.
570 *Nero.* Whether my passion or the people's will shall yield, I yet will prove.
Seneca. Nay, mildly please thy citizens.
Nero. A state is governed ill
When by the mob its ruler can be ruled.
Seneca. When with the prince its prayers have no avail,
575 Surely the state has reason to complain.
Nero. May one compel when prayers are no avail?
Seneca. 'Tis cruel to refuse.
Nero. 'Tis criminal to force a prince.
Seneca. Let himself grant their wish.
Nero. But rumor would report him overcome.
580 *Seneca.* Rumor is but a vain and empty thing.
Nero. Perhaps, but it brands many.
Seneca. Yet it fears the throne.
Nero. Yet none the less reproaches it.
Seneca. 'Tis easily suppressed. Let thy wife's youth,
Her modesty and truth, her father's gifts, prevail upon thee.
585 *Nero.* Cease to harass me,
Thou urgest me too much, I well may do
What Seneca condemns. The people's will
Already long ago I put aside,
She carries in her womb my pledge of love,
590 Why not tomorrow take her for my bride?

ACT III

Scene I

The Ghost of Agrippina.

Through the rent earth from Tartarus I come,
In my right hand I bear a Stygian torch
For that vile bridal, with such gloomy fires
As an avenging mother's hand prepares
₅₉₅ For the sad altars, shall Poppæa wed
My son. The memory of that murder dwells,
Even among the shades, within my heart.
Still it is unavenged, the dread reward
For all my favors was the rotten keel,
₆₀₀ That night on which I mourned the vessel's wreck
My payment for a throne! I would have wept
The murder of my friends, my base son's crimes—
There was not time for tears, but crime on crime
He heaped, and smitten by the sword, made foul
₆₀₅ By many wounds, my troubled life went out
Upon the sacred altars of the home;
Saved from the deep, my blood was not enough
To quench the hatred of my son, he wars,
The cruel tyrant, 'gainst the very name
₆₁₀ Of mother, seeks to overthrow my fame.
All the inscriptions and the statues raised
In honor of his mother he destroys
Through all the world, the world my hapless love
Gave, for my own destruction, to a boy
₆₁₅ To rule. In death my murdered husband's soul
Pursues me, presses in my hated face
The torch, he threatens, he attacks, imputes
His fate to me and murder to his son,
Demands the author of his violent death.
₆₂₀ Ah, spare, revenge is thine! I do not ask
For long; th' avenging goddess has prepared
Death worthy of the tyrant, coward flight,
Lashes, and penalties that shall surpass
The thirst of Tantalus, the heavy toil
₆₂₅ Of Sisyphus, the bird of Tityus,
The flying wheel that tears Ixion's limbs.
What though he build his costly palaces
Of marble, overlays them with pure gold?
Though cohorts watch the armored chieftain's gates,
₆₃₀ Though the world be impoverished to send
Its wealth to him, though suppliant Parthians kneel

And kiss his cruel hand, though kingdoms give
Their riches, yet the day shall surely come
When for his crimes he will be called to give
⁶³⁵ His guilty soul; when, banished and forlorn,
In need of all things, he shall give his foes
His life-blood. What availed my prayers and toils?
Whither has thine own madness and the fates
Borne thee, my son, that even thy mother's wrath,
⁶⁴⁰ Though by thy crime she died, should faint and fail
Before such evils? Would the beasts of prey
Had torn my vitals ere I brought thee forth
A little child into the light of day
And nourished thee; still innocent and mine,
⁶⁴⁵ Sinless and passionless thou then hadst died
Clinging to me; thou hadst obtained a place
Of everlasting peace among the shades,
Among thy father's fathers, mighty men,
Who now must feel perpetual grief and shame
⁶⁵⁰ Because of thee, base one. I too must mourn,
Who bore so vile a son. I who have brought,
As stepdame, wife, and mother, to my own
Naught but misfortune—wherefore should I cease
To hide my head in gloomy Tartarus?

Scene II

Octavia, Chorus.

⁶⁵⁵   *Octavia.* Oh, spare your tears upon this festal day,
Let not such love and kindliness toward us
Arouse the bitter anger of the king,
Let me not be a cause of woe to you.
Not for the first time do I feel the wounds,
⁶⁶⁰ More grievous have I borne. This day shall bring
The end of all my cares, mayhap my death.
I will not see my cruel husband's face,
The hated marriage chamber of a slave
I will not enter, I will be henceforth
⁶⁶⁵ The sister of Augustus, not his wife.
Let bitter pain and haunting fear of death
Depart. Ah, fool! Remembering his crimes,
Canst thou still hope for this? Too long preserved,
A victim to this bridal thou shalt fall.
⁶⁷⁰ But why perplexed and with wet cheeks look back
So often on thy home? Haste from its roof,
Forsake the blood-stained palace of the king.
   Chorus. The day long feared, long talked of, breaks at last,
When driven forth by Nero, Claudius' child

675 Forsakes her marriage chamber, even now
Victorious Poppæa there abides.
Our love falls off, our wrath is crushed by fear
And fruitless; where is now the Roman power
Which oft subdued great kings and gave just laws
680 To an unconquered land? With honors crowned,
The worthy citizens made peace and war,
Ruled barbarous nations, and imprisoned kings.
Lo, on all sides, before our saddened eyes
The image of Poppæa stands supreme,
685 With Nero's joined. Oh, cast it to the ground
With violent hands, too like herself it is;
And drag her from the chamber of the king,
Seek with destroying flame and cruel spears
The prince's palace.

ACT IV

Scene I

Poppœa, Nurse.

690   *Nurse.* O foster child, why fleest thou in fear
Thy husband's marriage chamber? Wherefore seek
With troubled look a solitary place?
Why wet thy cheeks with tears? The day long sought
With prayers and sacrifice now shines for us;
695 Thou to thy Caesar, whom thy beauty won,
Hast been united by the marriage bond.
Venus, Love's mother, mightiest of the gods,
Whom Seneca despised, has given him,
Captived, to thee. Dwelling within the court
700 How lovely wast thou on the princely couch.
The senate saw, amazed, thy loveliness,
When thou didst offer incense to the gods
And sprinkle on their altars holy wine;
Veiled wert thou with the filmy wedding veil,
705 Flame colored. Close beside thee walked the king,
Triumphant 'mid the people's favoring shouts,
In his proud face and carriage shone his joy.
So Peleas once took Thetis for his bride,
When from the foamy waters of the sea
710 She sprang; 'tis said the heavenly deities
And every ocean god with one consent
Honored their bridal. What has changed thy face
So suddenly? Why is it now so pale?
Tell me what mean these tears.
    Poppœa. Ah, nurse, my mind

715 Is darkened, troubled, and my senses fail
From fear of last night's visions terrible.
For when the happy day had left the sky
To darkness and the stars, I fell asleep
Encompassed by my Nero's loving arms;
720 But not for long might I enjoy sweet sleep.
It seemed as though a mourning company
Came to my marriage chamber; with loose hair
Rome's mothers, weeping, beat upon their breasts,
With dreadful oft-repeated trumpet notes;
725 The mother of my husband, with harsh threats,
Waved wildly in my face a blood-red torch;
When forced, by urgent fear, I followed her,
Earth yawned and suddenly a mighty gulf
Was opened for me whither I was plunged
730 Headlong, and there in wonder I beheld
My marriage-bed, in which I lay me down
Sore wearied. With a throng of followers, then,
I saw my former husband and my son
Coming. Crispinus, parted from me long,
735 Hastened to kiss me, take me in his arms,
When Nero madly rushed into my home
And buried in that breast the cruel sword.
At length my terror roused me from my sleep,
A fearful trembling shook my very bones,
740 My heart throbbed, and my voice was choked by fear;
Thy love and loyalty have strengthened me.
Alas, what threat these spirits of the dead?
Why have I seen my husband's blood poured forth?
    Nurse. Whatever trouble stirs the waking soul,
745 A swift, mysterious power of the mind
Recalls in sleep. What need to wonder then,
That circled by the arms of thy new mate
Thou sawest in a dream thy marriage-bed,
Thy husband? Did it trouble thee to see
750 Loose hair, breasts beaten on a festal day?
Within her father's and her brother's house
They mourn Octavia's divorce; that torch
Which thou didst follow, which the empress' hand
Upheld, was omen of the noble name
755 That hatred gained for thee; thy rest in hell
Promised thy marriage bond should be for ay,
That in his breast thy emperor plunged the sword
Presages that he will not stir up wars,
But sheath his sword in peace. Be calm again,
760 Be glad, I pray thee, put aside thy fear,
Go to thy marriage chamber.
    Poppœa. I will seek

The shrines and holy altars, offer there
The blood of victims slain unto the gods,
That all the ills that night and slumber threat
765 May be averted, and the things I dread
Be turned against my foe. Do thou adore
With pious prayers the gods, and offer up
Thy supplications for me, that my joy
May be abiding.

Scene II

Chorus.

770 If prating rumor's tales may be believed
Of all the amorous intrigues of Jove,
How, feathered like the swan, in his embrace
He held fair Leda, or, like fierce bull formed,
Bore on his back Europa through the waves,
775 He would desert the star where now he rules
To seek thy arms, Poppæa, whom indeed
He might prefer to Leda or to thee
Danae, who in wonder saw him once
Come in a golden rain. Let Sparta boast
780 Her daughter's beauty, Phrygia's shepherd joy
In his reward—she is more fair of face
Than child of Tyndarus who caused grim war
And whelmed the Phrygian kingdom in the dust.
But who is this who comes with troubled steps.
785 What message does his heaving bosom bear?

Scene III

Messenger, Chorus.

Messenger. The guard who watches at the emperor's gates
Must now defend his courts, the populace
Is roused against him. See, the prefects bring
In haste their cohorts to defend the town.
790 The people's fury, causelessly conceived,
Is not displaced by fear, but grows in strength.
  Chorus. What is the fury that disturbs their minds?
  Messenger. Filled with affection for Octavia,
And by great wrongs enraged, the crowd rush on.
795   *Chorus.* What have they dared to do and to what end?
  Messenger. They would give back again to Claudius' child
Her father's palace and the right she holds
As wedded to her brother, her due share
Of royal power.

  Chorus. These Poppæa holds.
   Messenger. This too great love has set their hearts on fire
And drawn them headlong into maddest deeds.
The images of marble and of brass
That have Poppæa's face lie overthrown
And broken by the mob's fierce hands and swords.
They drag the broken parts about with ropes,
And trample in the mire the shattered limbs.
Wild words and deeds are mingled, which my fear
Forbids my lips to speak. Now they prepare
To gird with flames the palace of the king,
Unless he yield to them his new made wife,
Restore to Claudius' child her former home.
That he himself may know of this revolt,
I have not tarried, but fulfilled in haste
The Prefect's bidding.
  Chorus. Wherefore have you stirred
In vain this cruel war? Invincible
Are Cupid's darts. He will o'erwhelm your fires
With the same flame wherewith he oft has quenched
The thunderbolts and carried Jove himself
A captive from the sky. You with your blood
Will pay the penalty, not patient he,
Nor easy to be ruled, when once rage-filled.
At his command Achilles smote the lyre,
He quelled the Greeks, he quelled Atrides, too,
And threw the realm of Priam in the dust,
Laid cities low; for what the ruthless god
With his wild might may do, my spirit fails.

ACT V

Scene I

Nero.

Too slow my soldiers' hands, too mild my wrath,
In view of crime like this. The people's blood
Should have put out the fires they light for me,
And Rome which bore such sons been made to reek
With slaughter of her citizens. Ah well,
The punishment of death is all too small,
Their lawless deeds deserve worse punishment;
But she for whom the angry citizens
Arose against me, my suspected wife
And sister, shall for their offence give up
Her life, shall quench my anger with her blood.
The city shall be wasted by my fires,

The guilty citizens shall be harassed
By flames, and ruin, and hard poverty,
Hunger, and bitter grief. The senseless mob,
Corrupted by the blessings of my reign,
Run riot, nor, ungrateful, comprehend
My clemency; they cannot be at peace,
But, restless, rash, and overconfident,
They rush to their own ruin. By hard means
They must be ruled, and by a heavy yoke
Subdued, that they may never dare like deeds,
Nor to my wife's fair face dare lift their eyes.
By heavy vengeance humbled, they shall learn
Through fear to give obedience to my nod.
But he whose singular integrity
And well-known loyalty have made him chief
Of all my army comes.

Scene II

Nero, Prefect.

Prefect. I come to say the fury of the mob
Is checked by slaughter of the few who long resisted foolishly.
    Nero. Is this enough?
Hast thou, a soldier, thus obeyed thy chief?
They have been checked? Is this the penalty
They owe me?
    Prefect. By the sword the leaders fell.
    Nero. Why are the rabble spared who dared attack
My home with fiery brands, who dared prescribe
A law unto their king, who from our couch
Dragged forth my lovely wife and with vile hands
And threatening words abused her? Shall not they
Endure just punishment?
    Prefect. Shall wrath prescribe
The penalty thy citizens shall pay?
    Nero. It shall prescribe a penalty whose fame
Shall never perish in the years to come.
    Prefect. Neither thy anger nor our fear should rule.
    Nero. She shall atone who first aroused our wrath.
    Prefect. Whom does thy vengeance seek? Spare not my hands.
    Nero. The murder of my sister, her vile life.
    Prefect. Such rigor with cold horror chills my soul.
    Nero. Art loth to do my will?
    Prefect. Why doubt my truth?
    Nero. Because thou didst not slay mine enemy.
    Prefect. And can a woman be thine enemy?
    Nero. When she is capable of crimes like hers.

Prefect. What proves her guilt?
Nero. The madness of the mob.
Prefect. Who shall restrain them?
880   *Nero.* She who stirred them up.
Prefect. Scarce any one, I think.
Nero. A woman can,
To whom was giv'n a spirit prone to ill,
A bosom filled with wiles for harming us.
   Prefect. She has no power.
   Nero. That not impregnable
885 She be, that wavering strength be crushed by fear,
By punishment that even now too late
Falls upon one too long at liberty,
To harm us, leave thy counsels and thy prayers,
Go do our bidding. Let her in a ship
890 Be carried to some distant shore to die,
That I at last may banish anxious fear.

Scene III

Chorus.

How dangerous is popular applause,
How terrible! With favoring breath it fills
The vessel's sails and carries it along,
895 Then in the deep and raging seas grows faint
And leaves it. The sad mother wept her sons,
The Gracchi, of distinguished family born,
Illustrious for piety and truth
And eloquence, brave hearted, to the laws
900 Attentive, whom the people's too great love
Destroyed. Such violent death was, too, thy fate,
O Drusus, not thy honors nor thy home
Protected thee—how many instances
Our present grief forbids us to recall!
905 The citizens may see her dragged to death
And torture, weeping, sad, to whom they sought
To give again her royal dwelling-place,
Her fortune in her brother's marriage-bed.
Well may the poor, beneath an humble roof,
910 Be happy, for the tempest often shakes
And Fortune oft o'erthrows proud palaces.

Scene IV

Octavia, Chorus.

Octavia. Where do you drag me? If I still may live,
Broken and humbled by my many ills,
What exile does the tyrant or his queen
915 Command? If he would crown my woes with death
Why does he harshly grudge that I should die
In my own land? Alas, there is no hope
Of safety, for I see my brother's ship,
Lo, in this vessel I shall be borne hence,
920 I, once his wife, now driven from his bed,
His wretched sister. No divinity
Protects the good from harm, there are no gods,
The sad Erinnyes rule the universe.
Who worthily may weep my misery?
925 With what lament can the sad nightingale
Answer my tears? Ah, would the fates might give
Her wings to wretched me! Then borne aloft
Upon bird pinions, I would flee afar
From sorrow, from the company of men,
930 From slaughter; in a solitary wood,
Sitting alone upon a slender twig,
I could pour forth my sorrowful lament
With querulous voice.
    Chorus. Mankind is ruled by fate,
And none may trust that his will be unchanged;
935 We need to fear each day that brings to us
Its varying fortunes. Strengthen then thy soul
With memory of the many instances
Thy house has seen. Ah, why should Fortune be
More harsh to thee? Thee first I must recall,
940 Child of Agrippa, by thy marriage made
The daughter of Augustus, Caesar's wife;
Thy name shone glorious over all the world,
Oft from thy fruitful womb thou broughtest forth
Pledges of peace, but soon thou sufferedst
945 Exile, the lash and chains, bereavement, grief,
And death at length with torture long endured.
Livia, wife of Drusus, in her sons
And husband fortunate, fell into crime,
She met her punishment.
950 Julia was followed by her mother's fate,
And though no crime was hers, was slain at last.
What power wielded not thy mother once?
She ruled within the palace of the king,

Was rich in sons and to her husband dear,
955 Yet, humbled by her handmaid, she was slain
By the fierce warrior's sword. What throne in heaven
Might Nero's noble mother not expect?
Yet she by sailors rude was first abused,
Then, wounded by the sword, she fell at length a victim to her cruel son.
960   *Octavia.* Behold,
Me also does the cruel tyrant send
To the dead spirits and the land of shades.
Why vainly linger in my misery?
Ye to whom fortune gave the power to slay,
965 Speed now my death. I call upon the gods—
Ah, fool, what wouldst thou? Cease to make thy prayers
To gods who hate thee. Tartarus, I call
Thee as my witness, and the goddesses
Of Erebus, avengers of all crimes,
970 And thee, my father.....
I do not dread this death. Prepare the ship,
Spread to the winds the sails, the lonely shores
Of Pandataria shall the pilot seek.

Scene V

Chorus.

Ye gentle zephyrs and soft breathing airs
975 That once from harsh Diana's altars bore
Iphigenia, hidden in a cloud,
Her also bear from such keen suffering,
To Hecate's temple carry her, I pray;
Milder is Aulis and the barbarous land
980 Of Taurus than this city, to the gods
The blood of strangers there is sacrificed,
In her own children's blood Rome takes delight.

THE END